Praise for

Basta Pasta, Ancora

"*Basta Pasta* occupies a special place in our Italian home, and I'm thrilled to have more stories and recipes with *Basta Pasta, Ancora*. Anita steeps the family dining experience in tradition, love, and good food, presenting recipes that are approachable for all levels of cooks. Another delightful compilation that is an asset to any kitchen!"

—Joan Arndt
Umbria, Italy

"I will welcome with open hands the second cookbook of Anita Augello. In addition to the wonderful family stories and recipes, [there are] the extra useful tips, many of which I have never before seen in other cookbooks. Brava, Anita!"

—Judy Bowman
Spoleto, Italy

"I am so thankful that I have the first cookbook that my grandmother put together for her grandchildren. Now that I have my own home in another state, I love having the cookbook so I can practice making some of her recipes. Cooking my favorite dishes from *Basta Pasta*, like sauce and meatballs, always reminded me of being at Nonna's house. Looking forward to the second cookbook because it will have even more of my favorite recipes that I can practice myself and share with others."

—Vince Campagna
Charlotte, North Carolina

"My wife and I have an extensive collection of Italian cookbooks. What set *Basta Pasta* apart [is] delicious recipes you won't find elsewhere: Acciuga Salsa, Vitello Tonato, Pasta con Sarde, Cotechino con Lenticchie. Add to that Anita's delightful family stories and the insightful anecdotes she provides with many of her recipes. This is family cooking, Italian style!"

—Ron G.
Norcross, Georgia

"*Basta Pasta* is a worthy addition to any cook's kitchen. Anita's recipes are simple to understand, simple to make, yet taste as if you [are] dining in Italy itself. Great recipes, traditional homestyle Italian cooking made simple, heartfelt family memories, and helpful hints everywhere you turn. *Mangia!*"

—Linda G.
Georgia

Basta Pasta Ancora

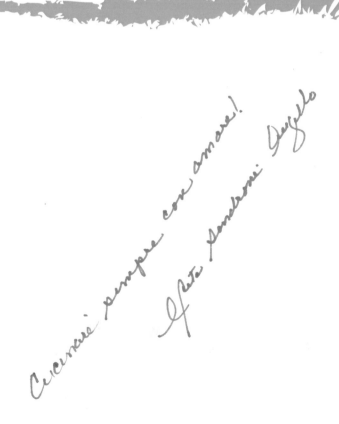

Cucinare sempre con amore!

Chita Sandroni Angelo

Basta Pasta

Ancora

More of Our Family's Favorite Recipes

Anita Sandroni Augello

For Our Children and Grandchildren

MOUNTAIN ARBOR
PRESS
Alpharetta, GA

ISBN: 978-1-63183-754-8 - Softcover
ISBN: 978-1-63183-755-5 - Hardcover

Printed in the United States of America   1 1 1 8 1 9

⊗This paper meets the requirements of ANSI/NISO Z39.48-1992 (Permanence of Paper)

I dedicate this cookbook first and foremost to my Father, who showed me through his own presence how to be a loving parent, and then to my Mother-in-Law, from whom I realized how to be a loving grandparent, possibly a prudent cook, and maybe, too, a good Mother-in-Law.

Also to my Grandparents, and all those brave but unknown, except for their stories, who through grit and some desperation, set the path for my relatives to achieve their dream and immigrate to America, allowing me the privilege of being born in this great country.

But, of course, it is my Husband, Charlie, whom I met in grade school, from whom I get my strength, as he always tells me I can accomplish whatever I set out to do. I tend to be a more serious spirit, but he helps me find the lighter side of life as we enjoy a glass of wine, converse, and laugh and dance around our kitchen. He's been my partner and best friend for fifty-eight years, so how could I ever have a doubt?

When Charlie and I gather our family together, and I look at our Children, Chuck, Andrea, Erica, Claudia, and their families, I know that I did—we did—accomplish something beyond my greatest dreams.

Charlie and me, Easter 1957

Contents

Acknowledgments

You will notice as you go through this cookbook that I defy the rule of grammar and capitalization whenever I refer to a member of my family. Somehow, I don't visualize these special people as ever being lowercase, and quite frankly, I find it disrespectful. So, they are capitalized!

Also, because this is a family cookbook and illustrates how our family enjoys eating, I have broken a food rule. "Pass the grated cheese" is added to almost every pasta recipe. In Italy, you would never have cheese in a dish where fish is included. However, food is meant to enjoy, not just to fill the stomach, so eat what you like and how you like it, and "Pass the cheese, please!"

Putting this cookbook together was much more involved than just submitting an assemblage of recipes to fill pages. Deciphering, translating, and interpreting notes, and adjusting and revising recipes to adapt them to suit the appetites of my family and friends has taken years. Before you is a culmination of many hours of work . . . but definitely a labor of love.

I want to sincerely thank the many people who indulged me by consuming my experiments—family and friends alike who sometimes, albeit unknowingly, were guinea pigs, yet always agreeable to try a new creation. Although there were many things that didn't quite turn out as illustrated or anticipated, my family (my ever-faithful victims) don't look the worse for wear through it all.

There are countless people who, in some way, unknowingly contributed to this book. Some I am able to thank, and others, for various reasons, I am not able to. But, this book helps to preserve their memory, too.

In deep gratitude for his friendship and with special thanks to Ron Scharbo,
who in his own inimitable way helped to make this book possible.

Even though each recipe has been read and reread, accidents are bound to happen. If there is something that you don't quite understand, just send me an email, and I'll do my best to set it straight: nycgal338@gmail.com.

With many thanks,

Anita

Our treasures and our hope for the future, 8/17/2019

Why Another Cookbook?

As I wrote in Basta Pasta, I always felt it was important for our Children to know their ancestry. And, I feel so strongly that I have to reiterate most of it again here in this new book. Our family is increasing, our Grandchildren are growing up, and we now have Great-Grandchildren. Yes, hard to believe, but we are now Bisnonna and Bisnonno! As luck would have it, I have uncovered another cache of old family recipes and other family favorites I have been garnering that are crying for publication and sharing.

I enjoy cooking. Cooking many of these familiar recipes connects me to my childhood, my family, my heritage, and people that I love. It grounds me and makes me happy. I'm hoping, at some point, it will have the same effect on our Children.

Now more than ever, I feel it is important for our Children to know their ancestry. When I was growing up, I thought of myself as being Italian, but by the same token, I knew without a doubt I was American. I was a fortunate American by birth, but my foundation was Italian to the very core.

Because I lived close to Grandparents, Aunts, Uncles, and Cousins, traditions were lived every day. Family lived downstairs, upstairs, next door, and not very far away. We ate traditional foods attached to stories, celebrated holidays in a traditional manner, and heard tales of my Parents and Grandparents growing up and immigrating to America. And, when I say holidays, I don't just mean Christmas, Easter, and Thanksgiving. I also mean baptisms, communions, confirmations, graduations, birthdays, engagements, weddings, Palm Sundays, New Year's Days, several feast days, and anything of importance in between!

When I am asked about my lineage, I am happy to say that my Mother was born in Torino, so I am in part Piemontese, and that my Father was born in Montefollonico, a hamlet in Siena, so I am, in part, Toscana, but most proudly, Senese. But, I am mostly proud to say that I am a flag-waving, anthem-singing American. And, that's what we want most of all for our Children, along with a little dose of their lineage.

For my Husband, Charlie, it was the same. Although he did not know his Grandparents, he was surrounded by many Aunts, Uncles, and Cousins who also lived upstairs, next door, up the street, and across the street. He repeats some of the stories told years ago at family gatherings. They were sometimes sad, but wonderful ones about brave people who left family behind for the unknown. They left with a dream of a better life for themselves and their families. They left with little more than the clothes on their backs and a few things in a tattered cloth bag. Our Children didn't hear these stories, and when we repeat them, it is not with the same intensity.

We want our Children to know who their ancestors are and understand their traditions. The best way I know how to do this is through the food in this cookbook. Charlie and I try to keep up traditions the same way our Parents and ancestors did: with food and love and stories. Try as we might, it does get diluted. This causes me to worry. In today's world, names for holidays are changed; rituals are overlooked or considered burdensome. To make matters worse, gender-neutral is becoming the norm. In years to come, how will my Children's Children know who they are and what their lineage is? Are we all to become known as global people?

Family dinners become impossible because of sports. Growing up, family gatherings were always a special time. You would never miss being at any of them. Without question, you were there, nicely dressed and on time, ready to pay respect to your elders and greet the young ones. But, more importantly, you wanted to be there. The world, I fear, is becoming blasé.

Cooking is becoming a thing of the past. We have store-bought, take-out, fast food, frozen food, meals you can drink, and on and on. Where is the food cooked with love and served to the family sitting around the table recounting the day's activities? Are any memorable mealtimes being celebrated? I want our Children to enjoy cooking and have a passion for putting something special on the table. I'm hoping familiar recipes will instill that in them. So, it is my hope that this cookbook, with its few little stories, will keep some of the traditions alive.

Our Children all have foods they cherish and expect to eat as we gather for family meals. They become more than foods; they become traditions; they become memorable meals. Our Children are familiar with most of these recipes as the time-honored foods we continue to prepare on holidays and special occasions. Other foods may bring back a memory of a family dinner or a relative no longer with us. Maybe, just maybe, they will be inspired to keep the flame lit for our Grandchildren and their Children's Children. I want them to cook with a passion to make dinner time enjoyable.

And that is why a cookbook!

So We Called It...
Basta Pasta

The name Basta Pasta, as I mentioned in my first book, comes from a funny incident that happened in 2004 when we took our entire family (fifteen from ages three and up) to Italy. While there, we visited my family in Montefollonico, a little town in Tuscany. Andrea, Cristina, and their boys, Lorenzo, Roberto, and Riccardo Sandroni, live in the same house that my Father and his family lived in before they immigrated to America.

After touring the little town and visiting the cemetery to pay our respects to our ancestors, we arranged a lunch for a small party of twenty-two at a local restaurant. We spent a good part of the afternoon there eating, drinking, and conversing with our Italian family. Our Children, who speak no Italian, conversed successfully and merrily with our relatives, who speak only Italian. It was a wonderful experience, and the food of many courses and wine was plentiful, and all arrived nonstop.

Pranzo with Italian family in Montefollonico, 2004

After some time, when the chatter seemed to quiet down, the desserts were enjoyed, and we were filled beyond the brim, two large plates of pasta arrived at the table. Apparently, our Children, in answer to a question from a waiter about wanting anything more, attempted to say basta, *which was interpreted as* pasta. *And so, out it came: two heaping platters of pasta, accompanied by several platters of patate fritte, which we incredulously finished. To this day, when we talk about our family visit, this story always comes up. So, that is why I chose the title* Basta Pasta; *it makes everyone smile.*

Charlie and I have been married for fifty-eight years. Our family continues to grow. We are blessed, and we don't take this for granted. As the Children grow and marry and bless us with Grandchildren and Great-Grandchildren, so do the foods we enjoy together continue to grow, as the Grandchildren now request certain foods they are familiar with and enjoy.

Every recipe is a small piece of our family. I don't want these foods and stories to be forgotten for them, either, so that is why Basta Pasta, Ancora *was born.*

House my dad was born in

13 Via Fedro Bandini

My Grandparents Nonno Ugo and Little Nonna Agnese were married sometime around March 1894, and around that same year purchased this house, #13, where my Father and my Uncle Dino were born. After several inquiries, I was told that it was built a little more than four hundred years ago. It is in the walled part of this ancient hamlet called Montefollonico. It sits on a charming cobblestone street.

As many times as I have visited Montefollonico, I always stroll down that street, stop, and take another picture. (Nothing ever changes, except the color of the door. However, it provides me with security that, yes, it is still there.) I have knocked on the door every time, hoping I would be able to speak to the present resident. I would ask if I could just take one step inside, passing over the threshold and through the doorway, as my Father did so many times and so long ago. I'll keep trying until I am successful.

338 before renovation with
Scribes Club on ground floor

338 East Forty-Third Street

This is the house my siblings and I grew up in. You can still see the sign for my Father's Scribes Club in the window on the ground floor. My Grandparents lived next door with my Uncles, Aunts, and Cousins. We also had Cousins living in 338.

My two older Sisters, Flora and Elena, shared a bedroom, and I shared a bedroom with my younger Brother, Gus, that was no larger than the closet I now have. We had bunkbeds and a five-drawer chest (top-two drawers were mine, bottom two were my Brother's, and we shared the middle one). There was a little desk, and if someone sat at the desk, you could not open the drawers in the chest. The closet door didn't open all the way, because it hit the bed. That was not a problem, because there was very little to hang in there.

We had one window for a breeze in summer that also let the city sounds in. They never kept us awake, even though we lived on the same street as the Hospital for Special Surgery, with ambulances and fire engines coming and going at all hours. Sometimes, late at night when everyone else was asleep, I would sit at the window and enjoy the excitement that one only finds in New York City in the wee small hours.

The building next door, 340, housed the Tudor City School, a private school strictly for resident Children of Tudor City. Mrs. Travers was the principal, and her husband, the gardener. Mr. Travers guarded the neighborhood park like a hawk, making sure my Cousins and I never set foot inside. Of course, just to taunt him, we would go in the farthest door from where he was working and run through the gravel path out the other. We were quite proud of ourselves. Our brownstone was surrounded by and in the midst of Tudor City, but we were not a part of Tudor City. My Nonno Ugo had purchased the two buildings as they were being built sometime in the 1920s.

Tudor City was festively decorated each year in time for Christmas with wreaths and illuminated trees. Every year just before Christmas, a yule log was burned in one of the parks, and Tudor City residents gathered around to sing Christmas carols. We could see and smell the fire from our opened window, and smugly, my Brother and I joined in singing the carols.

I can recall that on First Avenue, where the United Nations building now stands, there was a slaughterhouse for sheep. One night, when I believe it was already vacant of animals, it caught on fire. The fur from the sheep created sparks that exploded as far as the rooftops of 336 and 338. At that time, the roofs were tar paper and could have easily caught on fire from the sparks. For many hours, my Parents, Sisters, Uncles, and Cousins formed a water brigade, passing buckets of water up the metal ladder and through the hatch to the roof to keep it wet. My Brother and I witnessed it all from our bunkbeds, as our room opened to the hallway. We watched in fear and knew to be very, very quiet.

This is the house I lived in until Charlie and I were married

During the war years, I remember we had boarders in our house to help with expenses. We had a big backyard—unheard of in the city—where I played with my Cousins. My Uncles had their doctors' office downstairs in 336, and for a long while we had a pediatrician on the ground floor in 338. That later became an apartment. The front stoop was removed sometime around 1946 or 1947, and the entire building was remodeled along with 336.

In the early 1980s, the building was sold to Tudor City. With the exception of my Mother, who did not want to leave New York, we had all married and moved away, so it was time. My Mother remained in the building for several years, but eventually moved across the street into The Cloister, a Tudor City building with both a doorman and an elevator, which made life easier and more secure for her.

She lived there until she was ninety-two, making her regular visits as a volunteer to the St. Agnes Soup Kitchen. Then, she moved to California to live with my Sister Elena, until she died quite peacefully at the age of ninety-six.

The Market was established on September 30, 1986

E. 48th Street Market, Italian Food Specialties

When Charlie and I were growing up in New York City, we lived near small ethnic stores, where our families shopped on a daily basis. It was rare to shop at Safeway or A&P, the large supermarkets. Instead, we patronized the local butcher; the grocery store for fruits, vegetables, canned goods, cold cuts, and bread; and another little shop to purchase flour, cornmeal, dried or fresh pasta, and more bread. There was also the neighborhood fish market, where fish were kept chilled on ice on wooden tables outside the shop. The aroma was something I deeply dreaded.

After Charlie and I married, we moved to Baltimore. While not quite as convenient, the city had a very nice Italian section, where we could get the things we were accustomed to and needed. Other moves took us back to New York City, and then on to Smithtown, West Milford, Erie, and Andover. Again, we were able to purchase our Italian products in most places, though not as conveniently as a walk of a few city streets.

Everything was obtainable until 1981, when another corporate move settled us in our new home in a suburb of Atlanta. What we were accustomed to finding was not to be found. Every trip back to New York included a shopping trip, and every visitor to Atlanta was provided with a wish list of longed-for products. And, corporate life was becoming less enchanting.

While contemplating our strategy to transition from the corporate world to entrepreneurship, we gave much thought to what came next. Something to do with Italian food was at the top of our list—perhaps a grocery store or small restaurant. Fortunately, after much deliberation, grocery store won.

Now, the question was what we would like our Italian market to be. The plan we would work on called for a friendly neighborhood market, much like the ones we remembered from our youths and similar to one that had been owned by Charlie's Uncle Joe on East Forty-Eighth Street in New York City.

In 1985, Charlie arranged his separation from the corporate world. After much thought, planning, agonizing, and consideration, we opened E. 48th Street Market, Italian Food Specialties, in Dunwoody, Georgia, in September 1986.

Despite tremendous hard work and some lean years, it has been a rewarding experience to watch the Market evolve and grow. We began mainly as a grocery store with a small array of Italian delicacies ranging from family-recipe entrees to a variety of pastries, cold cuts, cheeses, olives, olive oils, vinegars, and a few years later, a small selection of Italian wines. In our planning, our top priority of specialty items was to be daily-made items, which would include fresh mozzarella, crusty Italian bread, Italian sausage, and fresh pasta. These have remained customer favorites throughout the years. A variety of specialty items were offered at holiday time. We began to make our own mozzarella. Sandwiches were served on crusty Italian bread. We developed our own recipe for the bread, which eventually led to our commercial-bread business and a selection of over a dozen different breads to choose from.

Many of our customers from 1986 remain our customers today. We have watched their Children grow and have families of their own. They still come in to shop. We share stories with them, both happy and sad. Through the years, we've laughed with them and cried with them. Many have become like family to us. We're very much involved and a part of the community.

The Market has evolved from the small grocery store to a full-scale market. Grocery shelves have been condensed to allow space for tables and chairs. Our customers brought us to this change, as they used our shelves to hold their drinks while eating their sandwiches! After a few years, even those tables weren't enough, so we expanded by building an outdoor patio, later enclosed with fans to cool in the summer and heaters to warm in the winter.

We now offer over a hundred different Italian wine selections. We arrange wine tastings, and have a wine bar with a selection of eight wines. We prepare special evening dinners on the enclosed patio, and cater *weddings, engagement parties, and corporate functions, to name a few. We have hot and cold entrees, and our sandwich board lists several dozen to choose from. Customers can dine-in or take-out. Pizza has become a big seller.*

Early on, our Son, Chuck, managed the front of the store. Now our Daughter Andrea is the manager. Through the years, every one of our Children—which would also include Daughters Erica and Claudia—and several of our Grandchildren could be found working at the Market. And, many a friend has jumped in to help at crunch time.

So, our dream has become a reality. We are truly a neighborhood market, approaching our thirty-third anniversary. It has truly been a labor of love.

Keep up with our latest developments by visiting www.E48thstreetmarket.com.

Giovanna Farm mid-1930s

Giovanna Farm

My Mother's parents, Antonio and Giovanna Ponzo Chiappone, were born in the Piedmont region of northwestern Italy. My Grandmother was born in Castel Nuovo Calcea in the province of Asti, and my Grandfather from Alessandria, a little town not too far away in an area known as the home of Asti Spumante, a renowned sparkling wine.

Because of meager living conditions and limited labor opportunities in Italy, it was decided they would immigrate to America. My Grandfather came first, found a job, and managed to earn enough money to bring my Grandmother to the States. Together, they worked long hours in a boarding house on East Forty-Fifth Street while living somewhere on the West Side near Thirty-Ninth Street in New York. They saved enough to then bring my Mother (Maria), Aunt Tillie (Metilde), and Uncle Antonio to America.

My Grandfather arrived on a ship named Chicago *in April 1912. My Grandmother arrived on a ship called* Duca d'Aosta *in May 1912, and the Children (my Mother, my Aunt Tillie, and my Uncle Antonio) arrived, accompanied by seventeen-year-old Aunt Agostina, in November 1912 on a ship named* America. *The Children were four, six, and ten years of age, and the voyage was a little more than three weeks on winter seas. My Mother would remember they slept in hammock-style beds and were each given one metal bowl. You washed and ate using the same bowl. The seas were rough most of the time, so everyone was forced to stay below. People got sick, and babies cried continuously. Men were separated* from women, although very young male Children did remain with their Mothers. My Mother didn't see her Brother until they reached America. She said she feared she would never see him again. The entire family (including my Grandparents) traveled steerage and came through Ellis Island.

I believe that before the Children arrived, my Grandparents had taken up residence in the boarding house at 203 East Forty-Fifth Street (a building they eventually bought, and it remained in the family until the early 2000s), and that is where my Mother lived until she and my Dad were married in 1925. My Dad lived with his family on the same street in 227.

Around 1923, my Grandparents bought a house on about one hundred acres in North Branch, New Jersey, just outside of Somerville. The house was large and rambling, with a two-story garage and a huge barn. I don't know the purpose of the house before they bought it, but they operated it as a pensione/restaurant. This is where I spent my summers until my midteens.

I always said I had the best of both worlds growing up: New York City life from the day after Labor Day until mid-June, and then barefoot and carefree all summer long. We took the Blue Coach from the Dixie Hotel on West Forty-Second Street, and two hours later, our stop was the Circle Inn on Old Route 17 in the middle of nowhere. No matter when we arrived, Happy, the black-and-white farm mutt, was always at the top of the long road to meet us.

The best things about the farm were the animals, the big barn, and the nearby watering hole.

My Grandfather died in 1943 and a family friend, Frank, was taken on as a working partner to help. Over the years, my Grandmother had chickens, ducks, a goat named Billy, rabbits, Happy, various strays, families of cats, and my favorites: pigs. I loved washing those little pigs and wheeling them around in the wheelbarrow like babies. I stopped naming the piggies once I realized they were not to be seen again when I returned the following season. Fortunately, for a long time, I didn't connect the missing little pigs with sausage and spareribs at the restaurant!

Billy only lasted one year. My Grandmother loved flowers, and they bloomed for her ferociously. However, Billy liked flowers, too, and after one time too many in Grandmother's flower garden, Billy was given away.

What animals my Grandmother didn't have, the neighboring farms did. There were cows I milked, horses I rode, and tractors I rode and later drove while baling hay or plowing the fields for corn.

For many of the years I spent on the farm, my Sisters, Brother, and Cousins were there with me. We spent the days walking the railroad tracks to two watering holes. The first was Silver Bridge, where we shared the creek with the cows (they came down to join us promptly at 4 p.m., and that let us know it was time to head back), and farther away there was a larger body of water deep enough to dive and swim in. The *funny story about Silver Bridge is that in our later years, when we would reminisce about swimming there, we always laughed and asked if the soft creek bottom was mud or if we had been stepping in cow cakes!*

Around the bend from Silver Bridge was Jim Hogan's stable and my favorite one-eyed Old Bob. There, we could rent horses and ride to our heart's content. On his ranch I liked to ride bareback. But off site, there had to be a saddle, and I always chose the one with the shiny silver horn. Old Bob couldn't be ridden, so after a few hugs and kisses, I mounted a gentle palomino and off I went. I've been on a horse since the age of three. When I was at least nine or ten, my Cousin Ric and I would hustle over to Jim Hogan's, muck a few stalls, and we could ride for free. What a deal!

Yes, that was the life. I can still remember flying down the stairs each morning and running straight out the squeaky screen door to the green grass, my animals, and blue skies before my Mother could catch me. Freedom! I could spend a whole day avoiding my Mother. My Father would come from the city each Friday evening, and Happy and I would run up the road to meet him. He always had some little treat in his pocket for me, like two-penny gum Chicklets or a tiny Hershey bar.

Even though I spent so many summers on the farm, I never did get to know my Grandmother Giovanna as intimately as my Little Nonna. My Mother's Mother was a fierce, self-taught cook and businesswoman. She didn't have time to get warm and fuzzy with her Grandchildren, something I didn't understand until I got older, but she did love all of us, and I did love her in a different sort of way.

After my Grandmother passed away, the property was sold and is now only a memory.

Nonna Giovanna and her chickens, 1940s

La cucina piccola fa la casa grande
(A little kitchen makes a large house)

Maria Graci Augello

My Mother-in-Law was a superb cook who could do wonders on this little stove in a tiny kitchen without modern conveniences. Today, when I am trying to organize a meal for our family dinners, I think back in amazement and marvel at what she did accomplish in that tiny kitchen on that little stove. I often watched her cook, sort of like private cooking lessons.

Before we were married, Charlie moved to Maryland after graduation to accept a position with Westinghouse. I stayed behind in New York and would have dinner with my soon-to-be In-Laws every Wednesday. I felt very comfortable making these weekly visits, because I had known them since my early teens and ate lunch with them on many a Sunday. From the first time my Mother-in-Law and I met, she was my biggest supporter. Charlie never had a chance. She raised four Children: Charlie's oldest Sister, May; Brother, Vinnie; Sister, Ann; and yes, Charlie was the baby, and she always lovingly referred to Charlie as "the baby."

While waiting for Charlie's Dad, Salvatore, to come home from work, we'd lean out on the windowsill watching for him, and she would tell me stories of life in Castrofillippo and immigrating to America, raising her Children, and life in general. Charlie's Dad was a laborer, so arrival time differed with the weather and the daylight. As soon as we saw him turn the corner, all talking stopped. Water was set to boil, pasta put in the pot, and once he had washed up and changed, his food was in front of him, always with his favorite fork and with great precision.

After dinner and a hot espresso (I could write a short story just about the coffee ritual), off he went to meet friends or play bocce at the courts by the United Nations on First Avenue and Forty-Second Street. Mama and I would continue cleaning up, and then I would accompany her as she walked to Holy Family Church, and I would continue on to meet friends or go home.

It was a beautiful time that I have come to appreciate more and more. I try to repeat stories about my Mother-in-Law to our Children, and hope maybe someday they will understand and repeat them. Unfortunately, they didn't have a chance to know her. What I saw in her was a loving Grandmother, and I hope I have achieved a little of this quality. But, mostly she was a wonderful Mother-in-Law, even before she was officially my Mother-in-Law, and I hope I have achieved a little of that quality, too.

Such a sweet Mother-in-Law.
She was always "Mama" to me.

Dad and me, summer of 1941

My Dad

My Father was born in Montefollonico, a small medieval village in the province of Siena, Italy. As a young boy, he immigrated to America with his family and settled in New York on Forty-Fifth Street between Second and Third Avenues. The family traveled steerage and entered through Ellis Island. Coincidentally, when my Mother immigrated to America, her family also settled on Forty-Fifth Street, and that is where they met and eventually married in 1925. But, a lot transpired during the years in between.

My paternal Grandfather was a wine-and-vinegar merchant. My Dad, as young as ten, would go to the livery, rig the horse to the wagon, and deliver wine and vinegar as far as 125th Street and collect the money. My paternal Grandmother, Little Nonna, told me this story herself, so I know it to be true. She said that in cold weather, she would fill a gallon jug with hot water and cover his legs with a blanket, and place the jug underneath to keep him warm.

My Grandfather depended on my Dad to the point that when my Father's dream of becoming a New York City policeman became a reality, he was told he could not accept. As the oldest son, his place was in the business, so that his two younger Brothers could be educated and eventually go on to medical school. I know my Dad was heartbroken, but he had no choice. He served in the US Army, and when he returned, my Grandfather had or would purchase two brownstones on Forty-Third Street. One would be given to my Dad for his part in the business. And, it was in that house, 338, where my Sisters, my Brother, and I were raised.

I know my Dad held many jobs to keep things going and spent long hours away from home. He ran a speakeasy called the Scribes Club with my Grandfather. He later owned a bar and then a restaurant on Forty-Fifth Street called Gus and Eddy's. He would leave early in the morning and come home late at night. By the time I was born, or maybe a little older, things settled down a little, and maybe that is why Dad and I were able to spend time together—time he could not spend with my Sisters and, for different reasons, with my Brother. Dad and I had a special bond, and we shared secrets and confidences.

If we were not going to New Jersey to my Grandmother Giovanna's farm, the two of us had Sunday outings. Together, we went to Yankee Stadium and ate Nedick's hot dogs ("Don't tell your Mother,") or to Ebbets Field to watch the "Bums," or to Coney Island to ride the wooden horses at the Steeplechase or the Parachute Drop. My Dad loved those "Bums," but when they left Brooklyn for California, he declared them traitors and never watched them again. He rooted for the Mets. Try as I might, I never could convert him to a Yankees fan!

Most Sundays we went to Central Park, where I would ride on the beautiful carousel. Dad would stand patiently at the rail and wave to me as I rode around trying to grab that elusive brass ring. We rode the Third Avenue trolley going, but always walked home. I was always anxious to get to the park; not so much to getting home! Walking home, we stopped at Cummings Bar, where I sat on the counter ("Don't tell your Mother,") eating cherries placed on the picks that resembled seals, complete with red balls balanced on their noses. Yes, many of our dates ended with "And don't tell your Mother." Yes, our secret.

Not all women are meant to be Mothers, and my Mother was one of those women. So, in the uncertain world of growing up with an overbearing Mother whose temperament and constricted rules changed with the weather, my Dad always offered the warmth and love that made me feel secure and happy. One thing my Mother was never able to threaten me with was "Wait until your Father comes home." Whenever possible, I would crawl up on his lap, and he would tell me made-up stories. I would tell him I wanted to marry him when I grew up, and he would call me sweetheart and tell me I would marry my Prince Charming. He was right!

I always felt that my Father was a good dancer, and I fondly remember the several times I danced with him—always a waltz. The first time I vividly remember our dancing was at a family wedding. I was eight or nine, and he twirled me around the floor like a princess. The last time was at my wedding—a beautiful last dance to remember with my Dad. Today, the waltz is still my favorite dance.

I shared his interest in sports and cooking, and some bits of local news, and always greeted him with a hug and a kiss. While I forever feared the wrath of my Mother, my goal was to never hurt or embarrass *my Father and always strive to please him and make him proud of me. For whatever reason, my siblings didn't have the window of opportunity I had, but it was mine, and I embraced it and have wonderful memories.*

Dad and me, graduation day 1957

Little Nonna and Nonno, circa mid-1930s

My Little Nonna, Agnese Del Mecio Sandroni

My Father's Mother, Nonna Agnese, was a tiny little woman, and she lived next door in 336 with my two Uncles and their families. Our two houses were connected by a door in the cellar or through the door in the backyard and, of course, the front doors. It was almost like one big house, because we had so many meals together. I don't think she ever weighed more than eighty pounds, if that, and reached only four feet ten inches in height. I always remember her in high-button shoes, long dresses, an apron, and her long gray hair neatly tied up in a bun.

She was a loving Grandmother, soft spoken, who raised three fine Sons and then a bunch of Grandchildren. Nonna lived next door, so I was very fortunate to be able to see her often, probably every day in my early years, and spend time with her. Sometime in my teen years, 336 was sold and Little Nonna went to live with my Uncle Bob, a doctor and her youngest son, on Long Island. She would come back to spend time with us or we would travel by subway to visit her. I feel certain that Little Nonna was the person most responsible for instilling Italian traditions in our families, and for that I am most thankful.

She only spoke Italian, so it was only with her that I spoke Italian. In our house, my Dad made sure we only spoke English, because he wanted us to go to school without any problems—problems he encountered until he left in the sixth grade—of a language barrier. But, to Little Nonna, it was only Italian.

Nonna was a wonderful, inventive cook who could make the most delicious meals with the simplest of ingredients. Her bread soup is a prime example. Especially during the war, she was always able to prepare something tasty with only a handful of ingredients. Whenever I see a spool of kitchen twine, I fondly remember she once knitted me a pair of socks out of white kitchen twine, because she knew we shouldn't wear shoes in the house, and these would keep my feet warmer than my cotton socks when I had no slippers.

She had a mean old cat named Topsy who loved to hide on the top shelf of the hall cabinet and attack me (and probably everyone else). Mostly, Topsy would swat the top of my head or paw my long braids as I passed by. One little scream, and out would come Nonna with the broom.

As I recall, Nonna didn't have a washing machine, but I do remember her washing clothes in the basement sink when it wasn't being used to soak baccalà! In nice weather, the clothes were hung out on a line that stretched across the yard from the kitchen window on the second floor to a very tall pole. There were four kitchens in the two houses, so most days—but never on Sunday—our clothes were sent out for all to see. When the weather wasn't cooperating, laundry was hung in the cellar.

Nonna lived to the age of ninety-four. I was in my teens when she passed away. I once asked her if it was fun to live so long to see so many changes. Nonna said she had to live many years without her Husband, and also buried a Son and a few other family members. That was the end of that discussion.

Nonno Ugo passed away just before I was three from malaria, which he developed while serving in the Italian Army in some obscure country. But, I do remember sitting on his lap and him giving me a chocolate-covered mint wrapped in silver paper after I recited a little poem.

Nonna went to sleep one night with a cold, and that was that and the way it should have been for someone so sweet and loving. I had never realized how much I would miss her. Somehow, when you are young, you think everything is eternal.

La buona salute e' la vera ricchezza
(Good health is true wealth)

Some Thoughts from Charlie

Being first-generation Italian, I was able to drink wine at a very early age during dinner with family. The wine for Children was a blend of Poppa's homemade red wine, Zinfandel, with cream soda. My Dad made wine religiously every autumn, usually starting the process around Columbus Day in the cellar at 321. My contribution to this process was to scrape the inside of barrels before the crush, and break up the wine crates to be used as kindling in our coal stove in the kitchen of our railroad apartment upstairs! At dinner, red wine was always on the table with our main meal, regardless of what variety of food was being served, and it always tasted good.

My Father also did make a very good white wine that my Wife enjoyed, remembers, and still raves about. Enshrined in one of our kitchen cabinets is a dusty bottle of his white wine—totally undrinkable today, but Anita likes to uncork it and let the aroma bring back a good memory!

Today, we are more knowledgeable about "tasting" wine, and pairing wine with food does make a difference to some people's palates. There are many references and guides that offer food-and-wine pairings. We all have had the experience of listening to a person presenting a wine prior to tasting, describing the nuances of the wine right down to the various flavors, weight, etc. However, when you took your first sip, your thoughts were, Really, I don't like this wine. So, who is the one to determine the perfect match? Yes, YOU are! Don't be apprehensive about making another selection. Don't concentrate too much on pairings. Drink what you enjoy.

There are some basic guidelines that might help, such as keeping flavors in balance (for example, mild foods with mild wines, or big flavors with big, bold, flavorful wines). Remember, what you like to drink takes precedence, regardless of the cost or the rating. Contributing undoubtedly to the enjoyment of wine is your mood, the ambiance, and family and the friends who are sharing the wine with you.

In Italy, always consumed with food are not only the reds and whites, but also the sparkling wines, such as Lambrusco and Prosecco, which go especially well with the salume and cheeses, as well as some desserts. Also, it is served to guests prior to the start of the meal.

Importantly, a good meal is meant to be more than delicious food or a great wine. A good meal is sitting around the table, sharing a meal cooked with love with those you love, and embracing the moment.

One of my favorite expressions about enjoying wine is *"**Life is too short to drink bad wine!**"*

Salute!

Sandroni home for well over one hundred years

Via della Madonnina 9
Montefollonico

One enters the small hamlet of Montefollonico by one of three archways: Porta di Follonico, Porta del Triano, or Porta del Pianello. Once inside the ancient walls of fired brick, one finds narrow and winding cobblestone streets, quaint houses, and a friendly medieval-style village seemingly trapped in a time warp. The first evidence of the area being inhabited goes back roughly 60,000 years because of the discovery of Lithic tools (believed to belong to the Neanderthal man) found in the area of the now-public park "II Tondo." However, the town's real development began somewhere in the 1100s.

Montefollonico sits in resplendent isolation majestically on top of a hill between Val d'Orcia and the Val di Chiana valleys southeast of Siena, Italy. The views are verdant, sweeping, and grand; a picture-perfect postcard image of rolling hills, olive groves, and vineyards. The people are very proud of their heritage and traditions. Their dialect is Sienese.

For a village that might never have had more than nine hundred residents, there are a surprising number of churches. Not all are in use on a regular basis. Chiesa di Triano (pictured on the cover of this book) is said to be built in 1609, and opens only on August 15 to celebrate the Assumption of the Blessed Virgin Mary (ferragosto). Oratorio della Compagna was built in 1640, while the Church of St. Bartolomeo was built in the eleventh century. One only opens at Christmas to display a large nativity scene.

Of greatest familial interest is Pieve di San Leonardo, built in the thirteenth century in the heart of the village. It is there where my Grandparents were married, possibly even baptized. My Father was baptized there, and with the help of my Cousin Lorenzo and the parish priest, I searched church records to record for my family the births and baptisms of many family members.

San Leonardo was built by Cistercian or Benedictine monks. The monks were known as "fullones" ("wool workers" in Latin), thus providing the village its name, Mons a Fullonica, later changed to Montefollonico. There is also a very small brick building that once was Chiesa di Santa Anna, built in the 1800s. It sits deconsecrated on a dirt road that was once surrounded by farmland.

One that has become of great interest to me is Conventaccio L'abbazia di Santa Maria a follonica on Strade del Vin Santo. Built in the 1100s as a Benedictine monastery, it is now reduced to ruins, but quite amazing to view. The original structure had a basilica with three naves. Of the original stone structure, in addition to the base of the bell tower, remains only a perimeter wall in which there are two portals and three pass arches. Its fortitude never ceases to amaze me. It seems to call out to me, and I have to walk to it every time I am in Montefollonico and take more pictures.

Montefollonico is lovingly referred to as the Town of Vin Santo. Enter any of the local homes and be warmly greeted with "Lo gradireste un goccio de Vin Santo?" ("Would you like a drop of Vin Santo?") This will most likely be followed with an offering of Cantuccini or Cantucci, a small, hard almond cookie used for dipping.

Vin Santo, traditionally bottled in November on All Saints' Day, is a delicious sweet wine served in small doses in small glasses. My Grandparents considered it a panacea for a variety of illnesses. Making Vin Santo is a labor of love. Each year there is a festival to honor Vin Santo, and the battle is on to claim the title of first prize for the best wine made that year. I can proudly report that several times my Cousin Andrea was the first- and also the second-prize winner. When we visit, he thankfully gives us a bottle or two, which I savor both for the taste and the fact that it comes from the town where my Father, Grandfather, and many other relatives were born. I remember my Grandfather making wine in wooden barrels in the basement of 336. He also made vinegar. But, I doubt that he ever could have made Vin Santo there.

Montefollonico, as small as it is, boasts several good restaurants, including a five-star restaurant housed in an old stone farmhouse and former mill. Via della Madonnina 9, in more recent years, was the home of my Cousins Andrea, Cristina, and their boys, Lorenzo (who is now a doctor and, thus, carrying out a Sandroni family tradition) and twins Riccardo and Roberto. It is in this house that I have enjoyed some of the most delicious meals.

Andrea has lovingly remodeled the house where my Father once lived just before immigrating to America. After he left, he would return many times, especially in his later years, as did my Mother. It had served for many years as a pensione named Pensione Anna operated by Mary and Giacomo (my Father's First Cousin) and later their Daughter-in-Law, Iris, and their Son, Dino, my Cousin Andrea's parents.

It gives me immense pleasure to visit this charming little hamlet. It gives me the greatest pleasure knowing that every day I can walk down a path that has thousands of years of history, and these are the very paths that my Grandparents, ancestors, and my Dad have traveled on, and when I am there and visualize walking on the same cobblestones as my Father did so long ago, I can sometimes feel his presence. It helps me to know who I am. It's just like being home.

Ruins of the Benedictine monastery built in the 1100s

Breakfast

Breakfast Coffee Cake

Topping:

1 Cup Walnut Pieces – chopped	⅓ Cup Flour
½ Cup Sugar	⅓ Cup Light Brown Sugar – packed
2 tsps Cinnamon	¼ tsp Nutmeg
1 tsp Kosher Salt	5 Tbs Butter – unsalted, melted

Line a baking sheet with parchment paper or wax paper and set aside. In a medium bowl, stir together walnuts, flour, sugars, cinnamon, nutmeg, and salt. Stir it just enough to form little clumps. Carefully sprinkle the topping onto the baking sheet and refrigerate while making the cake.

Cake:

½ Stick Butter – unsalted plus extra for pan	1 Cup Sugar
2 Eggs – room temperature	2 Cups Flour
1 tsp Baking Powder	1 tsp Baking Soda
1 tsp Kosher Salt	1 Cup Sour Cream
½ Cup Yogurt	

Butter the interior of a 9-inch cake pan and preheat oven to 350°.

In the bowl of an electric mixer, using the whisk attachment, beat the butter and sugar together on medium-high speed for about 8–9 minutes, until light and creamy. Scrape down the inside of the bowl occasionally while beating to make sure all is incorporated. Lower the speed and add the eggs one at a time.

Sift together the flour, baking powder, and baking soda. In a separate bowl, whisk together the salt, sour cream, and yogurt until very smooth. With the mixer on low, alternate adding the flour mixture and the sour-cream mixture to the butter-cream mixture. Again, scrape down the sides of the bowl to make sure everything is well combined.

Transfer the batter to the prepared baking pan, tapping it gently on the countertop to make sure it is evenly distributed and free of air bubbles. Remove the topping from the refrigerator and sprinkle all over the top of the cake, breaking up any very large clumps.

Bake for 55–60 minutes, or until a cake tester comes out clean. Cool in pan for 15–20 minutes before carefully removing it. If you can, make a sling with buttered parchment paper by lining the pan and leaving a 3-inch overlap on each side. Use the sling to remove the cake from the pan without disturbing the topping too much. Or, you can just cut into squares and serve from the pan.

Egg Soufflé Holiday Casserole

Our Traditional Christmas Morning Breakfast

1 Lb Sweet Italian Sausage or Breakfast Sausage – cooked and drained
8–10 Slices White Bread – cubed
4 Cups Milk

10 Ozs Grated Monterey Jack, Mozzarella, or Cheddar Cheese
8 Eggs
Pinch of Salt

Spray a 9" x 13" baking dish with Pam. Arrange sausage on bottom of pan, breaking up into clumps. Top with cubed bread. Sprinkle grated cheese over this. In blender, add eggs, salt, and milk. Blend well and pour over all in baking dish. Cover and refrigerate overnight. Place in cold oven and cook uncovered at 350° for 45 minutes until top is brown and all is nice and puffy.

Note: On Christmas morning we always had this with a blueberry breakfast bake. I still make a pan, and the family indulges as they come over for our marathon present-opening (we number 20 and growing), even though they might have made this at home for their own family breakfast.

French Toast Bake

½ Cup Melted Butter (1 stick)
1 Cup Brown Sugar
1 Loaf of Thickly Sliced Bread
4 Eggs

1½ Cups Milk
1 tsp Vanilla
Powdered Sugar for Sprinkling

Melt butter in microwave and add brown sugar. Stir until mixed. Pour butter/sugar mix into bottom of 9" x 13" pan and spread around. Beat eggs, milk, and vanilla. Lay single layer of Texas toast in pan. Spoon 1/2 of egg mixture on bread layer. Add second layer of Texas toast. Spoon on remaining egg mixture. Cover and chill in fridge overnight.

Bake at 350° for 45 minutes (covered for the first 30 minutes). Sprinkle with powdered sugar. Serve with warm maple syrup and your favorite toppings.

Fruit Cobbler

The Easiest Cobbler to Make

2 Cups Pioneer Biscuit Mix
2 Cups Sugar
2 Cups Whole Milk
2 Eggs – lightly beaten

¼ Cup Butter – melted and cooled 21 Oz
Can Fruit Pie Filling – your choice
½ tsp Cinnamon
Additional Sugar for Dusting

Preheat oven to 350°. Lightly grease a 9″ x 12″ baking dish (glass works best). Combine biscuit mix and sugar in a large bowl. Add milk and eggs and mix well—about 50 to 60 strokes. Pour batter into prepared baking dish. Pour melted butter evenly over surface. Spoon pie filling on top and sprinkle with cinnamon and sugar. Bake for 50–60 minutes until brown on top. When still warm, sprinkle with additional sugar or a mixture of sugar and cinnamon.

Note: This is another one of our Christmas breakfast favorites. It is also a great brunch cobbler and delicious when served as a dessert with ice cream.

Hummingbird Pancakes

1½ Cups Flour
½ tsp Salt
1½ Cups Buttermilk
½ Cup Crushed Pineapple – drained
3 Tbs Canola Oil
Sliced Fresh Bananas – for serving

2 tsps Baking Powder
½ tsp Cinnamon
1 Cup Mashed Ripe Bananas
⅓ Cup Sugar
1 Egg – lightly beaten
½ Cup Pecans – toasted and chopped

Stir together flour, baking powder, salt, and cinnamon in a large bowl. Whisk together buttermilk, mashed ripe bananas, crushed pineapple, sugar, beaten egg, and canola oil. Gradually stir this mixture into the flour mixture just until all the ingredients are moist and combined. Do not overmix or the pancakes will not be light and fluffy. Fold in the toasted pecans.

On a preheated hot griddle, pour ¼ cup of batter and cook until little bubbles form on top. Turn and repeat on other side. Place cooked pancakes on an ovenproof plate and keep warm in a 200° oven while cooking the remaining pancakes.

Note: This recipe makes about 16–18 pancakes.

Italian Cream Pancakes

What a Great Way to Start a Sunday Morning!

⅔ Cup Pecans – finely chopped
2 Cups Flour
1 tsp Baking Powder
Pinch of Salt
¼ Cup Heavy Cream
2 tsps Vanilla Extract

½ Cup Flaked Coconut – sweetened
⅓ Cup Sugar
½ tsp Baking Soda
1 Cup Buttermilk
2 Tbs Butter – melted
2 Eggs – separated

Preheat oven to 350°. Bake pecans and coconut in a single layer on a baking sheet until lightly toasted. Halfway through baking, give them a stirring so that they will bake evenly.

Stir together flour, sugar, baking powder, baking soda, and salt, all in a large bowl. In a separate bowl, whisk together buttermilk, egg yolks, heavy cream, and 2 Tbs melted butter. Gradually stir the buttermilk mixture into the flour mixture. Stir just until all is moistened. Do not overstir or the pancakes will not be soft and tender. You want the batter to be a little lumpy. Stir in toasted pecans and coconut. Beat egg whites with an electric mixer until stiff peaks form. Fold into the batter and let batter rest for about 10 minutes.

Pour ¼ cup of batter onto a preheated hot, buttered griddle. Cook for 3–4 minutes or until the tops of the pancakes have bubbles and the edges are getting slightly toasted. Turn and cook for an additional 3–4 minutes or until they are cooked in the middle and not runny. Place in a single layer on a baking sheet in a warm oven. Serve with the following recipe for a Cream Cheese Syrup or your favorite syrup.

Cream Cheese Syrup

4 Oz Cream Cheese – room temperature
¼ Cup Maple Syrup
1 Cup Powdered Sugar

¼ Cup Butter – room temperature
½ tsp Almond Extract – or to taste
¼ Cup Milk

Beat the cream cheese with the butter, maple syrup, and almond extract at medium speed until light and creamy. Gradually add 1 cup powdered sugar, and continue beating until all combined and smooth. Gradually add ¼ cup milk and beat until all is smooth. This is better served warm when poured over the pancakes.

Mennonite Cinnamon Bread

A Great Breakfast Bread

Batter:

1 Cup Butter – softened
2 Eggs
4 Cups Flour

2 Cups Sugar
2 Cups Buttermilk
2 tsps Baking Soda

Cinnamon/Sugar Mixture:

⅔ Cup Sugar

2 tsps Cinnamon

Preheat oven to 350°. Lightly grease and flour two bread pans.

Cream together butter, two cups sugar, and eggs. Add buttermilk, flour, and baking soda, and mix in well. Put **half** of the batter into greased loaf pans (¼ in each pan). In a separate bowl, mix together ⅔ cup sugar and 2 tsps of cinnamon. Sprinkle ¾ cinnamon mixture on top of the **half** batter in each pan. Add remaining batter to pans and sprinkle with the rest of cinnamon topping. Make sure to use a knife to swirl it in a little. Bake for 45–50 minutes. Let cool in pans for about 20 minutes before removing.

New York Crumb Buns

This Is Definitely a Recipe from Aunt May That We Have Enjoyed for Many Years

3 Eggs – large
3 Cups Flour – all purpose
1 Cup Milk
1 Cup Sugar

¼ Lb Crisco
4 tsps Baking Powder
2 tsps Vanilla
Crumb Topping

Cream together Crisco and sugar, add eggs one at a time, and beat until creamy. Add dry ingredients with milk and vanilla, starting with dry and ending with milk. Pour batter into a 10" x 15" baking pan lined with parchment paper and slightly greased. Sprinkle with Crumb Topping.

Crumb Topping:

½ Lb Butter – melted and slightly cooled
2½–3 Cups Flour – all purpose
⅓ Cup Light Brown Sugar
⅓ Cup Dark Brown Sugar

1 Cup White Sugar
1½ Tbs Cinnamon
Powdered Sugar for Dusting

Aunt May's sugar shaker

Mix dry ingredients and blend with cooled butter using a fork. Grasp by handfuls and crumble on top of batter. Bake at 350° for 30–40 minutes. Cool and sprinkle with powdered sugar. Cut into large squares.

This was a Sunday morning treat, if I was given money to go to Hanscom Bakery on Second Avenue somewhere between Forty-First and Forty-Second on the east side of the avenue. I would buy a half-dozen crumb buns after 9:00 Mass (try sitting through Mass with an empty stomach, thinking of crumb buns). Remember, my Mother didn't bake, so this was a real treat and didn't happen very often.

Piedmontese Cornmeal Cake

A Breakfast Treat down on the Farm

1¼ Cups Flour
½ Cup Polenta – fine yellow cornmeal
2 tsps Baking Powder
1½ Sticks Unsalted Butter – softened
1 Cup Sugar

5 Eggs – separated
2 tsps Lemon Zest – grated
½ tsp Nutmeg
Pinch of Salt – to taste
Powdered Sugar for Dusting

Sift together the flour, cornmeal, and baking powder. In a large bowl, beat the butter with an electric mixer until light and fluffy, gradually adding the sugar. Beat in egg yolks, one at a time, beating well after each addition. Add vanilla, lemon zest, nutmeg, and beat. Set aside.

In another bowl, beat the egg whites with a little salt until light and fluffy. Increase to high speed and beat until soft peaks form. Gently fold the egg whites into the egg mixture. Carefully fold in the dry ingredients, making sure they are well incorporated. Pour the batter into an 8-inch springform pan that has been greased and floured. Smooth top, and tap pan on counter a few times to eliminate any air bubbles.

Bake 35–40 minutes or until a tester inserted in the center comes out clean. Cool in pan on wire rack for 10 minutes. Loosen edges with a sharp knife, and release spring and unmold. Cool completely on wire rack. Sprinkle with powdered sugar just before serving.

My Grandmother was an excellent and very traditional cook. She didn't bake very fancy desserts, and she didn't bake often, but this was one of the things she enjoyed baking. Maybe it reminded her of a time past! But, we all enjoyed it, mostly for breakfast. My Grandmother surely did not have a springform pan, so I guess, as she did, you can use an 8-inch pan that has been greased and floured with parchment on the bottom. I haven't tried that. I'm sticking with my springform.

Appetizers

Baked Clams Oregano

2 Dozen Clams – rinsed well
¼ Cup Olive Oil
1 Garlic Clove – minced
1 tsp Chopped Fresh Parsley

1 Cup Breadcrumbs – seasoned or
unseasoned
2 Tbs Grated Parmesan Cheese
Salt and Pepper to Taste

Open clams over a bowl to save some of the juice. Do not discard the shells. Chop the clams and combine them with the remaining ingredients, adding enough strained juice to moisten slightly and add a little more clam flavor. Pile a small amount of mixture firmly on a clam shell. Set all the filled shells on a baking sheet. If looking a bit dry, sprinkle with a little more olive oil. Place under the broiler until crumbs brown nicely and are crisp.

This is most surely a recipe from our West Milford days. It was definitely an expected appetizer at our house, and we always served it during our shrimp/clam/chicken-boil parties. If you prefer Romano cheese, that works, too.

Bonati

Sausage, Olive, and Spinach Loaf

1 Lb Pkg of Fresh Pizza Dough
1 Lb Mild Italian Sausage – casing removed
1 (9 Oz) Pkg of Spinach – fresh and well rinsed
1 Large Onion – chopped
2 Cups Fresh Mozzarella – shredded
⅓ Cup Grated Italian Cheese – Romano or Parmesan

Salt, Pepper, and Garlic Powder to Taste
2 Cups Pitted Kalamata Olives – sliced (or Sicilian Oil Cured Olives – pitted and sliced)
1 Egg – beaten lightly with a few drops of water
Poppy Seeds – optional

Let pizza dough rest on a lightly floured pastry board, covered, for about 30 minutes until ready to use. Preheat oven to 350°. Cook the sausage until browned, but not too dry, in a few tablespoons of olive oil. Crumble with wooden spoon as it cooks, and then remove to a paper-towel-lined plate to drain. In the same pan, add a little more olive oil, and cook the onions until soft. Season with salt, pepper, and garlic powder. Stir and add the spinach. Cook until the spinach is wilted, and then stir all together. Add the grated cheese, olives, and the shredded mozzarella, and mix well.

Roll out the dough on a lightly floured surface into a 14" x 12" rectangle. Spread the cooked mixture down the center of the dough, keeping a border at all sides and ends. Roll up like a jelly roll, starting with the long end. Pinch the end seams to seal, and tuck under. Place seam-side down on a baking sheet lined with parchment paper. Brush with the beaten egg. Sprinkle poppy seeds, if using, and bake for 20 to 30 minutes until the top is golden brown. Let cool slightly before slicing.

This is a recipe adapted from my Mother-in-Law. A little has been lost in the translation, and freshly made dough would have been used instead of store-bought. Also, instead of one long loaf, my Mother-in-Law would make several small ones, 5 or 6 inches long. When she made these at Christmastime, she would make dozens in a small kitchen without modern appliances.

Farina Dolce

A Recipe from Berta's Chateau

1 Quart Whole Milk
6 tsps Sugar
1 Orange Rind – grated or zested
Unseasoned Breadcrumbs
¾ Cup Cream of Farina

1 Lemon Rind – grated or zested
2 tsps Butter
2 Eggs
Salt to Taste

Boil milk with sugar, pinch of salt, grated lemon, and orange rinds. Add the farina and stir, using a whisk constantly to prevent lumping. Lower heat after a few minutes and continue to cook for about 4 minutes until it has thickened.

Remove from the stove. Add the butter, a pinch of salt, and stir until well blended. Pour onto a greased cookie sheet, pat down, and let cool.

When cooled, slice into 1-inch strips. Dip in flour, eggs, and breadcrumbs, and deep fry in a heavy pot or electric fryer until golden brown. Oil should register about 375°. Do not add too many at a time, or the oil will cool, and they will not crisp and turn golden.

Berta's Chateau is a charming little restaurant in Wanaque, New Jersey, with a delicious menu of Italian food served in a friendly and cozy setting. We frequented there often when we lived in West Milford, New

Jersey, and always ordered Berta's Farina Dolce. It was started in 1925 by Santina and Pietro Berta in what was once a carriage house, and we were happy to learn recently that it is still in operation and celebrated their ninetieth anniversary. I'm not at all surprised. They were kind enough to share this recipe, which I am so pleased to have.

Mozzarella Marinara

1 Lb Fresh Mozzarella	1 Can (28 Oz) Italian Plum Tomatoes
2–3 Oz Fine Breadcrumbs	2–3 Garlic Cloves
¾ Cup Olive Oil	8 Fresh Basil Leaves
1 Egg – well beaten	Salt and Ground Pepper to Taste

In a frying pan, add ¼ cup of olive oil, garlic, and tomatoes (that have been pulsed in the blender for about 3–5 seconds), and cook all together for about 10 minutes. At the same time, in another frying pan, pour in the remainder of the oil. Slice the mozzarella into 4 nice slices about 1½-inches thick. Flour them, dip into the beaten eggs, and coat with the breadcrumbs.

Fry the breaded mozzarella in very hot oil. As soon as they get a nice golden color, turn and do the same on the other side. Serve at once on a plate with salt and freshly ground black pepper, and top with the tomato sauce and fresh basil. You can use either flavored or unflavored breadcrumbs—your choice.

Olive Bruschetta

1½ Cups Black Olives – pitted	⅓ Cup Extra Virgin Olive Oil
1 Garlic Clove – minced	24–30 Italian Baguette Slices – cut in ½"
1 tsp Dried Oregano	rounds and toasted
Pinch of Salt – or to taste	

Finely chop the olives and combine with the minced garlic. Stir in the olive oil, oregano, and salt in a small bowl and set aside. When ready to serve, spread about a tablespoon of the mixture on each toasted round, and serve.

Onion Pie

Preheat oven to 350°. Smear 6 Tbs of softened butter all over a 10-inch pie plate. Crush one full sleeve, plus about 6 crackers more, of Ritz crackers. Pour these into the buttered dish and press hard to make a fairly firm crust. Fry 2 cups of thinly sliced onions in 2 Tbs of butter for about 3–5 minutes, until soft. Take off heat and mix in 1½ cups Swiss cheese (actually, you can use any cheese you like, but this seems to work best), 2 eggs beaten until frothy, 1 cup milk, and salt and pepper to taste. Carefully pour all this into the pie shell, and bake for 1 hour, or until the top is golden brown. Let sit for 5 minutes before serving.

Note: This is one of my go-to recipes when I need an appetizer quick and easy.

Pizza Rustica

A Deep-Dish Meat-and-Cheese Pie

4 Eggs – large

1½ Lbs Italian Sweet Sausage – casing removed, cooked, and coarsely chopped

1 Chunk Mortadella – about 1-inch thick, coarsely chopped

1 Chunk Soppressata – about 1-inch thick, coarsely chopped

½ Cup Grated Parmesan Cheese

¾ Lb Mozzarella – cut into small cubes or shredded

½ tsp Sugar

Salt and Pepper to Taste

Preheat oven to 400°. Beat ricotta with the eggs by hand until smooth. Add remaining ingredients and mix well. Pour into a 9-inch springform pan lined with the pasta frolla. Recipe follows.

Pasta Frolla:

2 Cups Sifted Flour

¼ Cup Sugar

2 tsps Baking Powder

¼ Lb Butter – cubed

2 Eggs – large

1 Egg Yolk – beaten

Pinch of Salt

On a lightly floured board, combine flour, sugar, salt, and baking powder. Using your fingers, break the butter into the flour until the flour is meaty. Make a well in the center and break the eggs in it, and then beat with a fork in the well. Blend into the flour mixture, knead quickly, and gather into a ball. Set it under a bowl and let it rest for about 10–15 minutes. The dough will be soft and quite sticky, so lightly flour it on both sides as you roll it out. Using about ⅔ of the dough, roll it out to fit the 9-inch springform pan, allowing for a ½-inch hangover. Pour the cheese-and-meat mixture into the dough-lined pan. Roll out the remainder of the dough and place on top of the pan to cover completely, with a little overhang. Press the edges together as you would a pie crust, and then press down with the tines of a fork. Make some slits in the top crust to allow steam to escape. Brush the top with the beaten egg yolk. If necessary, thin the yolk with a little water. Place in oven and bake for 15 minutes. Reduce heat to 325° and cook for 45–50 minutes longer until the top crust is golden brown. Turn off the oven and let the pizza remain inside until cooled down. To serve, cut into small squares. This is better the next day and at room temperature.

Note: This is how this recipe was originally given to me—just jotted down in pencil on a piece of paper. It was before food processors, but I make the dough in my processor. Because this is a favorite, when I do make it around the holidays, I usually double the recipe and make two pizzas and freeze one. You can cut it up in small portions and freeze. Also, you can use any assortment of Italian cold cuts that you prefer. I have had it with cooked, chopped onions and roasted red peppers, which give it a totally different taste.

Ratatouille Pie

1 Cup Chopped Zucchini
½ Cup Chopped Tomato
½ Cup Chopped Onion
⅓ Cup Butter
½ tsp Dried Basil
Freshly Ground Black Pepper
1¼ Cup Milk
¾ Cup Bisquick or Pioneer Baking Mix
1 Cup Chopped Eggplant

½ Cup Chopped Yellow Pepper
1 Garlic Clove – crushed
1 tsp Salt
½ tsp Dried Oregano
1 Cup Shredded Cheese – your favorite
⅓ Cup Sour Cream – drained
3 Eggs – lightly beaten
¼ Cup Grated Romano Cheese

Preheat oven to 400°. Lightly grease a 10-inch pie dish. Cook zucchini, eggplant, tomato, yellow pepper, onion, and garlic in butter until crisp, but still tender. Stir in seasonings and mix well. Spread out in prepared pie dish (preferably glass) and sprinkle with your preferred cheese.

Add milk, sour cream, eggs, and baking mix to a blender, and blend for 15–20 seconds on high speed. Pour into pie dish, top with grated Romano cheese, and bake for about 30–35 minutes or until a knife inserted in center comes out clean. Let stand 10 minutes before serving, but best served warm.

Ricotta Fritters

1 Cup Fresh Ricotta – drained	**1 Cup Finely Diced Mortadella**
¼ tsp Nutmeg	**3 Tbs Butter – unsalted**
1 Cup Flour	**4 Eggs**
3 Cups Peanut or Canola Oil	**1 Cup Water**

In a medium-sized bowl, whisk together the ricotta, mortadella, and nutmeg, and set aside.

In a medium-sized saucepan, combine 1 cup of water and a pinch of salt, and bring to a boil over high heat. Reduce the heat to medium, add the flour, and stir constantly with a wooden spoon until the mixture is all combined and the dough pulls away from the sides of the pot and forms a ball. This happens fairly quickly, but stirring is important.

Transfer the dough to the bowl of an electric mixer fitted with a paddle. Let the dough cool in the bowl for few minutes, and then, with the mixer on a very low speed, add the eggs one at a time, making sure each egg is fully incorporated before adding the next. Continue mixing until the dough is smooth.

In a medium-sized saucepan or an electric frying pan, heat 2 inches of oil to 375°. A few at a time, fry a walnut-sized spoonful of dough in the oil, turning to evenly brown, until puffed and golden. Keep an eye on the heat to make sure that it does not drop below 375°, or the dough will not crisp and just be soggy.

Using a slotted spoon, transfer the fritters to paper towels to drain and cool. While hot, sprinkle with salt. Allow to cool. Make a slit in each fritter, and fill with about a tablespoon of the cheese mixture. Serve warm.

Clam Fritters

2 (6 Oz) Cans Chopped Clams – undrained
3 Tbs Butter – melted
2 tsp Baking Powder
½ tsp Ground Pepper

2 Eggs
½ Cup Clam Juice – or beer
½ tsp Salt
2 Cups flour

Drain clams, reserving ½ cup of clam juice. Whisk together the juice, eggs, and butter in a small bowl. Stir in the beer. Combine flour, baking powder, salt, and pepper in a large bowl. Whisk in the egg mixture and stir in the clams.

Heat a few inches of vegetable oil in a heavy-duty frying pan. Oil should reach 355–360° to fry properly. Scoop a heaping Tbs of the batter and slide it carefully into the hot oil. (If you dip the spoon in the oil first to cover it, the batter won't stick to the spoon and will slide off easily.) Cook for 3 minutes and turn. Both sides should be golden brown. You can fry them as little balls or flatten them slightly to make more of a little cake. Drain on paper towels. Serve with your favorite hot sauce.

Note: Serve these with Chili Mayonnaise.

Roasted Peppers with Anchovies

8–10 Anchovy Fillets – divided
2 Garlic Cloves – minced
2–3 Leaves Fresh Basil –
    torn into small pieces
3–4 Tbs Capers
Pinch of Dried Oregano
Freshly Ground Pepper to taste

6 Tbs Extra Virgin Olive Oil
1 Bag Fresh Greens – your favorite
Fresh Arugula – a handful
1 Jar Roasted Red Peppers
1 Dozen Black Olives –
    preferably Kalamata

In a medium-sized bowl, whisk together 4 anchovy fillets, garlic, basil, capers, oregano, oil, and pepper, and set aside. On a large platter, arrange the greens, including the arugula and roasted peppers (carefully pull each pepper out of the jar, and if large, just trim into a serving-sized piece), with remaining anchovies spread all around. Set aside to marinate at room temperature for a few hours. Just before serving, scatter the olives on top.

Roquefort Cheesecake with Fig Preserves

1 (8 Oz) Package Roquefort Cheese – chopped

2 (8 Oz) Packages Cream Cheese – softened

½ Cup Walnut Halves

½ Cup Sour Cream – drained

2 Tbs Fresh Chives – chopped

1 Tbs Fresh Parsley – chopped

2 Eggs

2 Tbs Flour

6 Oz Fig Preserves – more or less as needed

Crackers for Serving

Preheat oven to 350°. Bake nuts in a single layer until lightly toasted. Lower oven to 325°.

Beat cream cheese, Roquefort, sour cream, parsley, and chives on medium speed with an electric mixer. Add eggs one at a time, just until well combined. Fold in flour. Spoon mixtures into a lightly greased 7- or 8-inch springform pan. Bake at 325° for 1 hour or until completely set. While still hot, run a knife around the edge of cheesecake to loosen from sides of pan. Let cool in pan on a wire rack for 30 minutes. Cover and chill for 8 hours.

Remove sides of pan and transfer cheesecake to a platter, and spoon preserves over the top. Sprinkle with walnuts that have been very roughly chopped. Serve with crackers of your choice.

Torta Pasqualina

A Recipe from Rodolfo

Filling:

12 Oz Fresh Ricotta – drained

3–4 Tbs Flour

4 Oz Heavy Cream

2 Bunches Fresh Spinach – washed

4 Tbs Parmigiano Cheese – grated

5 Eggs

2 tsps Marjoram

1 Oz Butter

¼ Cup Olive Oil

Salt and Ground Black Pepper

Dough:

8 Oz Flour

1 Tbs Olive Oil

6 Oz Warm Water

Pinch of Salt

In a bowl, mix the flour with the oil, salt, and some of the water. Knead until you have a stretchy, soft dough, and put aside. Sauté the spinach in a skillet. Add the cream, ricotta, flour, a pinch of salt, Parmigiano cheese, marjoram, and 1 well-beaten egg, and mix all together until all combined.

Now, go back to the dough. Split the dough into 4 balls, making 4 very thin sheets of dough (one at a time). Oil a 9" round cake pan, and place one of the pieces of flat dough into it. Brush the top with olive oil and lay another piece of dough on top of the first piece. Pour the filling on top.

Make four holes in the filling and put one egg in each hole with some salt, pepper, and a little grated cheese. You can also add small pats of butter in with each egg. Cover the filling with another thin slice of dough and brush with some olive oil. Lay the last piece on top. Cut the dough around the rim of the pan as you would a pie crust. Brush the top crust with olive oil and bake in a 350° oven for 1 hour. When the torta has finished baking, brush one final time with olive oil and sprinkle with salt. Let cool and serve. Can be eaten hot, warm, or cold — your choice, but delicious however you choose to serve.

Note: Now, nobody in my family does this except me. I like to add some chopped onion (as much as you feel comfortable with) to the hot oil in the skillet and cook a few minutes before adding the spinach and continuing with the rest of the recipe. I think it adds to the flavor nicely.

Tuna and Bean Salad

½ Lb Cannellini Beans – or other dried Italian white beans
2 Garlic Cloves – peeled and crushed
3–4 Sage Leaves
2 (7 Oz) Cans Italian Tuna Packed in Olive Oil – drained

1 Small Red Onion – thinly sliced
Fruity, Good Quality Italian Olive Oil
Salt and Freshly Ground Black Pepper

Rinse the beans and then soak in a large bowl of water for at least 5 hours, or overnight. Drain beans and add to a pot with 6 cups lightly salted, cold water, adding the garlic, sage, and a splash of olive oil. Cover and bring to a simmer over medium heat. Reduce heat a little and continue cooking, partially covered, until the beans are tender but not mushy. This may take between 45 minutes to an hour. Drain the beans and put into a serving bowl with the sage leaves.

Season with salt and pepper, and set aside to let cool. Meanwhile, break the tuna up with a wooden spoon, but do not mash. Add to the beans. Spread onions over all, then drizzle with olive oil and season with salt and pepper. Toss again lightly.

Tuscan Bean Tuna Casserole

2 Cups Dried White Beans – rinsed and
   picked over (about 12 Oz)
⅓ Cup Olive Oil
12 Sage Leaves – fresh
1 Onion – small and finely chopped
5 Garlic Cloves

4–5 Slices of Pancetta – cut into small strips
1 Pinch of Salt
3–4 Tbs Lemon Juice – freshly squeezed
1 Can Italian Tuna – packed in oil and
   drained
Pepper – freshly ground

In a large bowl, soak the rinsed beans overnight in enough cold water to cover. If you can, rinse once or twice before going to bed. When ready to cook, preheat oven to 400°. Drain the beans and rinse well to remove some of the froth that might have accumulated. In a medium-sized casserole, combine the beans with the olive oil, sage, onion, garlic, pancetta, and salt. Mix well. Cover tightly and bake for 1½ hours, stirring once or twice during that time. If beans are not tender, cover and cook a little longer. Do not overcook or you will have mush. Remove from the oven, and stir in the lemon juice and the tuna. Bake uncovered for about ten minutes. Taste before seasoning with salt and pepper.

Note: This is a very Tuscan dish, and one that my Father made often. Instead of pancetta, he would sometimes add a large chunk of salt pork or pork skin. This dish cooks better in a heavy casserole, so I use a Le Creuset pot. It also works well without the tuna.

Uncle Mac's Shrimp

2 Lbs Medium Shrimp
3 Tbs Mayonnaise
6 Drops Tabasco

2 Tbs Curry
1 (8 Oz) Kraft Miracle French Dressing

Rub curry in with mayonnaise. Add French dressing and Tabasco, and beat with an eggbeater or electric hand-mixer until it increases in volume a little. For best results, marinate shrimp for several hours or overnight.

Note: Shrimp have to be steamed, peeled, and deveined. Or, you can buy shrimp already cleaned and cooked to save time. The longer they marinate, the better.

Warm Chickpea Salad

2 Tbs Extra Virgin Olive Oil
1 tsp Fresh Rosemary – diced or pulverized
2 Tbs Chopped Onion
1 Garlic Clove – peeled and chopped
1 tsp Balsamic Vinegar
1–2 Fresh Basil Leaves – torn

2 Cups Canned Chickpeas – rinsed and drained
2 Tbs Fresh Lemon Juice – divided
Salt and Pepper to Taste
Chopped Fresh Parsley for Garnish

Heat oil in a small saucepan. Add rosemary, onion, garlic, vinegar, and bring to a boil. Add chickpeas and 1 Tbs lemon juice, and cook for 5 minutes on medium heat. Stir in torn basil and cook for another minute. Remove from heat, add remaining lemon juice, and taste for salt and pepper. Stir well to make sure everything is combined. Pour into serving dish. Just before serving, garnish with chopped fresh parsley.

Soups

Bolognese Soup

4 Tbs Butter – unsalted
⅓ Cup Semolina Flour – plus some for dusting
4 Large Eggs
2 Cups Grana Padano Cheese – freshly grated
6 Slices Mortadella – finely chopped

1 Tbs Milk
¼ tsp Nutmeg
Sea Salt
5 Cups Chicken Broth – preferably homemade

Heat oven to 400°. Grease and flour 8" x 8" baking dish with butter, and then dust with some semolina flour. Shake out excess. In a large bowl, mix together butter, flour, egg yolks, cheese, mortadella, milk, nutmeg, and a pinch of salt. Stir until it forms a thick batter. In a different bowl, beat egg whites to soft-to-medium peaks. Fold into the egg mixture and pour into the prepared dish. Bake until the top is golden and a tester comes out clean (about 15 minutes). Remove from oven and cool on a wire rack until completely cooled. Run a spatula around the edges to loosen, and then cut into ½-inch cubes (removing them from the pan with a spatula). Add to the broth, and let the broth simmer until the cubes are soft (about 5 or 6 minutes).

Note: I don't know why we called this Bolognese Soup. The recipe was actually given to me from a friend in Lombardia. But, it is really easy, filling, and delicious.

Bread Dumplings Soup

(Canederli)

1–1½ Loaves Italian Bread – cubed (to make 3–3½ cups)
1 Cup Parsley – chopped
6 Eggs – beaten
5–6 Italian Sausage Links – casings removed
1 Cup Flour

6–8 Cups Broth – chicken, beef, or vegetable (or more as needed)
Salt and Pepper – freshly ground, to taste
Grated Cheese – your favorite for garnish

Place bread cubes in large bowl, and add the parsley and beaten eggs. Crumble up the sausage meat and add. Mix well until all the bread is thoroughly coated with the eggs, and then set aside.

Add the flour and one cup of the broth to the mixture, and mix well until it forms sort of a dough, adding more broth if necessary. Break off a small piece of the dough and roll it into a ball about the size of a walnut. Do this until all the little dough balls, or canederli, are formed, placing them on a platter as you go along. Meanwhile, in a large pot, heat up the broth and add the little dough balls carefully, a few at a time. Simmer for about an hour. Taste for salt and pepper, and then ladle into soup bowls and top with grated cheese.

During the war years, when meat was scarce, my Little Nonna (we always referred to this soup as Little Nonna's Bread Soup) would make this, often without the sausage. My Grandmother Giovanna had a farm, so eggs were usually available, and when we could get sausage meat, it was added. Either way, we enjoyed it and never felt deprived.

Canederli

The Italian Knödel

10 Oz Very Stale Bread – cubed
3 Eggs – lightly beaten
3 Tbs Italian Parsley or Basil – minced
3 Tbs Butter – unsalted
1 Onion – finely chopped
¼ tsp Pepper
12 Cups Broth

1 Cup Milk
½ Cup Flour
7 Oz Fontina – diced
1½ Tbs Olive Oil
½ tsp Salt
⅓ tsp Nutmeg – or to taste

Put the stale bread into a large mixing bowl and add the milk, eggs, salt, pepper, and nutmeg. Mix well and then let it rest for at least two hours, covered, in the refrigerator. Stir occasionally to make sure that the mixture is absorbing the liquid.

In the meantime, fry the finely chopped onion in oil and butter, slowly, for about 10 minutes, stirring occasionally. Set them aside to cool.

Remove the milk mixture from the refrigerator and add the flour, parsley or basil, and cheese. Mix gently and then add the cooled onions. Let this mixture rest, covered, for about 30 minutes.

Using your hands, form the canederli by pressing together enough of the mixture to make little balls the size of lemons. You should be able to produce about twenty little balls.

Heat the broth in a large pot and bring to a boil. Using a kitchen spider, carefully lower the canederli, a few at a time, into the stock, and cook for about 12 minutes. To serve, ladle a few in bowls and cover with broth. Pass some extra grated cheese.

Chickpea and Pancetta Soup

Zuppa di Ceci e Pancetta

1½ Cups Dried Chickpeas
  or 1 Can Chickpeas – rinsed
Salt and Pepper – to taste
¼ Cup Olive Oil
1 Large Onion – halved, sliced thin
2 Cups Cherry Tomatoes – halved

1 Sprig Rosemary

8 Cups Chicken Stock
3 Garlic Cloves – chopped
½ Lb Pancetta – cubed
Pinch of Red Pepper Flakes – or to taste

If using dried chickpeas, soak in a bowl filled with cold water for at least 12 hours, or overnight. Drain the chickpeas, and place them in a saucepan with rosemary and enough cold water to cover.

Add 1 Tbs of salt and bring to a boil. Reduce the heat and simmer for two hours. **If using canned chickpeas, skip all that soaking. Just drain and rinse the chickpeas.** Pour the chicken stock into a large pot and bring to a boil. In a saucepan, heat the olive oil and garlic, and sauté over medium heat. Add the onions and pancetta, and sauté until the onions brown, then slowly add the tomatoes, pepper flakes, and continue to sauté.

Once the stock comes to a boil, add the chickpeas and the onion-pancetta mixture. Add a pinch of salt (not too much, because there is salt in the pancetta), and simmer over low heat with the lid partially on for about 30 minutes. If you like a hearty soup, you can add some dry pasta, such as orzo, during the last 10 minutes of cooking. Ladle in soup bowls, sprinkle with a little extra virgin olive oil, and . . . pass the grated cheese for sprinkling!

Escarole Soup and Chicken Meatballs

1 Lb Ground Chicken
½ Cup Seasoned Breadcrumbs
½ Cup Grated Pecorino
½ Cup Grated Parmesan
1 Egg – slightly beaten
½ Cup Olive Oil
3 Garlic Cloves – sliced
2 Medium Onions – thinly sliced

1 Garlic Clove – minced
1 Small Onion – minced
¼ Cup Good White Wine
1 Bunch Parsley – minced
2 Large Heads Escarole – cored and cut
    into 2-inch pieces
8 Cups Chicken Stock – or more as
    needed

Mix chicken, breadcrumbs, grated cheese, ¼ cup oil, minced onion, minced garlic, parsley, salt, pepper, and egg in a bowl, and mix thoroughly. Form into thirty little meatballs and chill.

Heat remaining oil in a large soup pot over medium-high heat. Add the sliced garlic and onions. Cook until lightly browned (about 10 minutes). Add the wine and stir until the aroma of alcohol is gone. Add escarole. Cook until wilted. Add stock, bring to a boil, and then reduce heat to medium-low. Add meatballs and cook until the meatballs are thoroughly cooked, about 30 minutes. Season with salt and pepper.

Note: This soup is good served with crusty Italian bread toasted with a little olive oil, salt, and pepper. Or, you can serve it using cooked rice, pastina, or ditalini.

Italian Clam Chowder

1 Stick Butter – unsalted
4 Tbs Extra Virgin Olive Oil – divided
1 Red Onion – roughly chopped
1 Celery Stalk – chopped
Generous Pinch of Pepperoncini
3 Garlic Cloves – chopped
1 Lb Clams – cleaned and rinsed
1 Cup White Wine
1 Cup Clam Juice

2 Cups Heavy Cream
2 Medium Yukon Gold Potatoes –
    peeled and diced
2 Cups Fresh or Dried Cheese
    Cappelletti
1 Cup Milk
1 Tbs Flour
Chopped Fresh Basil or Parsley for
    Garnish

Melt the butter with 2 Tbs of the olive oil in a large pot over medium heat. Add the onions, celery, salt, pepper, and pepperoncini, and stir. After a few minutes, add the garlic and sauté for about 3 or 4 minutes. Stir constantly and do not let the garlic burn. Add the clams and stir for 2 minutes, and then add the wine. After the alcohol evaporates, add the clam juice. Mix everything well.

When everything starts to bubble, slowly pour in the heavy cream. Add the potatoes and cook for about 20 minutes. When the potatoes are almost done, add the cappelletti and cook on medium heat. Cook for about 10 minutes so that the pasta is al dente. Shortly before the pasta is ready, add 1 cup of milk with 1 Tbs of flour dissolved into it. This will thicken the soup to make it into a thick, creamy chowder. Taste for salt and pepper.

Note: You can substitute a short pasta such as gemelli, farfalle, orecchiette, or even pastina for the cappelletti, if you prefer, to make the soup just a little bit lighter.

Lemon Rice Soup

Minestra di Riso e Limone

6 Cups Beef or Chicken Broth
3 Large Eggs
½–⅔ Cup Arborio Rice

Juice of 1 Lemon – or more to taste
Salt and Pepper to Taste

Place the broth with the butter in a large saucepan and bring to a boil over high heat. When the water has boiled, add a pinch of salt, add the rice, stir a few seconds, and then reduce the heat to medium-low and simmer until the rice is al dente. Do not let the rice get overcooked.

Meanwhile, beat the eggs with a whisk, adding the lemon juice and a light sprinkling of salt and pepper. When the rice is done, stir the egg mixture into the broth, stir a minute or two to make sure all is well combined, and ladle into bowls. At this point, we pass some grated cheese. Either way, your choice.

Note: We all know that the basis for a great soup is a great broth, and the best broth, we also know, is homemade broth. Homemade broth is not difficult to make. It just takes time, but it will make your kitchen smell so good. And, if you take the time to make it, why not make a big batch and freeze most of it to have on hand? But, definitely there are some good store-bought broths out there, if you are pinched for time.

Lentil Soup

3 Tbs Extra Virgin Olive Oil
2½ Cups Onions – chopped
1 Cup Celery – chopped
Celery Leaves – for garnish
1 Cup Carrots – finely chopped
3 Garlic Cloves – chopped

1 Large Potato – cut into small cubes
1 ⅓ Cup Lentils – rinsed and picked over
1 Can (14½ Oz) Diced Tomatoes – with juice
Zest of 1 or 2 Lemons
6–8 Cups Chicken or Vegetable Broth

Heat oil in a large soup pot with a heavy bottom. Add onions, celery, carrots, and garlic. Sauté just until everything begins to brown, stirring often so as not to burn. Add 4 cups of broth, lentils, and the can of tomatoes, including the juice. Slowly bring to a boil and then reduce heat to allow the soup to simmer, just until the lentils are ready (about 30 minutes). Transfer 2 cups of the soup (trying to get mostly the solids) to a blender, and purée until smooth. Return purée to the soup pot. If it is too thick for your taste, you can thin it out by adding a little more broth. Season with salt and freshly ground black pepper. After ladling into bowls, garnish each bowl with a few celery leaves.

Note: Although this is not how my Little Nonna served it, we do add some grated cheese and sprinkle with some extra virgin olive oil over each individual dish.

Macaroni and Beans

Pasta e Fagioli

1½ Cups Dry White Beans
½ Cup Extra Virgin Olive Oil
2 Garlic Cloves – minced
1 Cup Canned Tomatoes – with juice
1 Cup Freshly Grated Cheese – your favorite
Extra Virgin Olive Oil – to drizzle

8 Cups Water
1 Onion – diced
1 tsp Fresh Rosemary – chopped
1½ Cups Small Pasta – ditalini or your favorite – cooked
Salt and Pepper to Taste

Soak the dry beans overnight, rinse well, and then cook over medium heat in 8 cups of fresh water (that should cover the beans by a few inches). Cook for about 1 hour until the beans are tender, and set aside, covered.

Heat the oil in a large soup pot over medium-high heat, and then add the onions, garlic, and rosemary. Stir occasionally and do not let the garlic burn. When the onions have softened, add the tomatoes, salt, and pepper. Cook until the liquid in the tomatoes has cooked off and the oil and tomatoes seem to separate (about 20 minutes).

Add the beans with the water to the pot and bring to a boil. Lower the heat to allow to simmer partially covered for about 2 hours. About 20 minutes before you are ready to serve, taste for salt and pepper, and then add the cooked pasta. Ladle into bowls and then drizzle with a little extra virgin olive oil. At the table, pass the cheese.

Note: Pasta e Fagioli has been called the "father" of pasta dishes. This dish is as basic as a recipe can get. As with most soup dishes, this is a great one to cook ahead and reheat, as it will taste better with time.

Minestra di Riso

Rice in Milk Soup

2½ Quarts Milk – not low-fat or skim
1 Tbs Butter
Sugar and/or Cinnamon Sugar – optional

1 Cup Arborio Rice
Salt to Taste

Pour milk into a large soup pot and slowly bring to a boil over medium heat. Add the rice and simmer for 14–16 minutes, checking for doneness about this time. You want the rice to be al dente, not mushy, so make sure to not overcook. Add butter and season with salt, if needed.

Note: This is a great dish for toddlers and young Children. I served this to my Children when they were young, sometimes for lunch with sugar and cinnamon, and occasionally for dinner, lightly salted. They might have had it for breakfast, too!

Mushroom Sherry Soup

Use Vegetable Broth and You Have a Lenten Meal

4 Tbs Butter – unsalted
3 Onions – thinly sliced
3½ Oz Fresh Porcini Mushrooms – sliced
2 Cups Stock – vegetable or chicken, your
    choice
2–3 tsps Sherry – a good quality you can sip
Salt and Pepper to Taste

3 Garlic Cloves – chopped
1 Lb Mixed Mushrooms – sliced
3–4 Tbs Fresh Parsley – chopped
3 Tbs Flour
1 Cup Half-and-Half
½ Cup Sour Cream

Melt the butter in a large soup pot over low heat. Add the garlic and onions, and cook, stirring so that the garlic does not burn, for a few minutes until the onions are slightly translucent and soft.

Add the mushrooms and continue cooking for about 5 more minutes. Add the stock then the parsley, and stir well. Taste and season, as needed, with salt and pepper. Slowly bring just to boiling. Reduce heat, cover, and simmer for about 30 minutes.

Put the flour into a small bowl and mix in enough half-and-half to make a smooth paste, and slowly stir into the soup. Cook and continue stirring for about 5 minutes, making sure that it has all combined smoothly into the soup. Stir in the remaining half-and-half and then the sherry, and continue cooking for a few more minutes. Remove from heat and stir in the sour cream. Return the pot to the heat and warm gently, and make sure the sour cream is well incorporated. Ladle into bowls and garnish with a little more parsley. Serve with slices of crusty Italian bread that have been sprinkled with oil and set under the broiler to toast until golden brown.

Note: Alternately, you can substitute sage in place of parsley, adjusting the amount to your taste.

Onion Soup from Piedmont

1 Stick Butter – unsalted
8 Large Yellow Onions – about 4 Lbs –
    sliced thin
2 tsps Sugar

12 Thick Italian Bread Slices – ½-inch
    thick
3 Tbs Extra Virgin Olive Oil

6 Cups Chicken Broth or Stock
2 Cups Red Wine

½ Cup Salted Mozzarella – grated or
    Asiago
Salt and Freshly Ground Pepper

Heat butter in a large soup pot and add the onions. Cover and cook over medium heat, stirring often to make sure they don't stick, for about 20–30 minutes, or until the onions are just soft and translucent. Transfer the onions to a large skillet and sprinkle with sugar. Cook uncovered over medium-high heat, stirring often, until the onions are a nice rich-brown color. This will take about 25–35 minutes. Stir in the flour and cook for a few minutes, stirring to make sure everything is evenly coated. Using a whisk, stir in 2 cups of the chicken broth gradually to prevent the flour from forming lumps. Return this mixture to the soup pot, making sure to use a spatula to get every little bit out. Stir in the remaining broth and wine, and taste for salt and pepper. Simmer uncovered over low heat for 40 minutes until the soup has reduced slightly.

In the meantime, preheat the oven to 400°. Put the Italian bread slices on a baking sheet and brush with olive oil. Bake for 10–15 minutes until nicely toasted. Remove from the oven and sprinkle the shredded cheese on top. Return to the oven and bake until the cheese melts and is slightly brown.

Ladle the soup into bowls and float a slice of bread on top. Pass a little more grated cheese.

Note: I confess that I have made this soup with white wine, although my Grandmother used mostly red wine in her soups. I remember a simple soup that she made by adding pastina to chicken broth and flavoring it with grated cheese and a little red wine after it was in our soup bowls. And, I also remember drinking 7-Up with a little red wine in it when I was very young.

Ribollita, a Tuscan Soup

Twice-Cooked Soup

¼ Cup Extra Virgin Olive Oil
4 Oz Pancetta – diced
1 Leek – rinsed and sliced
3 Garlic Cloves – minced
2 Celery Stalks – chopped
2 Carrots – peeled and chopped
1 Bunch Broccoli Rabi – cut in small pieces,
    tough stems discarded

2 Cups Tomatoes – chopped (or a small
    can of diced tomatoes)
1 Onion – thinly sliced
6–8 Cups Beef Broth – or more as
    needed
2 Cups Crusty Bread – torn into
    bite-sized pieces
Salt and Pepper to Taste

1 (15½ Oz) Can Cannellini or Navy Beans –
drained and rinsed

Extra Virgin Olive Oil for Serving
Freshly Grated Cheese for Serving

In a large saucepan, heat the oil. Add the onion, garlic, celery, and carrots, and cook for 8–10 minutes over medium-low heat. Stir often so as not to burn. Add the cabbage, tomatoes, potato, and mix all together. Pour enough stock or water over all this to cover all the vegetables. Bring to a boil. Lower heat to medium and cook for about 15 minutes. In another pot, bring 4 cups of lightly salted water to a boil. Add the rice and cook until almost done. Drain and stir into the pot with the vegetables. Add the parsley. Cook over low heat for about 5 minutes. Do not let boil. Taste for salt and pepper, and serve hot.

Note: This is a soup usually made when vegetables were in abundance, and enough would be made for many meals. So, the next time it was heated, it had been cooked twice, and that, I was told, is how it got the name "Twice-Cooked Soup." For a little crunch, before I add the bread to the soup, I like to drizzle it with a little olive oil and cheese and toast it in the oven.

Roman Eggdrop Soup

4 Eggs – large
1 Cup Grated Cheese – your favorite
6–7 Cups Chicken Broth

½ Cup Lemon Juice – freshly squeezed
1 Cup Breadcrumbs – seasoned or plain

Beat the eggs with a whisk. Mix in the lemon juice, cheese, and breadcrumbs. Bring the broth to a simmer and gradually add the egg-cheese mixture, stirring with a whisk constantly for about 5 minutes.

Ladle into bowls and serve immediately with crusty Italian bread slices that have been spread with extra virgin olive oil and toasted.

Scrippelle 'Mbusse

Soup with Sliced Crepe Strips

4 Eggs

2 Tbs Milk

1 Bunch Parsley – chopped

1 Tbs Freshly Grated Cheese – plus extra

3 Tbs Flour

Salt and Freshly Ground Black Pepper

6 Cups Chicken Broth – or more as needed

2 Tbs Extra Virgin Olive Oil

In a bowl, combine the eggs, milk, parsley, and grated cheese. Slowly mix in the flour, season with salt and pepper, and refrigerate for 30 minutes. Meanwhile, in a large pot, bring the chicken broth to a boil. In a skillet over medium heat, warm the olive oil, remove the egg mixture from the refrigerator, and drop by tablespoons into the skillet. Cook for 1 or 2 minutes on each side until golden. To serve, divide the scrippelle evenly among 4–6 soup bowls, roll them up loosely like an eggroll, ladle the chicken broth over the scrippelle, and sprinkle with more grated cheese.

Note: When I make this soup, I often have some chicken in the broth, too. I like to make this little crepe, roll it up, and cut it into slices about ⅓" wide, and then add it to the soup. Great filler for other soups, too.

Spicy Sausage and Chickpea Soup

¼ Cup Olive Oil

1 Lb Hot Italian Pork Sausage – casings removed

½ Cup Chopped Celery

4–6 Cups Chicken Broth – or more as needed

1 Can (15 Oz) Chickpeas – drained

6 Garlic Cloves

1 Cup Chopped Onions

½ Cup Chopped Carrots

1 Can (15 Oz) Crushed Tomatoes

½ tsp Black Pepper – or to taste

4 Cups Kale – chopped

Cook oil and garlic in a large saucepan over medium heat until the garlic begins to color and get soft. Remove and discard the garlic, but try to reserve about 3 Tbs of the garlic oil in a little bowl. Let the rest remain in the pan.

Increase the heat to medium-high. Add the sausage to the pan, cooking and stirring, and when browned and starting to crumble, remove the sausage from the pan and drain on paper towels. Add the onions and carrots back to the pan and cook until slightly tender, stirring occasionally.

Stir in the broth, tomatoes, chickpeas, and pepper. Stir well to combine, and then stir in the sausage, bring to a simmer, and cook for 30 minutes. Stir in the kale, which has been washed and torn into big pieces. Cook until the kale is wilted (about 10 minutes). If you are not fond of spicy, you can definitely use mild Italian sausage instead. And, if you are not fond of kale, you can use arugula, Savoy cabbage, or spinach. Lots of choices! Ladle into soup bowls and add a little of the reserved garlic oil on top of each bowl. In our house we always pass the grated cheese to sprinkle on top. But, that's just us!

Stracciatelli

Little Nonna's Special Soup

2 Eggs – lightly beaten
4 Tbs Parmesan Cheese – grated
3 Tbs Dry Breadcrumbs – seasoned or
    unseasoned
Pinch of Salt

Dash of Garlic Powder
⅛ tsp Nutmeg
5 or 6 Cups Chicken Broth
Fresh Parsley or Basil for Garnish

Mix eggs, cheese, breadcrumbs, salt, garlic powder, and nutmeg in a small bowl until smooth. Stir in ½ cup for the broth. Heat the remaining broth in a soup pot over medium heat, just until it begins to boil, then reduce heat to low. Stir another ½ cup of the hot broth into the egg mixture slowly, until well combined, and then gradually stir entire mixture into the remaining broth.

Cook, stirring constantly, until the egg mixture forms tiny specks or flakes. This will happen in about 5 minutes. Serve immediately and garnish with the freshly chopped parsley or basil, if desired.

My Little Nonna (she was never more than 80 lbs and very tiny) made this soup often, especially during the war times, when meat was difficult to get. We could get eggs because of my Grandmother Giovanna's farm in New Jersey. I can still picture her standing in front of the stove and stirring, stirring, stirring. I seem to remember that she sometimes added minced onions to the pot and browned them slightly before adding the broth. I've made the soup with and without onions, and it's delicious either way. The aroma was intoxicating, just because Nonna was making it. We all loved it.

Tomato Bread Soup

Pappa Pomodoro

¾ **Cup Olive Oil**
4 Garlic Cloves – minced
1 Onion – small and chopped
8 Sage Leaves – fresh and chopped
1 Lb Loaf Italian Bread – dense, cubed, approx. 8 cups

3 (14 Oz) Cans Italian Tomatoes – drained
6 Cups Beef or Chicken Broth – boiling
Salt and Pepper to Taste
Extra Virgin Olive Oil for Sprinkling

Heat oil in large, heavy pot and cook onion, garlic, and sage over medium heat until garlic starts to color and onion is translucent. Remove garlic if getting too brown, and add to drained tomatoes. Add bread cubes and toss frequently to make sure all are coated well and slightly toasted. Cook all together about 5–7 minutes. Meanwhile, place tomatoes in blender to purée, and then strain (to remove seeds and any thick skin pieces) into a pot with bread mixture. Mix all with wooden spoon until well blended. Stir into the boiling broth. Cover pot and set aside for one hour. Remove lid and stir again with wooden spoon to blend all and break up any large bread clumps.

Taste for seasoning, and add salt and pepper. Reheat, and then spoon into bowls and drizzle with extra virgin olive oil. Sprinkle with your favorite grated cheese, if you so wish.

This was another of my Little Nonna's soups. It brings back a sweet memory, as I can still visualize her standing at the stove in her apron, long cotton dress, and high-button shoes, white hair in a bun, stirring the soup with a wooden spoon. We ate it hot in the cold weather and at room temperature in the hot months. This is a very Tuscan-style soup and another that we ate often during the war years. During Lent, Little Nonna would have used a vegetable broth. I have to mention that when we ate these soups we didn't realize they had fancy names. To us, they were just Little Nonna's soups, and that's how we still refer to them.

Tuscan Farro Soup

1 Lb Farro – rinsed a few times in cold water
4 Garlic Cloves – thinly sliced
1 Medium Onion – halved, thinly sliced
1 Celery Stalk – thinly sliced
1 Can (28 Oz) San Marzano Tomatoes
6–7 Cups Chicken Broth
⅓ Cup Extra Virgin Olive Oil – plus extra
   for finishing

1 Medium Carrot – thinly sliced
6 Sage Leaves – julienned
Salt and Freshly Ground Black Pepper –
   to taste
1 Pinch Pepperoncini or Red Pepper
   Flakes – or more to taste

Heat the oil in a saucepan. Add the garlic, onion, carrots, and celery, and cook until the onion is soft, making sure the garlic does not burn. Stir often for about 10 minutes. Add the sage and stir to incorporate. Season with salt and pepper. Add the tomatoes to the pan slowly, squeezing the tomatoes firmly by hand before they enter the pot. Adjust heat to simmer.

In a separate pot, add the chicken broth and the drained, rinsed farro. Let it come to a boil for a few minutes, and then carefully stir the tomato sauce into the broth. Reduce the heat to low and simmer uncovered for about 40–45 minutes. Taste for seasoning. Add the pepperoncini or red pepper flakes. Simmer for a few more minutes. Ladle into bowls and sprinkle each bowl with a little extra virgin olive oil. In our house, we also pass the grated cheese. This is best served with thick slices of grilled Italian bread brushed with oil. Serves 6.

What exactly is farro? Farro is a healthy whole grain much like other whole grains, such as barley, whole wheat, and quinoa, but with a slightly nutty flavor and a little chewy. It is very adaptable and can be used in soups, stews, and salads. You can also cook farro like risotto. Farro contains more protein than most other grains, and is a healthy choice because it contains more fiber than other grains. Although it is considered an ancient traditional grain, farro is not commonly found in most pantries, but is enjoying a resurgence because of its nutritional aspects. Once you try it, you will enjoy its versatility.

Note: On a cool, crisp autumn day, nothing is better than a pot of soup simmering for dinner.

This is a Tuscan Farro Soup from my Father's native countryside near Siena. So, you know it will be delicious.

Passatelli

Passed Through

½ Lb Parmigiano Reggiano Cheese – grated

4 Eggs

Nutmeg – to taste

1¼ Oz Flour

7 Oz Breadcrumbs

¾ Oz Butter

8 Cups Chicken Broth

Salt – to taste

Work the eggs, the breadcrumbs, 5 Oz (150 g) of the Parmigiano, the butter, the flour, salt, and nutmeg together to form a dough. Cover with plastic wrap and leave to rest for 20 minutes. In a pan, bring the stock (preferably chicken stock) to boil.

With the aid of a potato ricer—in the absence of a special "iron" with a disk featuring larger holes—pass through all the mixture to obtain strips the length of a finger. Drop the passatelli straight into the boiling stock. Cook thoroughly and serve in soup bowls with the stock and a generous helping of grated Parmigiano Reggiano cheese.

Tuscan Fisherman's Soup

Fisherman's Soup

¼ Cup Extra Virgin Olive Oil

6 Garlic Cloves – peeled and coarsely chopped

1 Onion – peeled and roughly chopped

2 Carrots – peeled and finely chopped

2 Celery Stalks – roughly chopped

Pinch of Red Pepper – or to taste

2 Cups White Wine

5 Plum Tomatoes – roughly chopped

1 Cup Canned Tomatoes

2 Sprigs Fresh Thyme, 2 Sprigs Fresh Basil, 2 Sprigs Fresh Parsley – tied together in a piece of cheese cloth

½ Lb Squid – sliced into rings

1½ Dozen Clams – scrubbed and rinsed

2 Lobsters – halved, cleaned, and cut into 1-inch pieces

6 Large Shrimp – shelled and deveined

2 Lbs of a Hearty Fish – your favorite

1 Lb Mussels – scrubbed, debearded, and rinsed

½ Cup Chopped Parsley

Salt and Freshly Ground Black Pepper

6 Garlic Cloves

6–8 Thick Slices of Tuscan Bread – grilled with olive oil

Heat the olive oil in a very large saucepan. Add the garlic, onions, carrots, celery, and crushed red pepper, and cook over medium heat until the garlic begins to brown. Add the wine, fresh and canned tomatoes, and the cheesecloth bundle. Reduce the heat and simmer, covered, stirring occasionally, until the tomatoes are very soft, about 30–40 minutes. Using a wooden spoon, break up any tomatoes that are still whole. Add the squid to the mixture. Simmer, covered, for 30 minutes more. Remove and discard the cheesecloth bundle. Add the clams. Stir for a few minutes.

Add the lobsters, stir, and then add the shrimp, continuing to stir and cook for about 2–3 minutes more. Gently add your choice of the hearty fish, and simmer uncovered until the fish is thoroughly cooked through, about 5 or 10 minutes. Add the mussels and cook only until the mussels open (3 to 4 minutes). Season with salt and pepper. Taste for additional red pepper, and stir again. Cut the garlic cloves in half and rub the cut sides of the grilled bread. Serve immediately, discarding any of the shellfish that did not open.

Note: As always, use a good white wine that you will enjoy drinking while cooking and again with the meal.

Tuscan Rice Minestrone

A Good Summer Soup

½ Cup Extra Virgin Olive Oil	2 Tomatoes – seeded and chopped
1 Medium Red or White Onion – chopped	1 Large Potato – cut into small cubes
3 Garlic Cloves – chopped	⅓ Cup Barley
3 Celery Stalks – sliced thin	1 Cup Arborio Rice
10 Savoy Cabbage Leaves – chopped	Stock or Water
4–5 Carrots – chopped	¼ Cup Parsley – roughly chopped

In a large saucepan, heat the oil. Add the onion, garlic, celery, and carrots, and cook for 8–10 minutes over medium-low heat. Stir often so as not to burn. Add the cabbage, tomatoes, potato, and mix all together. Pour over all this enough stock or water to cover all the vegetables. Bring to a boil. Lower heat to medium and cook for about 15 minutes. In another pot, bring 4 cups of lightly salted water to a boil. Add the rice and cook until almost done. Drain and stir into the pot with the vegetables. Add the parsley. Cook over low heat for about 5 minutes. Do not let boil. Taste for salt and pepper, and serve hot.

Note: Instead of stock and chopped tomatoes, you can add one 28 Oz can of San Marzano peeled tomatoes. Crush the tomatoes by squeezing in your hand before adding to the soup pot.

Salads

Caesar Salad

3 Cloves Garlic – fresh	4 Anchovies – fillets
1 Egg – yolk only	½ Cup Croutons
½ Lemon – juice only	1 Tbs Parmesan Cheese – grated
3 Tbs Extra Virgin Olive Oil	1 Large Romaine Head
½ tsp Vinegar – red wine	Few Dashes of Worcestershire Sauce
½ tsp Dijon Mustard – or equivalent	Salt and Pepper to Taste

Crush the fresh garlic in a large salad bowl. Add lemon juice, mustard, salt, pepper, and a few dashes of Worcestershire sauce. Chop anchovies very fine or mash with fork. Add the yolk of one egg, and then combine all ingredients. Under steady stirring, add 3 Tbs of olive oil and ½ tsp of red wine vinegar.

Next, place the washed and dried romaine salad into the bowl. Add croutons and grated parmesan cheese and freshly ground pepper.

Next, with salad spoon in your right hand, fork in your left, go down to the bottom of the bowl with one tool while going up and over with the other. Toss the salad until every leaf shines with dressing.

Note: This recipe was given to me in the mid-to-late-1960s with the compliments of Waldemar Fitz, who was the captain in the Oak Room at Carl Hoppl's on Long Island.

Caprese di Farro

1 Cup Farro Perlato – pearl farro	1 Cup Cherry Tomatoes – halved
1 Ball Fresh Mozzarella	3 Scallions – diced
10 Kalamata Olives – pitted	2 Fresh Basil Leaves
2 Tbs Extra Virgin Olive Oil	Salt and Ground Black Pepper

Boil the farro in salted water until al dente, about 15–18 minutes, or according to the package directions. Drain the farro and let it cool. Wash, pat dry, and cut the cherry tomatoes in half. Clean and dice the scallions. Cut the mozzarella into chunks, about 1-inch dice.

In a bowl, add the cool farro, tomatoes, mozzarella, scallions, and olives. Add the olive oil, a pinch of salt, and freshly ground black pepper. Toss gently. Tear up the basil leaves and spread on top before serving.

Note: Farro is the grain of a certain wheat species such as barley, whole wheat, and quinoa, but with a slightly nutty flavor and slightly chewy. Farro is very adaptable and can be used in soups, stews, and even salads.

Creamy Coleslaw

¾ Cup Mayonnaise – preferably Hellman's
3 Tbs Sugar
1½ tsps White Wine Vinegar
⅓ Cup Canola Oil
¼ tsp Dry Mustard – preferably Coleman's
½ tsp Celery Seed
Freshly Ground Pepper

2 Tbs Lemon Juice
¾ Cup Half-and-Half – not low-fat
¼ tsp Salt
1 Small Onion – finely chopped
1 Large Head of Cabbage – finely
    shredded or chopped

Blend mayonnaise, sugar, vinegar, and oil. Add dry mustard, celery seed, lemon juice, half-and-half, salt, and pepper. Stir until smooth. Mix cabbage and onion in a large bowl and pour dressing over all. Toss well and let sit for several hours in the refrigerator to marinate. Stir well before serving.

Note: If you use a red onion, the coleslaw will be a festive pink.

Panzanella

A Bread and Vegetable Salad

8 Slices Crusty Italian Bread – a few days old
1 Lb Ripe Tomatoes – chopped
1 Ripe Cucumber – peeled and chopped
½ Bunch Fresh Basil – stems removed and
    chopped
½ Red Onion – chopped
Salt and Pepper to Taste

½ Cup Fresh Parsley – chopped
1 Red or Yellow Pepper – seeded and
    chopped
⅓ Cup Extra Virgin Olive Oil
2 Cloves Garlic – minced
3 Tbs Red Wine Vinegar

Cut bread into bite-sized pieces and put in a large bowl. Sprinkle bread with a little cold water to slightly dampen. Add tomatoes and their juice, cucumbers, peppers, onion, basil, and parsley to the bread and stir well. Add salt and pepper, and stir. Add minced garlic to the olive oil and drizzle over the salad. You do not want the salad to look soaked. Add vinegar and toss well. Let sit for at least 2 hours before serving. Taste for salt and pepper, and adjust. It should not look or be dry, but if it is, add a little more oil and vinegar. In a glass bowl, it makes a nice presentation.

Note: This is a rustic Italian salad made with day-old crusty Italian bread, very ripe tomatoes, and you can use the garden vegetables of your choice. Sometimes, I like to add a can of drained chickpeas. This is a joy to eat when the tomatoes are ripe and overflowing your garden. Add a can of Italian tuna for variety. But, either way, this will be a meal in itself.

Pear, Walnut, and Gorgonzola Salad

½ tsp Balsamic Vinegar
2½ Cups Romaine Lettuce – torn
1 Tbs Butter
½ Cup Gorgonzola Cheese – crumbled

1 tsp Extra Virgin Olive Oil
1 Large, Firm Pear – sliced
Walnuts – shelled and in large pieces

Romaine should be torn into bite-sized pieces. Combine the vinegar and oil, toss with the torn romaine, and set aside. Melt the butter in a skillet. Add the pear slices and walnuts. Sauté until the pear slices are lightly browned. Add the pear slices and walnuts with the butter to the lettuce, and toss lightly. Top with gorgonzola cheese. This is a great salad for a luncheon.

Rice Salad

Insalata di Riso Agrodolce

2 Cups Arborio Rice
2 Large Onions – minced
1 Tbs Sugar
2 Ripe Tomatoes – peeled, seeded, chopped

5 Tbs Olive Oil
3 Tbs Balsamic Vinegar
Salt and Freshly Ground Pepper
4 Fresh Mint Leaves

Bring 2 quarts of lightly salted water to a boil in a large pot. Add the rice to cook, checking after about 15 minutes to make sure the rice is tender, but not overcooked. When the rice is done, pour into a strainer and rinse with cool water. Set it aside to drain completely. While the rice is cooking, chop the tomatoes. Sprinkle with a bit of salt, toss, and set aside.

In the meantime, in a large skillet, warm the olive oil over medium heat and add the onion. Sauté gently until the onion is just soft. Stir in the vinegar. Salt and pepper to taste.

Drain the tomatoes of any extra juice, and then add them to the onions. Stir and remove from the heat.

When the rice has cooled, transfer to a large serving bowl, pour the onion-tomato mixture over, and stir gently to combine, but not mash down, the rice. Garnish with fresh mint leaves, or you can use basil leaves instead. For a little crunch, I like to sometimes add ⅓ cup roughly chopped celery.

Warm Summer Vegetable Salad

1 Small Red Onion – thinly sliced
¼ Cup Red Wine Vinegar
1 Lb Yukon Gold Potatoes – peeled and cut into eighths
2 Yellow Squash – sliced in rounds
⅓ Cup Basil – chopped

Salt and Ground Pepper 2 Anchovy Fillets – mashed
2 Small Zucchini – sliced in rounds
½ Lb String Beans – cut in half
¼ Cup Extra Virgin Olive Oil
1 Garlic Clove – minced

Bring a large pot of salted water to a boil. In a large bowl, toss the onion with the anchovies and vinegar. Add the potatoes to the boiling water and cook for 5 minutes. Add the beans and cook for an additional 5 minutes, then add the zucchini and yellow squash, and cook for 5 minutes longer. Drain the vegetables well in a strainer so that all the liquid is released. Stir the olive oil, basil, and garlic into the onion mixture. Gently add the vegetables to the bowl, coating the vegetables and allowing the potatoes to break up a little. Season with salt and freshly ground black pepper, and serve warm or at room temperature. A small squirt of balsamic vinegar adds a nice finish.

Note: Sometimes instead of potatoes, I add cooked rice or a tiny pasta, like orzo or farro.

Vegetables

Asparagi Parmigiana

1 Bunch Fresh Young Asparagus	6 Tbs Parmigiano Cheese
4 Tbs Butter	Salt and Ground Pepper

Put asparagus in a large pan, cover with lightly salted water, and bring to a boil. Take off the heat and let cool. In a sauté pan, melt the butter and heat the asparagus, stirring it around in the melted butter. Sprinkle with Parmigiano cheese and serve.

Note: I have an old Corning percolator coffee pot. Once I trim the bottom of the asparagus, I stand them up in the pot filled partway with lightly salted water, and cook. The bottoms get soft, and the tops still have a little crunch in them.

Baked Cabbage

1 Head Cabbage – halved, sliced, cored	1 Stick Butter – salted or unsalted
1 tsp Sugar – or to taste	1 Onion – sliced
1 Garlic Clove – sliced	Salt and Pepper to Taste
Garlic Powder – to taste	Olive Oil – as needed

Put sliced cabbage in a baking pan with about 1 inch of water on the bottom. Pour olive oil over the cabbage. Sprinkle with salt, pepper, some garlic powder, and a little sugar, and toss well, using your hands. Mix in the sliced garlic. Cover and bake for about 45 minutes total in an oven preheated to 350°.

After 15 minutes, slice the butter and spread all over the top of the cabbage. Cover and return to oven. After another 15 minutes, uncover and toss again so that the melted butter is distributed.

If, for some reason, the cabbage seems dry, add a little more oil and toss. After 45 minutes, or whenever cabbage is wilted but not mushy, taste and adjust for seasonings. Uncover and cook for 10 minutes just to brown the top layer a bit.

Note: This is a great recipe for a crowd, and baking the cabbage does not allow the cabbage smell to permeate throughout.

Beans with Pork Skin

Fagiole con le Contiche

1 Lb Pork Skin (Rind)
2 Carrots – peeled and minced
4–5 Garlic Cloves – minced
¼ Cup Dry White Wine
6 Cups Barlotti Beans – cooked and drained
½ Cup Extra Virgin Olive Oil

2 Celery Stalks – minced
2 Cups Tomatoes – fresh or canned, peeled and chopped
2 Cups Meat Broth – or as needed
Salt and Pepper to Taste

In a saucepan, combine the pork skin with cold water to cover and bring to a boil. Cook for about an hour to tenderize and boil off some of the fat. Drain and rinse under cold running water, and then cut into short strips.

In a soup pot, warm the olive oil on medium-low heat. Add the pork skin and sauté until it gets lightly colored. Stir in the onions, carrots, celery, and garlic, and continue to sauté until the vegetables have softened, about 10 minutes. Stir in the tomatoes, mix well, and add the wine. Cook, stirring until the alcohol evaporates. Add the broth and stir until all is well combined, and then add the beans. If the mixture seems too dry, add more broth. Bring all to a simmer and let cook slowly for about an hour. Season with salt and pepper, and ladle into warmed serving bowls. Sprinkle with a little olive oil and enjoy. This is a very typical Umbrian dish.

Note: Three cups dried beans will yield six cups of cooked beans when simmered in a pot of lightly salted water for about an hour. Before boiling, beans should be rinsed a few times.

Cheesy Broccoli Casserole

1 Can Cream of Broccoli Soup
½–¾ Cup Half-and-Half
2 tsps Yellow Mustard – optional
1 (16 Oz) Bag Frozen Broccoli Florets – thawed
1 Cup Shredded Cheddar Cheese – or your favorite

½ Cup Breadcrumbs – plain or flavored, your choice
3 Tbs Butter – melted
¼ Cup Onion – finely chopped

Mix the onion with the soup and stir in. Mix half-and-half and mustard together with the soup mixture in a 1½–2-quart casserole dish. Add the broccoli and mix well. Mix the breadcrumbs with the melted butter and sprinkle over the broccoli mixture. Bake at 350° for 30 minutes or until hot and a little bubbly.

Note: In place of breadcrumbs, I also use Ritz cracker crumbs. Take a sleeve or two and pulse in a food processor until coarse. Pour in melted butter and then spread that over broccoli.

Eggplant Meat Casserole

My Very First Company Meal

1 Lb Ground Beef Round
6 Italian Mild Pork Sausages – removed
   from casing
3 Tbs Butter
3 Onions – chopped
2 Cups Tomato Purée
½ tsp Basil
½ tsp Oregano
½ Cup Chopped Yellow or Orange Pepper

1 tsp Salt
Pinch of Freshly Ground Black Pepper
1 Clove Garlic – crushed
2 Eggplants – large, peeled, and sliced
   thin
2 Eggs – beaten
⅔–1 Cup Vegetable Oil
½–¾ Lb Mozzarella

In a skillet, sauté the beef in butter. Add onions and cook until golden. Then add the tomato purée, basil, oregano, yellow or orange pepper, salt, garlic, and pepper. Remove from heat. In another skillet, sauté sausage meat until browned. Peel and slice the eggplant, thin. Dip slices into eggs and sauté in hot oil until both sides are golden brown. Drain on paper towel. Arrange ⅓ of the meat sauce and ⅓ of the mozzarella. Then, top with ⅓ of the sausage meat. Repeat until all is used, ending with mozzarella on top. Bake at 350° for approximately 1 hour.

Note: If you prefer, you can brown sausage links whole and then slice and add over the mozzarella, as you would the sausage meat. We married in June and immediately after returning from our Bermuda honeymoon, we moved to Maryland. This was my very first attempt as a young bride at cooking for company when we lived in Maryland, and it always made a hit, so I stuck with it.

Eggplant Pie

1 9" Deep Dish Pie Crust – unbaked
¼ Cup Butter
2 Cups Eggplant – peeled and cubed
¾ Cup Onion – chopped
Grind of Black Pepper to Taste

3 Garlic Cloves – minced
8–10 Oz Sauce – homemade or canned
¾ Lb Ground Beef
¼ tsp Dried Oregano
1 Cup Fresh Mozzarella – divided

Preheat oven to 375°. Heat pan over medium heat and melt butter. Add eggplant, cover, and cook for 5 minutes. Remove eggplant from the pan and set aside.

To the pan, add beef, onion, and garlic. Cook, stirring until beef is browned and large chunks are broken up. Drain liquid from pan. Add tomato sauce, oregano, and pepper. Continue cooking over medium heat, stirring for about 6–8 minutes. Stir in eggplant. Remove the pan from the heat. Stir in ½ of the cheese, and spoon the mixture into the pie crust.

Place in preheated oven and bake for about 45 minutes, or until the pie is golden brown. Sprinkle the remainder of the cheese on top and bake a few minutes longer until the cheese is completely melted.

Eggplant Stew

3½ Cups Vidalia Onions – thinly sliced
4 Garlic Cloves – thinly sliced
1½–2 Cups Tomato Sauce – divided

3½ Lbs Eggplant – cut in ½-inch slices
Salt and Ground Pepper
A Bunch of Torn Basil – divided

Preheat oven to 300° and grease a 2-quart casserole dish. In a large skillet, add a thin coating of oil. Add sliced onions and cook over medium heat, stirring frequently until golden brown and caramelized. Halfway through their cooking, scrape the sides of the skillet to scrape down any little bits that may have stuck to the sides. When the onions are thoroughly caramelized, remove the skillet from the heat and allow to cool.

In another large skillet, heat a little oil, and when hot enough, carefully add half of the garlic and several slices of eggplant, and cook until golden brown on each side. Make sure the pan is not crowded, or the eggplant will just absorb the oil and not brown. While the eggplant is frying, season with a little salt and pepper to your taste. (I like to add a little garlic powder to the mix.)

Remove the eggplant from the pan and repeat with remaining eggplant and garlic until all is cooked.

Spread ½ cup of sauce on the bottom of the prepared casserole dish. Add a layer of the caramelized onions and then a layer of eggplant (which I sometimes cut in half crosswise). Sprinkle with a little torn basil. Continue until you have used up all the eggplant and onions. Top with a good layer of sauce. A topping of shredded mozzarella is good, too. Cover with foil and bake until hot all the way through.

When ready to serve, sprinkle with a little torn basil. Serve hot or at room temperature.

Fava alla Pecorino

2 Lbs Fava Beans – removed from pods
2 Garlic Cloves – sliced
3 tsps Olive Oil
Salt and Freshly Ground Pepper

3 Oz Pecorino Cheese – crumbled
1 Tbs Red Wine Vinegar
1 Tbs Fresh Basil – torn

Remove the beans from the pods and put them in a pot of water in which they are covered by two inches, and add some salt. Bring to a boil and let boil for 1 minute. Remove the pot from the heat and let the beans soak in the water until they are cool. Drain and put into a bowl. Add the pecorino, garlic, vinegar, olive oil, basil, salt, and pepper. Give it a good toss and let sit for a few minutes before serving.

Note: This is a traditional dish to serve when celebrating the Feast of St. Joseph on March 19.

Fresh Tomato Frittata

3 Tbs Extra Virgin Olive Oil
½ tsp Kosher Salt – divided
⅓ Cup Heavy Cream – room temperature
1¾ Cup Fresh Mozzarella – diced or shredded

1¼ Cups Cherry or Grape Tomatoes – halved lengthwise
7 Large Eggs – room temperature
½ Cup Basil Leaves – roughly chopped

Preheat the broiler to high and place the oven rack in the middle of the oven. Heat an 8-inch ovenproof, nonstick skillet over medium heat. Add the olive oil and tomatoes. Season the tomatoes with ¼ teaspoon salt and cook until they are soft and beginning to fall apart, about 3 to 5 minutes.

In the meantime, whisk the eggs in a large bowl. Add the heavy cream, basil, and remaining salt, and whisk all together until light. Pour the egg mixture over the tomatoes, sprinkle with mozzarella, and cook for 2 or 3 minutes. Using a rubber spatula, loosen the cooked eggs from the sides and bottom of the pan, and tilt the pan to allow the raw egg to run underneath. Cook another minute and repeat until there are no runny eggs. Place the whole pan under the broiler and cook for 5 or 6 minutes, or just until you are sure the eggs are set. Slide the frittata onto a board, slice, and serve.

Fried Potato Cakes

2 Cups Mashed Potatoes
1 Small Onion or Several Green Onions –
   chopped
1 Cup Flour

1 Egg – possibly 2, if loose
¼ tsp Black Pepper – can use cayenne
1 tsp Garlic Powder
1 Cup Oil – for frying

Mix all ingredients, except the oil, into the potatoes. Make into patties. Fry in hot oil until browned on both sides. Makes about 12 patties. Enjoy!

Note: We love fried potato cakes. I always use leftover mashed potatoes to make them. The family enjoys them, so when I make mashed potatoes, I always make a lot extra and save for making these little cakes. They are a good side dish for another dinner, and they are great for breakfast with eggs.

Fried Potatoes and Onions

4 Large Russet Potatoes – can use
   Yukon Gold
2 Tbs Extra Virgin Olive Oil
½ tsp Dried Dill Weed
¼ tsp Black Pepper

1 Large Onion – sliced thin
4 Tbs Butter – more if needed
½ tsp Garlic Powder
¼ tsp Salt

Peel and slice potatoes about ⅛-inch thick or thinner. Slice onion very thin. In a large frying pan on medium-high heat, melt butter and add olive oil. When hot, add sliced potatoes and onions. Cover and fry for 10 minutes. Using a spatula, turn the potatoes and onions over carefully so they do not break apart. If potatoes appear too dry, add some additional butter.

Sprinkle with granulated garlic powder, dried dill weed, salt, and pepper, and continue to fry with cover removed for another 5 minutes, or until potatoes begin to turn slightly brown, turning occasionally. Serve hot with your meal.

Note: You may use 2 or 3 large garlic cloves (chopped small) instead of granulated garlic powder. Add to the potatoes after the first 10 minutes of cooking time.

Home Fries

2 Lbs Yukon Gold Potatoes	**2 Tbs Peanut or Canola Oil**
1 Onion – ¼-inch diced	**Salt to Taste**
3–4 Tbs Butter – unsalted	**Freshly Ground Black Pepper**

Cook potatoes in a large pot of very lightly salted boiling water for 22–25 minutes. Drain, then rinse under cold running water until cool enough to handle. Peel and cut into ½-inch cubes.

Heat oil in a large skillet over medium heat until the oil is starting to ripple. Add onion and sauté, shaking pan frequently until softened, about 4–5 minutes. Add potatoes, salt, and pepper. And toss to combine. Increase heat to medium-high. Add butter to the skillet, tossing occasionally until the potatoes are nicely browned, but still tender, about 10 minutes. Serve hot.

Lemon Broccolini

1 Cup Italian Bread – cubed	**1½ Lb Fresh Broccolini**
2 Tbs Butter	**1 Tbs Olive Oil**
2 Tbs Basil – chopped	**Salt and Freshly Ground Black Pepper**
1 Garlic Clove – minced	**Red Pepper Flakes – optional**
2 tsps Lemon Zest	**2 Tbs Lemon Juice**

Process bread in a food processor for about 1 minute until it is coarse and crumbly. Preferably, use a bread that is a day or two old. Melt the butter with the garlic in a large skillet over medium heat. Add the breadcrumbs and stir while cooking for 2 or 3 minutes, or until golden brown. Stir in the lemon zest and the basil, and remove from heat. Meanwhile, cook broccolini in boiling salted water for 3–5 minutes, or until crisp-tender. Drain well. Toss the broccolini with the lemon juice zest, olive oil, salt, and freshly ground pepper. Add red pepper flakes now, if using. Transfer to a serving platter and sprinkle with the breadcrumb mixture. Keep warm until ready to serve.

Lentils for New Year's

½ Lb Lentils
3 Garlic Cloves – peeled
1 Cup Broth – vegetable or chicken
Garlic Powder – to taste
2 Sprigs of Rosemary – optional

⅓ Cup Extra Virgin Olive Oil
Salt and Pepper to Taste
Pinch of Red Pepper Flakes – for
    warmth (optional)

Soak the lentils for 1 hour in cold water. Rinse and drain well two times. Place in a 2-quart pot and cover with cold water. Add the rosemary, if using, together with the garlic cloves. Bring to a gentle boil and simmer for 15–20 minutes. Drain and discard the rosemary. Mince the garlic and add to heated olive oil in the pot. Cook until you can smell the aroma, but be careful not to burn. Cook over low heat. Add the lentils back to the pot with the broth, salt, pepper, red pepper flakes, and a little garlic powder (if you love garlic, like I do). Stir well and add 1 Tbs tomato paste (also optional). Cook until most of the liquid has been absorbed, about 20 minutes, adding more broth along the way if needed. Adjust the seasonings. If you are serving the lentils with cotechino, while the cotechino is cooking, exchange some of that water to the lentils for a little more flavor.

In traditional Italian families, as in Italy, lentils are usually on the menu on either New Year's Eve or New Year's Day. Lentils are perceived as a symbol of good luck and prosperity. While the main accompaniment with lentils is usually cotechino, many Italian families have their own favored dishes. But, if you haven't tried it with cotechino, you are missing out on a delicious meal.

Melanzane alla Prezzemono

Eggplant with Parsley

1 Medium Eggplant – cubed
1 Tbs Fresh Italian Parsley – chopped
4 Tbs Olive Oil

1 Garlic Clove – chopped
4 Tbs Parmigiano Cheese – shaved
Salt and Ground Black Pepper

In a large pan, heat the olive oil over medium heat and sauté the eggplant, stirring occasionally. When the eggplant starts to brown, add the garlic, and continue browning the eggplant while stirring and making sure the garlic does not burn. Add the parsley, salt, pepper, and shaved cheese. Toss and coat well.

Onion Rice Casserole

3 Lbs Onions – thinly sliced
   (should be 16 cups)
1 Cup Long Grain Rice
1½ Cups Cheese – grated (Colby, Swiss, or
   Monterey Jack)

1¾–2 Cups Light Cream or
   Half-and-Half
Salt and Pepper
8 Tbs Butter – unsalted (one stick)

Sauté onions in butter until limp. Meanwhile, boil rice in two cups of water for only five minutes, and then drain. Mix together the onions, rice, cheese, and light cream. Taste for salt and pepper. Place in oblong, greased casserole. Bake uncovered at 325° for 1 hour, or until the top is crusty. Check halfway through the baking, and if looking a bit dry, add more cream or half-and-half.

Note: Casserole can be baked a day ahead, stored covered in refrigerator, and then reheated before serving. However, if you do it this way, you definitely need to add extra half-and-half, or it will be very dry.

Oven-Baked Crispy Potatoes

3–5 Lbs Yukon Gold Potatoes – peeled
Olive Oil
Salt and Freshly Ground Black Pepper

Garlic Powder to Taste
Butter to Taste

Cut the potatoes in quarters or good serving-size pieces. Put in a plastic bag and sprinkle a few tablespoons of olive oil over all, and shake. Then sprinkle with salt, pepper, and garlic powder. Mix around in bag, making sure the potatoes are well coated. Spray a large baking dish with cooking spray or lightly grease with olive oil. Arrange the potatoes in it, but don't crowd them, as they will not crisp. Bake in preheated 425° oven for about 20 minutes. Top with butter and continue baking until brown and crisp.

Note: The same way we would not have a meal without bread, we would not have a meal where we serve meat that we wouldn't have this potato dish. The secret is in the butter.

Potato Cake alla Montefollonico

4 Eggs
¼ Cup Ricotta – drained
½ Cup Parmigiano – freshly grated
1 Cup Pecorino – freshly grated
4 Tbs Butter – unsalted
1 Lb Fresh Mozzarella – cubed, ¼ inch

½ Cup Milk
4 Lbs Potatoes
½ Lb Soppressata – diced
¼ Cup Parsley – finely chopped
½ Cup Fresh Breadcrumbs

Heat oven to 450°. In a medium bowl, lightly beat the eggs. Add the milk and ricotta, and set aside.

Boil the potatoes until tender, about 35–45 minutes. Drain, peel, and pass through ricer while they are still warm into a very large mixing bowl. Use a spatula to fold in the parmigiano and pecorino cheeses. Add the soppressata and parsley, and stir just enough to evenly mix. Gently stir in the egg mixture. (Do not overstir at this point, or it will become too stringy. Be very careful. Just gently stir in the egg mixture.)

Butter a 12-inch springform pan with 2 Tbs of the butter, and dust with some of the breadcrumbs. Spoon half of the potato mixture into the pan gently, and smooth it all the way to the edges. Sprinkle the mozzarella over the potato mixture to within ½ inch of the edge. Top with the remaining potato mixture. Smooth to fit to edge. Sprinkle with remaining breadcrumbs and dot with remaining butter.

Bake until a light golden-brown (25–30 minutes). Remove from oven and let rest for 15 minutes at a minimum. Unmold and serve warm, in wedges.

Potato Pancetta Frittata

2 Oz Pancetta – diced
7 Tbs Butter – unsalted and divided
8 Eggs – extra large
¾ Lb Gruyere Cheese – grated
⅓ Cup Flour
2 tsps Kosher Salt
6 Fresh Basil Leaves – julienned

1 Tbs Olive Oil
2 Cups Yukon Gold Potatoes – ½-inch diced
15 Oz Ricotta Cheese – drained
½ Cup Whole Milk
¾ tsp Baking Powder
1 tsp Freshly Ground Pepper

Preheat oven to 350°. In a 10-inch ovenproof pan (preferably an omelet pan) over medium-low heat, cook the pancetta in the olive oil for about 8–10 minutes until browned. Remove the pancetta from the pan with a slotted spoon and set aside.

Don't wipe the pan, but melt 2 Tbs of the butter in the pan. Add the potatoes and fry them for about 8 minutes, or until cooked through and slightly browned, turning occasionally. Melt the remaining 5 Tbs of butter in a small dish in a microwave.

Meanwhile, whisk the eggs in a large bowl, then stir in the ricotta, gruyere, melted butter, and milk. Combine the flour, baking powder, salt, and pepper, and stir into the egg mixture. Add the basil.

Put the pancetta back into the pan with the potatoes and pour in the egg mixture. Place the pan in the center of the oven for about 50–55 minutes, or until the frittata is nicely browned and puffed, and a knife inserted into the center comes out clean.

Roasted Garlic Broccoli

1½ Lbs Broccoli Crowns – cut into florets
(about 8–9 cups)
4–4½ Tbs Olive Oil – divided

2 Garlic Cloves – minced
Dried Crushed Red Pepper to
    Taste

Preheat oven to 450°. Toss broccoli and 3 Tbs of olive oil in a large bowl to coat. Sprinkle with salt and pepper. Transfer to rimmed baking sheet that has been lightly sprayed. Roast for 15 minutes.

Stir remaining olive oil, garlic, and red pepper in a small bowl. Drizzle garlic mixture over the broccoli. Toss to coat. Roast until broccoli is beginning to brown, about 8 minutes longer. Season to taste with salt and pepper. Serve while still hot.

Sausage and Potato Stew

A Tuscan Peasant Recipe

4 Tbs Olive Oil
3–4 Sage Leaves
3 Celery Ribs – roughly chopped
1 Large Red Onion – cut into chunks
Cups Broth
½ Lbs Italian Sausage – cut on
    diagonal into ½" slices

3 Garlic Cloves – sliced
¼ tsp Crushed Red Pepper – or to taste
2 Carrots – roughly chopped
⅓ Cup White Wine
2 Cups San Marzano Tomatoes
2 Lbs Potatoes – peeled and cut into chunks
Salt and Pepper – to taste

Heat the oil in a large heavy-bottom pot. Add the garlic, sage, and red pepper, and sauté slowly just until the garlic starts to turn color. Add the celery, carrots, and onion. Season with salt and pepper, and cook until all the vegetables start to get soft. Next, add the sausage and cook for about 10 minutes, then slowly add the wine. Cook until the wine is reduced a bit. Add the tomatoes, potatoes, and 2 cups of broth. Simmer for 1½ to 2 hours, checking occasionally and stirring to make sure that the stew is not getting too dry. If it is, add a little more broth.

When the potatoes are very tender (but not falling apart), the stew is done. Serve in bowls with crusty bread.

Sautéed Escarole

1 Lb Escarole – salt to taste
2 Garlic Cloves – smashed

3 Tbs Extra Virgin Olive Oil
Pinch of Red Pepper Flakes

Tear the escarole into manageable-sized pieces and rinse several times in cold water. Escarole can be gritty; drain very well. In the meantime, bring a large pot of water to a boil. Add salt and the escarole leaves. Cook only until wilted, about 5 minutes. Drain well and allow to cool. Squeeze out all excess water with a towel. Chop escarole into bite-sized pieces. Heat the olive oil and the garlic in a large pan. When the garlic is fragrant and slightly golden (do not let it burn), add the hot pepper flakes and sauté for a few minutes. Add the escarole and mix well so that all the leaves become well coated. Sprinkle with salt and mix again. Serve immediately or at room temperature.

Note: Escarole is a tasty addition to soup.

Savoy Cabbage and Sausage

2 Lbs Mild Italian Sausage	2 Tbs Olive Oil
¾ Cup Yellow Onion – finely chopped	2 Tbs Butter
1½ Cup Dry Red Wine	12 Garlic Cloves – sliced
1 Savoy Cabbage – about 3 Lbs	3 Tbs Salt Pork – roughly chopped
1 Can (16 Oz) Crushed Tomatoes	Salt and Pepper to Taste

With the tip of a sharp knife, pierce the sausages in several places and place in a deep dish. Scatter garlic slices around the dish, and then pour one cup of wine over all. Cover well and set aside to marinate.

Separate the cabbage leaves, wash thoroughly in saltwater, and rinse. Cut off the thick part and core of the heavy leaves. Set aside to drain. Put the olive oil, butter, and chopped salt pork in a 6-quart pot. Cook over moderate heat. Add onions, and brown until the onions are transparent.

Drain the sausage and save the wine marinade. Add sausage to the pot and cook until lightly browned. Add wine marinade and simmer until the wine is partly evaporated. Add tomatoes, cabbage, and additional ½ cup of wine. Cover and cook, stirring occasionally. Cabbage will add additional liquid as it wilts. Continue cooking until the cabbage is tender, about 35–40 minutes.

Adjust for salt and pepper, and serve in soup bowls with crusty Italian bread.

Special Corn Pudding

3 Large Eggs
⅓ Cup Sugar
½ Cup All-Purpose Flour
1½ tsps Baking Powder
3 Cups Heavy Cream

2½ Cups Frozen Corn – thawed
2 Tbs Butter – melted
½ tsp Nutmeg
Salt and Pepper

Preheat oven to 375°. Spray or lightly grease a 2-quart baking dish. In a large mixing bowl, beat the eggs with the sugar on medium speed for 3–4 minutes. Add flour, baking powder, and nutmeg, and beat for an additional few minutes. Slowly add the cream and mix just to combine. Add a pinch of salt and freshly ground pepper. Add the corn and melted butter, and stir by hand so that you do not mash the corn. Pour the mixture into the prepared dish and bake for 45–50 minutes. Depending on the size and/or depth of your dish, it might take as long as 60–75 minutes or longer. But, it should be lightly browned, puffed on top, and set in the center. Cool on a wire rack for 15–20 minutes before serving. The top will deflate a little and settle.

Note: You can use half-and-half instead of the heavy cream, but since we only have this about twice a year, I go with the heavy cream. It does give a little creamier texture. I did try making it with milk and adding a little flour for body, but it didn't work out and was quite liquid. And, everybody complained.

Spicy Garlic Broccolini

1 Lb Broccolini – rinsed well
Salt to Taste
⅓ Cup Extra Virgin Olive Oil

½ tsp Red Pepper Flakes
½ Cup Pecorino Romano – freshly grated
4 Garlic Cloves – slivered

Trim off the bottom ⅓″ of the broccolini. Bring a large pot of water to a boil. Add the broccolini and about 1 Tbs of salt. Cook until just tender, about 5 minutes. Quickly drain and add to a large bowl of ice-cold water to stop the cooking, and drain well again. Heat the olive oil in a large frying pan. Add the garlic and red pepper flakes. Cook just until all is aromatic. Stir in the broccolini, sauté 5 minutes, and pour out onto a serving platter. Sprinkle with the grated cheese.

Stuffed Bell Peppers

Peperoni Imbottiti

1 Onion – chopped
½ Lb Ground Beef
2 Cups Dry White Wine – divided
⅓–½ Lb Shredded Fresh Mozzarella
4 Bell Peppers (Green, Red, Orange, or Yellow) – your choice
8 Tbs Extra Virgin Olive Oil

½ Lb Ground Pork
2 Tbs Fresh Parsley – chopped
1½ Tbs Salt
Pinch of Garlic Powder
Freshly Ground Black Pepper
½ Cup Grated Cheese – your favorite

Cut off the tops of the peppers, reserve, and remove the seeds. In a saucepan over medium heat, sauté the onion in olive oil until translucent. Add the ground meats and cook slowly for about 15 to 20 minutes. Sprinkle with a little salt and pepper. Add 1 cup of wine and continue cooking for another 15 minutes.

Transfer the meat to a large bowl and add the parsley, grated cheese, shredded mozzarella, salt, pepper, and garlic powder. Mix well and allow mixture to cool.

Preheat oven to 300°. Arrange the peppers standing up on a baking sheet that has been lightly oiled. (Actually, I prefer to do this in a baking dish or two bread pans. Don't crowd them.) You can scrunch up some foil and place in between the pepper for stability. Divide the meat mixture evenly among the peppers and close with the tops on. Drizzle the peppers with some additional olive oil and the remaining 1 cup of wine. Bake for 1 hour.

Tomato-Potato Gratin

1 Large Yellow Onion – thinly sliced
12 Roma Tomatoes – seeded, cut into chunks
Pinch of Dried Oregano
1 Cup Grated Mozzarella
Olive Oil – for sautéing

2–3 Tbs Garlic – minced
Pinch of Fresh Rosemary – or to taste
4 Russet Potatoes – peeled, thinly sliced
½ Cup Grated Parmesan or Romano Cheese
Salt and Freshly Ground Black Pepper to Taste

Preheat oven to 450°. Sauté the onion in a few tablespoons of the olive oil just until soft. Stir in the garlic and cook just until it is starting to get aromatic. Add the tomatoes, oregano, and rosemary. Cook until most of the moisture has evaporated, about 10–12 minutes.

Spray a large casserole dish with cooking spray. Layer half of the potatoes in the casserole and sprinkle with salt and freshly ground black pepper. Top the potatoes with half of the tomato mixture and half of the cheese. Sprinkle some of the grated cheese on top. Repeat the layers, ending with the grated parmesan or Romano cheese topped with the mozzarella.

Cover with foil and bake for 30 minutes. Remove the foil and continue baking for an additional 15 minutes, letting the cheese brown, but not burn. Let sit for 10–15 minutes to let the cheese set before slicing.

Note: This is a great dish to make on a chilly day, and a very versatile one at that. It works great all by itself or as a side dish. Sometimes I add some Italian sausage (that I remove from the casing and partially cook) between the layers, and it makes a full meal.

Zucchini Pancakes

2 Zucchini – about ¾ Lb total	**3 Tbs Red Onion – grated**
2–3 Eggs – lightly beaten	**8 Tbs Flour**
1 tsp Baking Powder	**1 tsp Kosher Salt**
Freshly Ground Black Pepper	**Butter and Vegetable Oil**

Preheat oven to 275°. Grate zucchini into a bowl using the large grating side of the grater. Immediately stir in the onions and eggs. Stir in flour, baking powder, salt, and pepper. If batter seems too thin, add a little more flour.

Heat a skillet over medium heat, and melt the butter and oil in the pan. When all is hot but not smoking, lower the heat to medium-low and drop heaping tablespoons of batter into the pan, pushing the center down lightly to help them spread evenly. Cook for 2–2½ minutes on each side until browned. Place pancakes on a baking pan and keep warm in the oven while you continue to cook the remainder.

Pasta
Polenta
Rice

A Quick-and-Easy Tomato Sauce

¼ Cup Olive Oil
1 Medium Onion – sliced thin
3 Garlic Cloves – peeled and sliced thin
1 Lb Italian Sausage – crumbled
1 (28 Oz) Can San Marzano Tomatoes
   – drained

½ Cup Fresh Basil Leaves – torn
Salt and Pepper to Taste
1 Pinch Dried Oregano
Chili Flakes or Pepperoncini to Taste
¼ Cup White Wine

In a large pan combine the olive oil, sliced onion, and garlic. Cook on medium heat just until the onions are translucent. Stir often to make sure that the garlic does not burn. If it gets too brown, remove. Add sausage and cook until browned. Raise heat and add white wine, stirring up any bits of meat or onions that might be stuck to the bottom of the pan. Continue stirring until you can no longer smell the aroma of wine. Add tomatoes. You can put the tomatoes in a blender and blend using a few quick on-and-off turns. I prefer to break up the tomatoes with my hand as I slowly pour the tomatoes into the pan. We like lumpy sauce. As soon as sauce bubbles a little, reduce heat to medium-low and add salt, pepper, and chili flakes (or pepperoncini) to your taste. Stir, and a few minutes later, add oregano and basil. I prefer to tear the basil rather than chop, and sometimes I just leave it whole.

Note: Use the same wine that you will drink while cooking. Use red if you prefer, but it does change the taste. Serve with your favorite pasta and pass the cheese. Our family prefers Romano, and we top with extra fresh basil.

Anchovy Garlic Sauce for Pasta

1 Lb Pasta – your favorite
2 Oz Anchovy Fillets – minced
3 Garlic Cloves – minced
½ Cup Olive Oil

3 Tbs Seasoned Breadcrumbs
2 Tbs Fresh Basil – torn
Grated Cheese – your favorite

Cook pasta according to directions to make it al dente. Drain well and set aside. While the pasta is cooking, sauté anchovies and garlic in hot olive oil for a few minutes. Pour over the drained hot pasta. Stir in the breadcrumbs and basil. Serve immediately. Pass the cheese.

Note: You can do this without the breadcrumbs, if you prefer. But they do add a certain kind of texture. As I always say, I don't like to chop basil; I prefer to tear it. Gives out more flavor when torn, and that sage bit of information I got from my Grandmother!

Arancini

Saffron Rice Balls

3 Tbs Olive Oil	½ Small Yellow Onion – minced
½ Small Carrot – minced	½ Rib Celery – minced
3 Oz Ground Beef	3 Oz Ground Pork
1 Cup Tomato Sauce – your favorite	2 Tsp Tomato Paste
1 Small Red Onion – minced	1½ Cups Arborio Rice
¼ tsp Crushed Saffron	2 Eggs
2 Tbs Grated Parmesan Cheese	¼ Cup Flour
2 Cups Breadcrumbs	Kosher Salt
Canola Oil – for frying	Black Pepper

Heat 1 Tbs olive oil in a large skillet over medium-high heat. Add onions, carrots, and celery, and cook, stirring often until soft, about 10 minutes. Add beef and pork, and cook, stirring until browned. Stir in tomato sauce (homemade or our favorite) and paste. Reduce heat to medium-low and cook until thickened, stirring occasionally. Transfer meat filling to a bowl and let cool. Refrigerate until chilled.

Heat remaining oil in a 2-quart saucepan over medium heat. Add red onion and cook, stirring until soft. Add rice and stir to coat. Stir in saffron and 1½ cups water. Bring to a slow boil, cover, and remove from heat. Let sit for 20 minutes. Remove lid and stir in parmesan cheese, salt, and pepper. Spread rice out on a plate to cool.

Meanwhile, whisk together flour, eggs, and ½ cup water in a shallow bowl until smooth. Place breadcrumbs in another bowl and set both aside.

To Assemble:

Place 1 heaping Tbs of rice in the palm of your hand. Flatten into a disk. Place 1 tsp of chilled meat filling in center of disk and form rice around filling to encase it completely. Press gently to form a small ball. Roll ball in batter and then in breadcrumbs until evenly coated. Transfer to parchment paper–lined baking sheet. Repeat with remaining rice and meat mixture, batter, and breadcrumbs. Refrigerate for 20 minutes to firm up. You should have about 22–26 balls.

Pour oil into a 6-quart frying pan that has a depth of 2 inches, and heat over medium-high heat until a deep-fry thermometer reads 360°. Working in small batches, add rice balls to the oil and fry until golden and heated through, about 3–4 minutes. Using a slotted spoon, transfer rice balls to paper towels to drain. Let cool for 5 minutes before serving.

Arancini Quick and Easy

Rice Balls

1 Cup Uncooked Rice	1½ Cups Chopped Pepperoni – or cooked
2½ Cups Mozzarella – shredded	Italian sausage meat
8 Oz Ricotta – drained	⅓ Cup Grated Cheese
2 Cups Breadcrumbs – flavored	Pinch of Ground Black Pepper
Egg Wash – 2 eggs and 3 Tbs water	Vegetable Oil – for frying

Cook the rice and set aside to cool. Place finely chopped pepperoni (or cooked and drained sausage meat) in a large bowl. Add mozzarella, grated cheese, egg, ricotta, black pepper, and rice, and mix well.

Roll small portions of the rice mixture into golf-ball size. Make firm balls. Dip into egg wash, then dredge to coat liberally with breadcrumbs. Fry in deep fryer set at 350° until golden-brown, about 1½–2 minutes. Serve with your favorite marinara sauce.

Baked Rigatoni with Bechamel Sauce

1 Stick Butter – unsalted, sliced	1 Cup Grated Fontina
½ Cup plus 2 Tbs Flour	3–4 Oz Pancetta – sliced and rough
1 Quart Whole Milk – room temperature	chopped
Pinch of Nutmeg	1 Lb Rigatoni
Sea Salt and Freshly Ground Pepper	2 Tbs Butter – unsalted, diced

Bechamel:

In a small pan, cook the pancetta just until translucent. Do not let it crisp. In a 2-quart saucepan, melt the stick of butter over medium heat. Add the flour and whisk until smooth, about 2 minutes. Always stirring, gradually add the milk and continue to whisk until the sauce is smooth and creamy. Simmer until it is thick enough to coat the back of a spoon. This will take approximately 10 minutes. Remove from the heat and stir in the nutmeg, ½ cup Fontina, pancetta with its drippings, and taste before seasoning with salt and pepper. Set aside. Stirring and whisking is very important or the sauce will scorch, stick to the bottom of the pot, and all is lost.

Pasta:

In a large pot, bring about six quarts of water to a boil. Add the salt and rigatoni. Stir well so that the pasta does not stick to the bottom of the pot. Continue to cook for about 5 or 6 minutes. You do not want the pasta to be too cooked, because you will continue to bake it in the oven. But, it should have a little softness to it. Drain the pasta and return it to the pot. Pour in the bechamel sauce using a wooden spoon. Mix it well, making sure that all the pasta is coated with the sauce.

To Bake:

Into a greased 9" x 13" baking dish, pour the pasta, scraping the pot to make sure you get all the cream sauce. Smooth the top and sprinkle the remaining ½ cup of Fontina over all. Dot with diced butter and bake in the oven at 425° for 25–30 minutes until the top is golden brown and bubbly. When serving, pass some freshly grated cheese.

Note: If you would prefer this dish to be a bit more creamy, just increase the bechamel recipe by one-half.

Beach Pasta Surprise

*This Is More of a Story Than a Recipe,
but Somewhere in the Story Is Sort of a Recipe*

Each year, starting, I believe, in 1995, we have taken the entire family to the beach so that we all could have a week of relaxed togetherness. It started with one house, and as the family grew, so did the size of the house. We now are a family of over twenty, so we are in two houses side by side. This is especially great for the Grandchildren, as they get to spend time with their Cousins. It's an even better time for me, as I get to have my entire family together for a week.

We never go out to eat. In the summertime, with a family of over twenty, that would be an impossible situation. Besides, we are a family of cooks! Each night, a different family cooks while the rest of us enjoy Aperol Spritzers. The Grandkids help with the cleanup. The main thing is that we all sit down to enjoy dinner together. The meals have been nothing short of delicious. Breakfast is prepared in the morning, and a multitude of sandwiches are made soon after in sort of production-line fashion. Generally, we are on the beach by 10:30. It's a day of games, reading, napping, and swimming.

I wanted our Sunday meal to be similar to our traditional spaghetti-and-meatball meal. So, three years ago, we hauled the sauce, pasta, big pots, and frozen meatballs, etc., to the beach. All well and good, but still a lot of work. Last year I came up with a Sunday Beach Recipe—all things I can get done in advance. During the week I made the sauce, but instead of regular-sized meatballs, I made them the size of ping-pong balls or a bit smaller. On Friday, I made a few very large pasta casseroles and imbedded the meatballs throughout the layers of pasta and cheese— ricotta and shredded mozzarella—almost like a lasagna. I topped the casseroles with sauce and packed them well, first with Saran, then foil, and then refrigerated them. I placed them in the cooler just before leaving for the beach very early Saturday morning with a few containers of extra sauce and grated cheese, and all was ready for our Sunday night traditional dinner.

It was a success, so on the list to do again every year!

Bucatini, Calabrian Style

1 Lb Bucatini	4 Tbs Olive Oil
2 Garlic Cloves – diced	½ Cup Onion – chopped
½ tsp Dried Chili Flakes	4 Oz Prosciutto – chopped
1 Can (28 Oz) Crushed Tomatoes	1 Bunch Fresh Parsley – chopped
1 Bunch Basil – torn	Pinch of Kosher Salt – or to taste
Caciocavallo or Romano – grated	Freshly Grated Pepper to Taste

Cook pasta according to package directions (al dente). Meanwhile, in a large skillet, combine olive oil, garlic, onion, and red chili flakes. Cook on medium heat for a few minutes. Add prosciutto and cook for 5 minutes, while stirring well to coat. Add the tomatoes and bring to a boil, and then reduce the heat and let it simmer for 30 minutes. Stir in half of the parsley.

When the pasta is cooked, reserve two cups of the pasta water. Drain the pasta, and quickly add the pasta and some of the reserved water to the skillet. Stir in the remaining parsley, basil, salt, and pepper. Cook the pasta in the skillet on low, stirring constantly until the water is evaporated. If the pasta looks too dry, add a little more water until you get a consistency you like. Stir in the cheese and ladle into bowls. Of course, pass more cheese.

Note: If you want this dish to be authentic, you have to choose a bucatini that is egg-free, because in Calabria, pasta is made egg-free.

Cacio e Pepe Rice with Guanciale

4 Oz Guanciale – diced
Freshly Ground Pepper to Taste
4 Cups Cooked Arborio Rice

6 Tbs Butter – unsalted
1 tsp Sea Salt or Kosher Salt
Grated Cheese – for sprinkling

In a food processor, pulse the guanciale until it is ground. (Guanciale is made from the entire jowl and cheek from a pig. You can find it in Italian specialty stores.)

Boil enough rice to make 4 cups cooked, and reserve ¾ cup of the water while keeping the rice warmed.

Family grinder used for the grinding of pepper and also coffee beans

Heat butter in a large saucepan, and when starting to sizzle, add the guanciale and coarsely ground pepper, salt, and up to ¾ of the rice water a little at a time. Stir in the rice and cook just until heated, and then ladle into bowls and garnish with a little more freshly ground black pepper and grated cheese.

Note: In Italy, rice is cultivated in water, planted in April, and ready to harvest by September. The rice is grown along the Po Valley in Piedmont, Lombardy, Emilia, and Veneto. Italian rice, when cooked, releases a good amount of starch, which enables the grains to cling nicely without becoming glutinous.

To give this dish just a little twist, add three cups, packed, of chopped baby arugula into the pan with the guanciale, and toss for a few minutes. Do this just before adding the rice. After adding the rice, if it seems to be a bit dry, add some of the reserved rice water a little at a time until you get the right consistency.

Cavatelli Dough Recipe

Victor's Recipe

4 Cups Flour
¾–1 Cup Water

¼ Cup Olive Oil
2 tsps Baking Powder

Mix flour and part of the water, and knead, adding more water slowly. Dough should not be soft; it should be a little on the dry side, but not crumbly. After mixing, form into a disc, cover with Saran, and let rest for 30 minutes. Roll out to desired thickness and cut into 1½-inch wide strips. Put through Cavatelli machine. Let dry on cloth for a little while, and put slowly into salted boiling water, separating the strands.

Holiday specialty rolled out on very thin needles

Crepes for Making Lasagna

12 Eggs	**1 Cup of Flour**
3 Cups Water	**Large Mixing Bowl**

Beat eggs. Add water. Slowly add flour while constantly mixing. Use a good crepe pan. Depending on the size of the pan, you may want to cut them in half after rolling. Heat pan to medium-to-high heat, then lightly grease the pan with either fatback or olive oil.

I have an electric crepe maker, but you can use a 10-inch crepe pan. Add about half a soup ladle of batter and roll it around quickly so it spreads evenly. It should be very thin. Lift the edges of the crepe, and when the edges start to curl, pick it up quickly with your fingers, if possible, and turn it over. It only takes about a minute or less on each side. Let each one cool for a minute or two before stacking them on top of each other. One dozen eggs should make about 40 10-inch crepes. If it is easier, you can just make 6-inch or 7-inch crepes; it just will take much longer. Make them a day ahead, stack on a cookie sheet with layers of wax or parchment paper in between, seal, and refrigerate. But, they must be completely cooled to do this.

To make lasagna, layer all over bottom and up the sides of your dish with a big overhang that will fold over and cover the top of the lasagna. On each layer, put very little of each of the following: your favorite sauce; chopped, cooked sausage; mozzarella; grated cheese. Dip each crepe quickly in a mixture of egg and milk, let excess roll off, and place in pan. Top layer should be crepes completely covering the lasagna. Make a few slits in the lasagna, and with a teaspoon, add a little of the excess egg liquid, but not too much. Top with a little bit of mozzarella, sauce, and grated cheese.

Note: Using crepes instead of the traditional lasagna noodle results in a much lighter lasagna. This recipe was given to me from the aunt of an old friend.

Fettuccine e Gamberi

1 Lb Fettuccine	**1 Pint Cream – reduced**
20 Medium Shrimp – cleaned	**2 Garlic Cloves – chopped**
1 Cup Flour	**½ Cup White Wine**
Salt and Ground Black Pepper	**4 Tbs Olive Oil**

Reduce the cream by cooking it down until it has reduced somewhat. Heat the olive oil in a sauté pan. Flour the shrimp and sauté until they start to become pink. Add the white wine, salt, and freshly ground black pepper. Add the garlic and cook for about three minutes. Add the cream and continue cooking over low heat.

Meanwhile, cook the pasta in a large pot of salted water until al dente. Drain and spread the cooked pasta over the sauce in the pan. Add a pat or two of butter and some Parmigiano cheese for a little extra flavor. Toss well and serve, maybe with a little extra freshly ground black pepper.

Fettuccine con Funghi

½ Oz Imported Dried Porcini
1 Lb Fresh Mushrooms
3 Tbs Butter
1 Clove Garlic – finely chopped
1 Lb Fresh Fettuccini

½ Cup Grated Parmigiano
2 Cups Heavy Cream
Salt and Ground Black Pepper
1 Tbs Extra Virgin Olive Oil

Soak the dried porcini in a cup of lukewarm water for a minimum of 30 minutes. Remove the mushrooms without stirring the water. Filter the porcini water through cheesecloth into a cup, and set aside. Quickly rinse the fresh mushrooms in cold water and carefully dry. (For best results, without getting the mushrooms too wet, I dampen a paper towel and just lightly clean off the mushrooms.) Slice the mushrooms very thin, together with the stems.

In a sauté pan large enough to accommodate the cooked pasta, pour in the olive oil and refreshed porcini mushrooms and their filtered water. Cover and cook over low-to-medium heat until the water has completely boiled away. Add the thinly sliced fresh mushrooms, salt, and pepper to the pan, and cover. Cook for 15–20 minutes. If at the end of that time there is still liquid in the pan, remove cover and continue to boil the liquid away over a higher heat.

Add chopped garlic and cook for 5 minutes. Add heavy cream, adjust the heat to simmer, and reduce the cream until it thickens. Reduce heat while pasta is cooking.

Cook fettuccini al dente in salted, boiling water. Drain well and stir into the cream sauce. Add butter and Parmigiano, and stir into the pasta. Ladle into bowls. Serve immediately, and pass more black pepper and grated cheese.

Fried Polenta

4–6 Cup Cooked Polenta – room temperature   **Olive Oil**

Place cooked polenta on a wooden board that is covered with wax paper. With a heavy wooden spatula, press down on the polenta until it is square or pie-shaped—whichever you prefer, but still thick. Heat enough olive oil to lightly cover the bottom of a cast-iron pan or heavy skillet. Heat almost until oil starts to smoke. Lifting with the wax paper from the board, carefully place the polenta onto the skillet and discard the wax paper. Watch out for splatter. Fry polenta, pressing down with the wooden spatula until it is even all around and sits firmly on the skillet. Cook on medium heat until the polenta is crusty and brown on the bottom. Turn the polenta over in the pan, adding a little more oil if needed, and cook that side until crusty and golden. Turn out onto a serving plate, and cut into squares or wedges.

During my childhood, we ate polenta often. It was a staple in our house, especially during the war. It usually was not served in a bowl, but turned out onto a board. Extra always was made, because we enjoyed it fried the next day and considered it a treat. For some reason, it was passed down from my Grandmother that one should only use wooden utensils when working with polenta.

Gnocchi Sorrentina

Gnocchi:

1 Medium-Sized, Dry Potato – like russet   **1 Cup Flour**
Pinch of Salt   **1 Egg Yolk**
1 Tbs Extra Virgin Olive – plus extra for   **A Sprig of Fresh Basil**
    greasing casserole dish

Sauce:

½ Cup Tomato Sauce – your favorite   **2 Oz Mozzarella - cubed**
Basil Leaves – a few torn   **¼ Cup Parmesan Cheese – divided**

Wash the potato. Boil it in salted water until cooked through (approximately 30 minutes). Wait a few minutes until the potato is cool enough to handle, and then peel it, mash it with a potato ricer, and then allow it to cool some more on a slightly floured board.

Make a well in the center of the potato pile and sprinkle some flour on the outer edge. Put the egg yolk in the well with salt and the olive oil. Mix lightly with your hands, incorporating the flour into the potato and egg until you have a soft, manageable dough. You may not need all the flour, and there is a slight chance you might need a bit more. The mixture should not be sticky when you roll it into a ball.

Roll the ball in a bit of flour, flatten it a bit, and then slice into 5 or 6 pieces. Roll each piece into long logs that are no thicker than a hot dog, using a minimal amount of flour. Cut each log into ½-inch pieces, and using your thumb, slide each piece over the tines of a fork to produce ridges. These ridges will capture the sauce.

Cooking the Gnocchi:

Cook the gnocchi in salted, boiling water for a few minutes (stirring lightly to keep them moving and not sticking together) until they rise up to the top of the pot. Scoop out with a large slotted spoon or kitchen spider, and place gently in a large frying pan with some of the sauce on the bottom so that the gnocchi don't stick. Top with shredded mozzarella, a sprig or two of basil, and sauté for a few minutes. Place the pan in an oven preheated to 350° and bake for about 15 minutes. Sprinkle with the remaining parmesan cheese and serve.

Basic Gnocchi

2¼ Lbs Mealy or Dry Potatoes – like russet	2½ Cups Flour
1 Egg	Generous Pinch of Salt
2 Egg Yolks	

In a pot of salted, boiling water, cook the potatoes for about 25 minutes. Remove from the water and let the potatoes cool slightly to let the steam escape from them. When cool enough (but not cold) to handle, pass them through a potato ricer and salt lightly.

Knead together the potatoes, egg, and egg yolks. Slowly work in as much flour as needed to produce a smooth, supple dough that does not stick to your fingers. Gnocchi should be fluffy and delicate.

On a floured work surface, form finger-width logs from the dough. Cut each log into ¾-inch pieces, and gently roll each one over the back of a fork (because genuine gnocchi must have grooves to better hold the butter or sauce) to give each one their characteristic ridged texture.

Lay out on a very lightly floured cloth. Bring a large pot of salted water to a boil and cook the gnocchi in small portions, lest they all stick together, until they rise to the surface. While they are cooking, stir occasionally and slowly just to keep them separated. Remove with a slotted spoon (pouring into a colander will make them fall apart) and prepare in your favorite way.

Note: If you would like to give the gnocchi a little lemon flavor, add freshly grated lemon zest from two lemons to the egg yolks and beat in with a fork before adding to the dough. There is really no precise guideline for the ingredients of this recipe, since the amount of flour depends on the type of potato used and the adeptness of the cook. This recipe was the guideline my family followed.

The Story of Gnocchi

Our one-and-only serving spoon used for gnocchi, polenta, and pasta

Gnocchi (gnocco, which literally means "dumpling," and also means "dunce" in the vernacular, is the singular form and very rarely used, as nobody eats just one!) are a classic part of Italian cuisine, particularly in Northern and Central Italy. They are an exquisite delicacy, despite the simplicity of the ingredients and method of making, which requires a distinctive feel and knack. But, there is nothing better than delicate gnocchi dressed in melted butter and freshly grated cheese.

The gnocchi family is varied and large, depending on the region and town. They can be made from the most usual dry "potatoes," as well as pumpkin, semolina, corn, or chestnut flour. In Trentino, they are made with a potato dough and red beets, and finished off with poppy seeds. In an area near the Austrian border, they are stuffed with dried plums. In Trieste, they also make sweet gnocchi called "Gnocchi al Cacao" from potato gnocchi with bittersweet chocolate and candied fruit, and are served for dessert. In Piedmont, they are made from durum wheat semolina, and are topped with cheese and then baked in the oven. In Lombardy, they are referred to with the unflattering name of "malfatti," which translates to "badly made." Verona hosts a gnocchi festival each year during carnival time (referred to as "Baccanale del Gnocco" or "Funzione dei

Gnocchi"). On Carnival Friday, a "Papa del Gnocho" is chosen, and as Pope of the Bacchanalia, he leads a festive procession through Verona, riding on a donkey and holding a giant fork on which a huge gnocco is skewered. In Venice, gnocchi is usually finished with a lobster sauce.

But, there is nothing better than potato gnocchi
dressed in melted browned butter and freshly grated cheese!

Farfalle al Carciofi

1 Lb Bowtie Pasta	20 Marinated Artichoke Halves
2 Roasted Peppers – sliced into strips	1 Cup Black Olives
10 Fresh Basil Leaves	¾ Cup Extra Virgin Olive Oil
1 tsp Red Pepper Flakes	2 tsp chopped garlic
1 tsp Oregano	Salt and Freshly Ground Black Pepper – to taste

Cook pasta in 4 quarts of salted, boiling water just until al dente. Drain and run cold water through the pasta until chilled. Drain well. Place pasta in a large bowl. Stir all other ingredients into the pasta and mix well. Refrigerate for 2–3 hours for maximum flavor.

Gorgonzola Cream Sauce

A Great Sauce for Lots of Dishes

2 Tbs Butter – unsalted	½ Cup Gorgonzola – crumbled
1 Half-Pint Whipping Cream	½ Cup Parmesan Cheese – grated

In a heavy-bottomed sauté pan, over medium heat, add the butter to melt but not to get brown. Add the whipping cream slowly while stirring, and when all incorporated, add the gorgonzola and bring the sauce to a simmer. Stir to reduce the cheese crumbles and to become creamy and smooth. Remove from heat and serve.

Note: This sauce will make anything extra special. You can pour it over pasta, sautéed chicken, baked potatoes, and other vegetables. It just is a handy little secret to have in your recipe collection.

Homemade Egg Pasta

Pasta Dough for 4 People

2 Large Eggs   **½ tsp Salt**
1½ Cups All-Purpose Flour – unbleached

Put the flour on a flat surface or in a bowl, and form a well that will be deep enough to hold the eggs. The sides should be high enough to prevent the eggs from running out. Break the eggs into the flour well, add the salt, and with a whisk, beat the eggs lightly. While doing this, begin to incorporate a little bit of the flour from the inside of the flour well. Keep incorporating the eggs into the flour until the eggs are no longer runny. A good technique for doing this is to hold the outside wall of the flour with one hand while whisking with the other. If you feel more comfortable, you can use a fork to do this. My Grandmother just used her fingers to mix the eggs in, and of course, she was making much larger portions.

When all the flour has been incorporated, make a ball with the dough. Put the ball on a flat, lightly floured surface, and start kneading. With the heel of your hand, push down firmly into the center of the dough, giving the dough a slight turn and pushing down and turning again. Have flour-dusted hands as you knead. Kneading will take about 7 or 8 minutes. When nice and smooth (and not sticky), rest the dough under a bowl for about 15 or 20 minutes. Cut the ball in half, and while keeping one half covered, roll out the other half on a pastry board with a large rolling pin to about ⅛-inch thickness. Flour as necessary, but not too much, as this will make the dough tough.

You can now pass the dough through your pasta machine or roll the dough up like a jelly roll, and slice into thin slices to make tagliatelle or fettuccine. Open the sliced pasta and dry out on a cloth-lined board until ready to cook. Fresh pasta cooks much faster than dried pasta. So, watch the pot.

Hot Rice Salad

Insalata di Riso Calda

2 Cups Arborio Rice   **3 Tbs Olive Oil**
1 Tbs Butter   **½ Cup Fresh Parsley**
Juice of 2 Lemons   **Salt and Freshly Ground Black Pepper to Taste**

Bring 4 quarts of water to a boil in a large heavy-bottomed pot. When the water has boiled, add some salt and butter, give it a swirl, and then add the rice. Cook until the rice is al dente and not overcooked. When done, remove from the heat and drain, pressing down a little on the rice to remove as much liquid as possible. Add the rice to a bowl and drizzle with a mixture of the olive oil and lemon juice. Taste and adjust salt and freshly ground black pepper. Sprinkle the parsley on top and toss again. Serve at once.

Lasagna al Forno

3 Tbs Olive Oil
1 Lb Ground Chuck
1 Can (6 Oz) Tomato Paste
1 Large Onion – chopped
3 tsps Crushed Oregano
2 Lbs Whole-Milk Ricotta – drained
1½ Cups Romano Cheese –grated
Salt and Freshly Ground Pepper

6–8 Fresh Lasagna Sheets
3 Eggs – lightly beaten
3 Garlic Cloves – minced
¾ Lb Italian Sweet Sausage – removed from casing
2 Cans (28 Oz Each) Crushed Italian Tomatoes
8 tsps Fresh Basil – chopped
1½ Lbs Fresh Mozzarella

In a large sauce pot, heat olive oil until hot. Add onions and garlic, and cook until just tender. Add beef and sausage meat, and sauté until browned, stirring occasionally to break up the chunks.

Pour off the excess fat. Stir in the tomatoes and tomato paste, and simmer, covered, for 30 minutes. Stir in the spices and simmer for another hour. Stir frequently, reaching all the way down to the bottom to prevent it from sticking. Cool a little before using.

Preheat oven to 350°. Lightly oil a 13" x 9" pan. In a good-sized bowl, beat the eggs, add a pinch of salt, a grinding of black pepper, ricotta, and ½ cup of grated cheese. For easier spreading, add a little of the cooled sauce to thin the mixture out a little.

Put a thin layer of sauce on the bottom of the baking dish. Fit one fresh lasagna sheet on top of the sauce. Spread with a layer of the ricotta mixture, dot with a little more sauce, and sprinkle with shredded mozzarella. Repeat with as many layers as your pan will hold, usually 4. On the top layer, do not add any ricotta; just top with a good amount of sauce, a good amount of shredded mozzarella, and ⅓ cup of grated cheese. Drizzle with a tiny bit of extra virgin olive oil.

Bake for 20 minutes. Let stand for 15 minutes at the least before serving. Pass hot sauce, additional grated cheese, and some torn fresh basil at the table.

Lasagna, Tuscan Style

Lasagna:

1 Lb Lasagna – dry or fresh sheets   2 tsps Sea Salt
1 tsp Olive Oil

Preheat oven to 350°. Generously grease the bottom and sides of a 9" x 12" x 13" baking dish. If using dried lasagna noodles, bring water to a boil in a large pot and add 2 tsps of sea salt and oil. Add pasta and stir gently for a few minutes to make sure they don't stick together. This is the only time I add oil to pasta water. Pasta is ready when it is still very al dente, because you will be cooking it again. Drain the pasta, and with tongs, lift the strips out and place on towels to dry a little. If you are using fresh pasta, skip all that and just cut the fresh sheets to a size to fit the baking dish. You do not need to cook the fresh pasta sheets, even though you may be tempted to.

Lasagna Filling:

1 Cup Onions – coarsely chopped   4–5 Fresh Basil Leaves – torn
2 Garlic Cloves – coarsely chopped   2 Cans (28 Oz) San Marzano Tomatoes
½ Lb Ground Beef Chuck   1½–2 Lbs Ricotta – whole milk
2 Lbs Italian Mild Sausage – casing removed ½–⅔ Cups Italian Cheese – freshly grated
Pinch of Ground Nutmeg   ½–¾ Lb Fresh Mozzarella – shredded
Salt and Pepper to Taste   Olive Oil

In a large pot, heat the oil, add the onions and garlic, and cook until translucent. Do not let them burn. Add the ground chuck and sausage meat, breaking up the meat clumps as the meat cooks. Add salt and pepper to taste, and stir well. Add the nutmeg. When the meat is cooked but not too dry, add the tomatoes and basil. You can put the tomatoes in a blender and quickly pulse beforehand, if you like. I like to break up the tomatoes with my hand as I put them into the pot. It does make for a lumpier sauce. Lower the heat and simmer for about an hour or a little more, making sure everything is well blended.

Assemble the Lasagna:

Lasagna Sheets   Ricotta, Mozzarella,
Sauce   and Grated Cheese

Spread a thin layer of the sauce on the bottom of the baking dish. Add a layer of the lasagna noodle of your choice over the sauce. Cover it with a little sauce, ricotta, shredded mozzarella, and grated cheese. Repeat, making as many layers as your baking dish will hold, ending with just sauce, shredded mozzarella, and grated cheese, in that order. Bake for 30–45 minutes until piping hot and a little bubbly. Let rest for 10–15 minutes before serving. Pass more sauce and cheese.

Note: To make the ricotta a little easier to spread, I like to mix it with a beaten egg and a little sauce. Also, if you are using fresh pasta sheets and you have any sheets left over, or even the scraps when trimming to fit the baking pan, cut these up in little strips and freeze to add to soup at a later date.

Lemon Gnocchi

1¾ Lbs Dry Potatoes – like russet or Idaho
3 Zested Lemons – save some of the juice
3 Tbs Extra Virgin Olive Oil
Freshly Grated Romano or Parmesan Cheese
  – for sprinkling (optional)

2 Eggs – room temperature
1½ Cups Flour (approximately)
2 Tbs butter

Bake the potatoes for about an hour at 400°F, or until they are soft. After they cool a bit and you can handle them, peel them while they are still a bit warm. Put the potatoes through a potato ricer (or grate them) into a mound on the counter. Make a well in the center, and break two eggs into the well. Add the lemon zest to the eggs, and beat them with a fork a little bit. Slowly incorporate the potatoes into the eggs, and start adding some of the flour; a pastry scraper helps with this. Work the flour in until a nice dough forms. Don't overwork the dough. Add just enough flour so the dough is not too dry. You want the dough to be slightly sticky. Pinch off some of the dough and roll into a long, thin log. Cut the log into 1-inch pieces and gently roll each piece off the tine of a fork to create wedges. The smaller the pieces, the easier they are to handle.

(We set the gnocchi out on a cloth as we make them. This is where having little Grandchildren comes in handy. They think sorting them is fun, and Gianna and Olivia take this job very seriously.) If you are not going to cook them in the next 20 minutes or so, place on a tray covered loosely with wax paper, and refrigerate until it is time for them to be cooked.

Bring a large pot of water to boil. Add salt, and slowly add the gnocchi. Reduce the heat so that the water is not boiling too rapidly, and stir gently; the gnocchi are fragile. As they rise to the top, taste one for doneness. When they are done to your likeness, remove from the pot with a large slotted spoon and gently add to the dish you will serve from.

In a small pan, heat the olive oil, butter, and some lemon juice until the butter is slightly brown. Stir in the zest, and then pour over the gnocchi and toss gently. Serve at once. Pass the cheese. Serves 2–3 as a main, 6 as a side dish.

Note: I like to use a potato ricer to make the gnocchi, but you can grate the potatoes on a box cheese grater, if you don't have one. This is a little more tedious, because the potatoes tend to crumble unless you grate slowly.

Lemon Pasta with Crab and Chili

½ Lb Linguine
4 Tbs Extra Virgin Olive Oil
2 Cloves Garlic – sliced
¼ Cup Fresh Basil Leaves – shredded

½ Lb Crab Meat
1 Chili – seeded and chopped
Juice and Zest of 1 Large Lemon

Cook the pasta in salted water until al dente. In the meantime, in a medium-sized bowl, combine all the remaining ingredients (except the basil) and toss well. Season with salt and pepper.

Drain the pasta, reserving a cup of the water as a backup. Add the drained pasta back to the pot, and add the crab mixture and toss. If the pasta looks a little dry, now is the time to keep stirring some of the reserved pasta water back into the pasta until you get the desired consistency. Taste for a little more salt and pepper, maybe a dash of olive oil. Sprinkle with the shredded basil, and pass the cheese.

Linguine in a Sausage Lemon Sauce

(Pasta di Cascia)

1 Egg
Zest of 1 Large Lemon
1½ tsps Grated Nutmeg

½ tsp Black Pepper – freshly ground
Juice of ½ Large Lemon
¼ Cup Heavy Cream

Zest from ½ Large Lemon
4 Tbs Extra Virgin Olive Oil
2 Links Italian Sweet Sausage – crumbled
Freshly Grated Romano or Parmesan Cheese
   – for serving

2 Oz Pancetta – diced
½ Lb Fresh Pasta – preferably linguine

In a medium bowl, beat together the egg, pepper, nutmeg, lemon juice, zest, and cream. Mix well so that all is incorporated, and set aside.

In a large heavy-bottomed pan, add 1 Tbs of the olive oil and heat. Add the pancetta and cook until it just starts to crisp. Do not overcook. Remove pancetta from the pan and put in separate bowl.

Add the sausage to the pan and cook until browned. Add to bowl with pancetta. Drain off all excess fat and add remaining olive oil to the pan. Set aside.

In a large pot, bring water to a boil. Add the salt and the pasta, and stir. Cook pasta until al dente and then drain pasta, reserving about a cup of the pasta water. Fresh pasta cooks quickly, so watch carefully.

While the pasta is cooking, reheat the pan, and return the sausage and pancetta to it to warm. As soon as the pasta is ready, drain it and add it to the pan. Toss it with the sausage and pancetta.

When all is mixed in, remove pan from the heat and add the egg mixture. Stir quickly, making sure the egg mixture coats all the pasta. Transfer from the pan to a warmed bowl, or serve directly from the pan. If you think it is too dry, add a little of the reserved pasta water. Pass the cheese and the pepper mill.

Linguine with Fresh Clams

Charlie's Version

4 Tbs Extra Virgin Olive Oil
4–5 Garlic Cloves – sliced
½ Tbs Red Pepper Flakes
4 Tbs Sliced Shallots
24 Little Neck Clams – scrubbed well
1 Lb Linguine

2 Tbs Butter – unsalted
1 Tbs Butcher Pepper
2 tsps Oregano
½ Cup Dry White Wine
4 Tbs Chopped Parsley or Basil
Salt to Taste

In a heavy saucepan, heat olive oil with butter until the butter melts. Add the garlic and stir just until the garlic starts to color. Add salt, pepper, red pepper flakes, oregano, and sliced shallots. Stir until well combined and the shallots are soft. Add the white wine and stir in.

Add the clams to the pot and gently boil for 6–8 minutes. Discard any clams that did not open. Stir in the chopped parsley. Remove clams with a slotted spoon and place in a bowl, covered.

Cook pasta in 4 quarts of salted, boiling water. Stir and cook just until al dente.

Drain pasta and ladle into the saucepan with the clam sauce, and heat for about 2 minutes. Then portion pasta and place the clams on top of the pasta. Garnish with additional chopped parsley or basil, if desired.

Anita's Note: Charlie won't put "Pass the cheese" in his recipe. However, in our house, we sure do pass the cheese!

Montefollonico Tomato Sauce

2–3 Cups Grape Tomatoes – rinsed and cut in half	Dried Oregano – pinch or to taste
3 Tbs Olive Oil	2 Garlic Cloves – finely chopped
1 Medium Onion – finely chopped	Salt and Pepper to Taste
A Few Fresh Basil Leaves – roughly torn	1 Tbs Butter – unsalted
Pinch of Red Pepper Flakes	1 Lb Pasta – your favorite
Grated Cheese – to pass	Fresh Basil – for garnish

Heat olive oil in a large pan. Add onions and garlic, and cook over medium heat until both are translucent. Add the cut tomatoes, and sprinkle with salt and pepper. Cook over medium-low heat, stirring occasionally until the tomatoes are soft. Stir in basil, oregano, and red pepper flakes, and cook for about 10 minutes on medium-low heat. When the tomatoes are very soft, add the butter and stir well to mix in. Cook pasta al dente, drain well, and add to the pan with the tomatoes, stirring to make sure all is well combined. Serve and pass the cheese, some extra virgin olive oil for topping, and some fresh basil.

Note: While visiting my family in Montefollonico, Cristina made this simple but totally delicious sauce one noonday for our pranzo. It has become one of my favorite spaghetti sauces.

My Very First Spaghetti Sauce

The Recipe I Always Count On

3 (28 Oz) Cans San Marzano Crushed Tomatoes

1 Large Onion – chopped (softball size)

3 Garlic Cloves – peeled and sliced

1 tsp Salt – or to taste

1 tsp Crushed Red Pepper – or to taste

¼ Cup Romano Cheese – grated (or one good cheese rind)

1 tsp Sugar

4–5 Basil Leaves – large

1 tsp Oregano

⅛ Cup Olive Oil

Heat olive oil in a large pot. Add onion and sauté over medium heat. When onions begin to get soft, add garlic and stir. Do not let the garlic brown or burn, as it will taste bitter. When garlic is just starting to color, add tomatoes and stir well, making sure you get down to the bottom of the pot. Slowly bring to a good simmer. If you have not used San Marzano tomatoes and the sauce looks a little pale, you can at this point add 2 heaping tsps of tomato paste. Stir well and then add all the seasonings. After 5 minutes, adjust the heat to low, and cover and cook for one hour. Stir occasionally and never let the sauce come to a boil. If you are adding meatballs and other meat, add after the sauce has cooked for about 30 minutes. After you have browned the meatballs (I brown in the oven/broiler), save a good portion of the drippings, add to the sauce, and stir in well. This is where you will get most of your flavor. Sauce is better when cooked early in the day or the night before.

Note: Pieces of pork, country-style spareribs, and Italian sausage are good meats to add and enrich the flavor. I cook these in the oven before adding, along with a little of the accumulated juices. Chicken can be added, although it will give the sauce an entirely different flavor. If making a sauce using only chicken parts, brown 6 slices of chopped pancetta in with the onions and garlic. This will intensify the flavor a little.

This is the basis for the spaghetti sauce I learned by watching my Mother-in-Law. There were usually pork pieces in with the meatballs (and not chicken). Of course, over the years, it has probably changed a little as I accommodate my family. What I learned was a sauce for 4, and oftentimes I find that I am making sauce for 20 for a family gathering.

Orecchiette with Sausage and Herbs

¾ Lb Orecchiette
1 Cup of Chopped Onion
1 Lb Italian Sausage Meat
1½ Cups Chicken Broth
1 tsp Fresh Sage – chopped
3 Tbs Capers – drained
3 Tbs Basil – freshly chopped

2 Tbs Olive Oil
4 Garlic Cloves – sliced
½ Cup Dry Red Wine
2 tsps Fresh Rosemary – chopped
2 Tbs Butter
½ Cup Parmigiano-Reggiano Cheese

Cook the pasta according to the package directions only until al dente. In a large skillet, combine olive oil, onion, and garlic, and cook on medium heat for about 5 minutes. Do not let the garlic burn. Add the sausage meat, salt, and pepper, and cook for about 10 minutes, stirring to prevent sticking and to break up the sausage a little.

Add wine, broth, rosemary, and sage. Mix in well and bring to a slow boil. Reduce to simmer and cook for about 8 minutes. Add capers and butter, stirring to mix in well. Drain the pasta and add to the skillet, along with the grated cheese and chopped basil. Toss well, ladle into bowls, and pass more cheese!

Pasta alla Carbonara

½ Lb Linguine or Fettuccine
⅓ Cup Butter – melted
½ Cup Heavy Cream
2 Egg Yolks – lightly beaten
Olive Oil

⅔–1 Cup Parmesan Cheese – plus extra
  for serving
4 Oz Pancetta – chopped
Salt and Pepper to Taste

Bring 4–5 quarts of water to boil in a large pot. Just before adding the pasta, add a generous amount of salt to the water. Add the pasta and stir for a minute or two to avoid clumping. While the pasta is cooking, warm the butter and heavy cream in a small pot. Remove from the heat and allow it to cool slightly so that the eggs won't curdle when added. Using a whisk, slowly stir in the egg yolks and mix well. In a saucepan that will be large enough to hold the cooked pasta, cook the pancetta in a very small amount of olive oil, just until starting to crisp. Once the pasta is cooked al dente, drain well, and add to the pan with the pancetta, mixing well to coat the pasta with the pancetta. Pour the cream mixture over all and mix well. Add half of the grated cheese and toss well over low heat, making sure all the pasta is well coated. Taste for salt and pepper. Pass the remaining cheese for topping.

Note: There are many versions of carbonara, but this is my favorite. Some recipes omit the heavy cream, but increase the butter, and some recipes add peas. Probably the traditional way would be without the cream and with the peas. Don't be concerned about the raw eggs, because the heat of the cream mixture and the heat of the pasta will cook the eggs.

Pasta Carbonara

Charlie's Version

1 Lb Tagliatelle – or your favorite
4–6 Oz Pancetta – sliced thin and chopped
1 Cup Parmigiano or Pecorino – grated
¼ Cup Chopped Italian Basil or Parsley –
    for garnish

2 Tbs Extra Virgin Olive Oil
3 Egg Yolks
1–2 Tbs Freshly Ground Black Pepper

Prepare the sauce ahead of time.

Heat olive oil over medium flame. Add the pancetta and sauté, adding the black pepper and stirring periodically until lightly crisp. Remove from the heat and set aside.

In a separate bowl, add the egg yolks and ½ cup of the cheese. Mix in until well combined, and set aside.

In a large pot of salted water, cook the pasta al dente. Before draining, reserve 1 cup of the pasta water to use if needed. Drain the pasta and place in the pan with the pancetta, heating over a medium flame for about 2 minutes, and then tossing to make sure all is mixed in. Remove from the heat and add the egg-cheese mixture. Toss while adding the remainder of the cheese and a little more black pepper. If the pasta seems a bit too dry, add a bit of the reserved pasta water a little at a time until you are satisfied with the consistency. Toss again, ladle into bowls, and garnish with basil or parsley. (Anita says to "Pass the cheese!" We do in our house, but that's up to you.)

Pasta con Sarde

A Traditional Sicilian Christmas Eve Dish

¼ Cup Olive Oil

¼ tsp Dried Oregano

4 Medium Yellow Onions – thinly sliced

1 Onion – roughly chopped

2 tsps Tomato Paste

½ Can (28 Oz) Italian Tomatoes – crushed, in juice with basil

3–4 Basil Leaves

2 Cloves Garlic – finely chopped

Salt and Pepper to Taste

1½ Lb Fresh Sardines – filleted and chopped

2 Tbs Flour

4 Anchovies – finely chopped

1 Cup Golden Raisins – soaked for 30 minutes in warm water and drained

¼ Cup Pine Nuts

1 Lb Pasta – your favorite

2 Tbs Fresh Parsley – finely chopped

1 Large Fennel Bulb – thinly sliced

Heat 2 Tbs of olive oil in a large saucepan over medium heat. Add oregano, chopped onion, garlic, and cook until soft. Add tomato paste and continue cooking until caramelized, being careful to not burn. Add all the tomatoes, breaking up the tomatoes by hand as you add to the pot, but only half the juice. Cook until reduced, about 30 minutes. Stir in basil, season with salt and pepper, and set aside.

Bring another pot of salted water to boil. Add the fennel and cook until tender, about 30 minutes. Stir in basil, season with salt and pepper, and set aside.

Bring another pot of salted water to boil. Add the fennel and cook until tender, about 5 minutes. Drain the fennel and set aside.

Heat ¼ cup of oil in a large skillet over medium-high heat. Toss sardines in flour, add to skillet, and cook until golden brown, about 4 minutes. Add remaining oil, sliced onions, drained fennel, and anchovies. Cook until very soft, about 15 minutes. Add tomato sauce, drained raisins, and pine nuts. Cook for about 10 minutes until flavors are well blended. Cook pasta al dente in salted, boiling water. Drain well and add to pan with sardine sauce, and toss well. Transfer to large serving bowl and sprinkle with parsley. My Mother-in-Law would never have passed cheese with this dish. Yes, in our house, we do.

Note: This is also served on the Feast of St. Joseph and often during Lent.

Pasta d'Padre

The Priest's Pasta, Charlie's Version

2 Tbs Extra Virgin Olive Oil
½ Lbs Italian Sausage – out of casing
Red Pepper Flakes – optional
Pecorino Cheese – freshly grated

½ Cup Onions – sliced
6 Tbs Mascarpone Cheese
Basil – optional
1 Lb Penne or Rigatoni

In a large pan that will accommodate the pasta, heat the olive oil on medium heat and caramelize the onions. With a chef's knife, chop the sausage meat in several directions and place in the pan with the onions. Cook all together for 3 or 4 minutes, and with a wooden spoon, break the sausage down into smaller pieces. Do not overcook. Remove from the heat and set aside.

Cook the pasta until al dente in a pot of lightly salted, boiling water. When the pasta is done, drain and add to the pan with the sausage and onions, and cook over medium heat for 2 or 3 minutes.

Remove from the heat, add the mascarpone cheese, and toss until the pasta is well coated. Ladle into bowls, add some torn basil (optional), and at the table, pass the cheese!

Pici

12 Oz Flour – sifted
Pinch of Salt

Several Tbs Water

Knead all the ingredients together to form a very pliable dough. The kneading is very important to make sure that everything is incorporated. However, you don't want to overwork the dough.

Cover and let sit for about an half hour. Roll the dough out (preferably in a rectangle so that it is about ¼-inch thick). Then, cut into strips about ½-inch wide. Take each of the strips and roll them on the board, twisting and pulling as you do this so that you will end up with a very long, twisted pasta. Cook in salted, boiling water until al dente. Serve with your favorite sauce. It is best served with a thick, meaty sauce.

Note: Pici is known as a poor man's pasta, because the ingredients are so simple. However, it is very time consuming to make, but well worth the effort. I was taught to make Pici by the

Grandmother of my Cousin Andrea's boys, Lorenzo, Roberto, and Ricardo, Nonna Rina, during a recent visit to Montefollonico.

Pasta Povera

Poor Man's Pasta

1 Lb Pasta – your favorite
3 Cups Breadcrumbs – plain or Italian style (your choice)

2–3 Garlic Cloves – minced
Red Pepper Flakes – a pinch or to taste
¼ Cup Extra Virgin Olive Oil

Cook pasta in salted water, al dente. Meanwhile, heat the oil in a large skillet over medium heat and sauté the breadcrumbs, garlic, and pepper flakes until the crumbs are golden brown. Drain the pasta, and with a slotted spoon, remove the breadcrumb mixture and spread over the pasta. Add as much of the oil as necessary. Mix well and add more of the oil, as necessary. This works best with homemade breadcrumbs, because they are not as fine as store-bought.

Note: Growing up, we could not eat meat on Friday. On the first Wednesday of every season, we couldn't eat meat, either. For Catholics, these were called Ember Days. So, this was a good, basic, meatless meal. For variety, sometimes anchovies were mashed and cooked with the breadcrumb mixture. My brother and I, being cheese lovers, always topped our pasta with grated cheese, as does my family now.

Pasta with Fresh Tomatoes, Garlic, and Mozzarella

1 Lb Short Pasta – your favorite
1 Large Tomato – very ripe
2 Cloves Garlic – sliced
¼ Cup Extra Virgin Olive Oil

7–8 Fresh Basil Leaves – torn
1 Small Onion – minced
1 Cup Fresh Mozzarella – shredded
Salt and Pepper to Taste

In a bowl, add the olive oil, garlic, basil, and onion. Chop the tomato and add to the mixture.

Then, add the basil and stir. Add a little salt and pepper, stir, and cover. Let the mixture marinate for several hours out of the fridge. When ready, boil the pasta al dente. Drain well and add to the tomato mixture. Quickly add the shredded mozzarella and stir well so that all the cheese melts. Serve immediately.

Note: The mozzarella melts and gets nice and stringy. This is a family favorite and so easy. It is always on our beach menu.

Pasta with Sausage, Lemon, and Nutmeg

Pasta Salsiccia con Limone e Noce Moscata

1 Egg – beaten
¼ tsp Ground Nutmeg
Zest of 1 Large Lemon
4 Tbs Extra Virgin Olive Oil
2 Links Sweet Italian Sausage
¾ Lb Bucatini

Good Pinch of Ground Pepper
Juice of ½ Large Lemon
⅓ Cup Heavy Cream
2 Oz Pancetta – diced
Pinch of Salt

In a bowl, beat the egg until frothy, and then whisk in the pepper, nutmeg, lemon juice, lemon zest, salt, and cream.

In a heavy-bottomed skillet, add 1–2 Tbs of the olive oil over medium heat. When hot, add the pancetta and cook until it starts to color, moving it around the pan so that it does not stick and burn. When cooked, remove from pan and place in a bowl. Next, add the sausage meat (removed from the casing) and cook, stirring until it is not pink in color. Drain off some of the excess fat from the pan and add the sausage to the bowl with the pancetta. Add the remaining olive oil to the pan and keep near the stove.

Bring a pot of salted water to a boil and add the pasta, stirring so that it does not clump. While the pasta is cooking and is almost ready, return the pan to the stove to warm up the oil. Cook the pasta al dente, and when done, remove and reserve one cup of pasta water and drain the pasta.

Return the sausage and pancetta to the warmed pan and stir around to warm again. When the pasta is fully drained, add it to the pan with the sausage and pancetta mixture. Mix well and then quickly stir in the egg mixture. Remove from the heat. Not to worry about the eggs being uncooked, as the heat of the pasta will cook the egg.

You can serve directly from the skillet, as we do, so that it stays warm, or you can turn it all into a warmed bowl. If the sauce seems too dry, you can now add a little of the reserved, warm pasta water a little at a time, until you are satisfied with the consistency. Adjust seasonings to your taste. Serve immediately, and as always, pass the cheese.

Note: This recipe is from Cascia, a mountainous city in Umbria, where legend has it that this dish originated from. To be totally traditional, you should use bucatini, but of course, you can use your favorite pasta, if you wish.

Polenta alla Fontina

8 Oz Instant Polenta
8 Tbs Parmigiana Cheese – grated or shaved
Salt and Ground Black Pepper

8 Oz Shredded Fontina
½ Stick Butter

Prepare polenta according to package directions. Scoop out of pot, spread in a baking dish, and let cool. (Calculate the size of the dish so that when the polenta is cooled, you can slice it into three even layers.) When polenta is cool, remove from dish and slice into three layers. Butter a baking pan (use the one the polenta cooled in). Put in one layer of polenta, and top with ½ of the fontina, a little Parmigiana, and some butter. Repeat with another layer, and top the final layer of polenta with the remaining Parmigiana and butter. Bake at 375° for 15–20 minutes. Let rest for a few minutes, and then cut into serving-sized pieces and serve.

Polenta with Cabbage Mushroom Sauce

1 Pkg Instant Polenta
1 Lb Mixed Mushrooms – thickly sliced
2 Lbs Head Savoy Cabbage – core removed,
    sliced ⅓-inch thick
½–1 tsp Pepperoncini – or to taste
6 Oz Pancetta – cut into ¼-inch pieces

1 tsp Coarse Salt
⅓ Cup Extra Virgin Olive Oil
½ Cup Sliced Garlic Cloves –
    about 7 or 8 cloves
1¼ Cup Vegetable or Chicken Broth, or
    Water

Pour olive oil into heavy-bottomed pot. Add garlic and pancetta, and cook until garlic slightly colors and pancetta is starting to crisp. Add pepperoncini and stir it in, letting it cook a few minutes to release flavor, and then add mushrooms and cabbage. Sprinkle with a little salt and pepper, and stir all in to incorporate. Cover pot and cook for about 5 minutes over medium heat.

Continue cooking for about 45 minutes to 1 hour, stirring every so often to make sure nothing is sticking to bottom of the pot, and adding ½ cup of broth or water to the pot whenever vegetables seem to be getting dry.

Uncover the pot and cook for an additional 30 to 45 minutes, until the cabbage is completely soft.

Cook polenta according to package directions. Turn out onto large platter or wooden board. Put a serving in each dish, and pour Cabbage Sauce over all.

Polenta with Mushrooms

5 Tbs Butter
1 Garlic Clove – minced
3 Sprigs Basil – finely chopped
9 Oz Instant Polenta
Salt and Pepper to Taste

1½ Oz Dried Porcini
3 Sprigs Parsley – finely chopped
4½ Cups Chicken Stock
⅓ Lb Mascarpone

Soak mushrooms in 1 cup of warm water for about 30 minutes. Drain. Melt 2 Tbs butter in a skillet. Add garlic and mushrooms, stir well, and cook over low heat for about 5 minutes. Add parsley and basil, and cook for another 3–4 minutes. Season with salt and pepper, and keep warm.

In a large pot, cook the instant polenta according to package directions in the chicken stock. Just before serving, stir in 3 Tbs of butter.

To Serve: Spoon hot polenta into individual bowls. Top with mascarpone and a spoonful of the mushroom mixture.

Porcini Sauce for Polenta

1 Oz Dried Imported Porcini – soaked in warm water for 30 minutes	1 Can (28 Oz) Imported Plum Tomatoes – pulsed for 3 seconds
1 Cup Extra Virgin Olive Oil	16 Oz Fresh Mushrooms – cut into halves
1 Sprig Rosemary	2 Garlic Cloves - chopped
1 (9 Oz) Pkg Instant Polenta	Salt and Pepper to Taste

Pour ½ cup of olive oil in a sauté pan and add the porcini, along with the water they have soaked in. (I do strain the water through some cheesecloth or a coffee filter to eliminate any grit.) Cook until almost all the water has evaporated. Add the tomatoes, bring to a slow boil, and simmer for 20–30 minutes.

Meanwhile, pour the other ½ cup of oil in another sauté pan, and over high heat, sauté the mushrooms with the rosemary. When the mushrooms start to look cooked, add the garlic and cook for about 3 minutes. Add the fresh sautéed mushrooms to the tomato and porcini sauce.

Cook for 5 minutes, adjust for salt and pepper, and serve hot over the polenta.

Processor Pasta Dough

Aunt May's Recipe

4½ Cups Flour	1 Tbs Olive Oil
Pinch of Salt	¼ Cup Water
4 Eggs – to equal 1 cup	

Beat eggs, and add salt and oil. Put flour in food processor, and with the motor running slowly, add the egg mixture. Then, slowly add enough water for the dough to be elastic and pull away from the side of the bowl. If necessary, add more water in drops a little at a time. On a board, form into a ball and store under a bowl for a few minutes to rest until you are ready to use.

Family board used for pizza and/or pasta dough, well over ninety years old

Ragu di Salsiccia

⅓ Cup Olive Oil
1 Cup Tomato Purée
1½ Lbs Italian Sweet Sausage – removed
    from casing
2 Celery Stalks – chopped
¼ tsp Sugar

Salt and Freshly Ground Black Pepper
    to Taste
Grated Cheese – for topping
2 Garlic Cloves – sliced
1 Onion – large, chopped

Heat the olive oil in a large saucepan, and add the onion and garlic. Cook slowly for a few minutes until both are soft, and then add the celery. Stir often, and after a few minutes, add the sausage meat. Cook slowly, breaking up the pieces and making sure that nothing is sticking to the bottom of the pan and burning. When sausage is cooked through, but not brown, add the tomato purée and ½ cup of very hot water. Stir until all is incorporated. There should be enough liquid to just cover all the ingredients. If not, add a little more water. Season to taste with the salt and pepper, and simmer for one hour, checking often to make sure that it is not getting too dry. Serve over your favorite cooked pasta, and pass the grated cheese.

Note: My Grandmother (Nonna Giovanna, who owned the Pensione in New Jersey) used to make this with the very thin Italian sausage that was roughly ground and, I think, contained garlic, basil or parsley, and not cheese. That is difficult to find now, so regular Italian sweet sausage will have to suffice.

Rice Torta

1 Cup Long-Grain Rice	**3 Eggs – large**
6–8 Tbs Olive Oil	**½ Cup Parmesan Cheese – grated**
1 Medium Onion – finely chopped	**Freshly Ground Black Pepper**
1 Tbs Cornmeal or Polenta	**Salt to Taste**

Bring 2 cups of salted water to a boil and add the rice. Stir once, cover, and reduce the heat to low.

Cook until rice is tender, approximately 20 minutes. Set aside to cool. In the meantime, heat 2 Tbs of the oil in a small skillet over medium heat. Add the onions and cook until golden, about 7 or 8 minutes. Let cool. Preheat oven to 450°. Grease an 8″ x 8″ baking dish with some olive oil, and then evenly coat the bottom and sides with the cornmeal or polenta. Beat 2 eggs in a medium bowl. Add the onions, 4 Tbs of the olive oil, and all but 1 Tbs of the cheese. Mix well. Fluff the cooled rice with a fork and fold into the cheese mixture. Taste for salt and pepper. Transfer to prepared dish and smooth the top. Beat the remaining eggs in a small bowl with 2 tsps of water, remaining oil, and 1 Tbs of cheese. Mix well and pour over rice. Bake for 5 minutes, and then reduce heat to 350° and continue baking for about 30 minutes, or until the torta is golden brown and is set in the center. Set aside to cool, and serve at room temperature.

Rice with Sweet Sausage

Riso alla Salciccia

2 Tbs Unsalted Butter
2 Cups Arborio Rise – do not rinse
A Few Fresh Basil Leaves – torn

2 Links Sweet Italian Sausage – 10 Oz each
1 Cup Romano or Parmesan Cheese –
    freshly grated

Place the butter in a large skillet over medium heat. Cut the sausages into small pieces. When the butter gets foamy, add the sausages and sauté gently until done, but do not let the butter burn.

In the meantime, bring a large pot of salted water to a boil. Add the rice and cook, checking for doneness at around 16–18 minutes. The rice should be al dente. Make sure to not overcook and let the rice get too soft or mushy. When the rice is done, remove from the heat and drain thoroughly.

Place the rice in a large serving bowl. Add the sausages, basil, and grated cheese, toss gently, and serve immediately.

Note: You can either cut the sausage into small rings and cook, or if you prefer, remove from the casings, crumble the meat, and cook.

Rigatoni alla Amatriciana

A Recipe from Rodolfo

1 Lb Rigatoni
8 Oz Pancetta – sliced thin and chopped
1 tsp Dried Oregano
5 tsps Freshly Grated Romano Cheese
1 Can (28 Oz) Italian Plum Tomatoes

1 Medium Onion – chopped
½ Stick Butter
Salt to Taste
Freshly Ground Black Pepper

Coarsely chop the sliced pancetta, and sauté with the onions until partially cooked in a large pan that will hold the cooked pasta. Drain off the excess fat. Pour into the pan the tomatoes that have been blended for about 4 or 5 seconds, and simmer until 80 percent of the liquid has evaporated. Set aside.

Cook the pasta in a pot of salted, boiling water just until al dente. Drain well and pour the pasta into the pan with the sauce mixture. Add the butter, oregano, cheese, salt, and pepper. Stir until all of the pasta is coated with the sauce. Ladle into bowls and serve immediately. Pass extra grated cheese.

Optionally—and this is just what we do—sprinkle some torn, fresh basil on each serving.

Note: Pancetta is Italian bacon that is cured pork belly, and can be found in most supermarkets and always in Italian specialty markets.

Rigatoni with Broccoli and Anchovy

Rigatoni con Broccolo alla Acciuga

6 Cups Broccoli Florets
3 Flat Anchovy Fillets
1½ Tbs Capers – salt packed
3 Tbs Italian Parsley – finely chopped

1 Lb Rigatoni
2 Garlic Cloves – thinly sliced
3 Tbs Extra Virgin Olive Oil
½ Cup Grated Cheese – your favorite

In a large pot of salted, boiling water, cook the small broccoli florets until tender, about 5 minutes.

Using a slotted spoon or a kitchen spider, transfer the florets to a large bowl. Return the water to a boil and add the pasta, cooking just until al dente.

Meanwhile, coarsely chop together the anchovies, garlic, and capers. Add to the bowl with the broccoli and toss.

In a large skillet, heat 2 Tbs of olive oil over medium-high heat. Add the broccoli mixture. Cook, stirring frequently for a few minutes, and then remove from the heat. Reserve ¼ cup of pasta water when draining pasta. Transfer the pasta to a large serving bowl. Add the broccoli mixture, pasta water, and remaining 1 Tbs of oil and the parsley. Taste for seasonings and adjust. Serve in bowls and pass the cheese.

Risotto con Sugo

2 Tbs Butter – unsalted
4 Cups Chicken Stock – or as needed
1 Cup Bolognese Sauce

Romano or Parmesan Cheese – freshly grated
1 Cup Arborio Rice
Salt and Freshly Ground Black Pepper – to
taste

Heat butter in a deep heavy-bottomed pot. Add rice and cook, stirring constantly until rice takes on some color. Add 1 cup of broth, salt and pepper to taste, and cook uncovered over moderate heat, stirring constantly. Add more stock as needed. When rice begins to soften at about 15 minutes, add Bolognese Sauce, and continue to stir constantly. When ready, rice should be tender, but firm; in other words, al dente.

Serve hot with grated cheese.

Risotto Milanese

1 Cup Arborio Rice
2 Cups Chicken Broth
2 Tbs Butter
1 Small Onion – chopped

⅓ Cup Parmigiano Cheese – grated
⅓ Cup White Wine – your favorite
1 Cup Hot Water
1 Envelope Saffron

In a large saucepan, melt the butter. Add the onion to the melted butter and sauté over medium heat. Add the rice and stir until the rice is completely coated with the butter. Now, add the wine and saffron. Stir constantly until the wine is absorbed. Continue stirring, adding broth a little at a time as it is absorbed by the rice. Cook until the rice is al dente, adding additional water or broth if needed. When the rice is ready, remove from the heat and stir in the grated cheese. This is a good partner for Osso Bucco Milanese.

Risotto Verde

¾ Lb Arborio Rice
6 Oz Fresh Spinach Leaves –
rinsed and chopped

1 Quart Chicken Broth
4 Tbs Butter
4 Tbs Olive Oil

1 Small Onion – chopped
1 Celery Stalk – chopped
1 Small Carrot – chopped

6 Tbs Parmigiano
Salt to Taste
Freshly Ground Black Pepper

Sauté the spinach, carrot, onion, and celery in olive oil in a saucepan. Add the rice and cook for 1 minute, stirring constantly. Add the broth a little at a time, and only when the previous addition of broth has been consumed. Stir well to make sure the rice does not stick to the bottom of the pan. When the rice has absorbed the liquid and is al dente, add the butter and Parmigiano cheese. Stir well and serve in bowls.

Sage Almond Pesto

1 Garlic Clove – crushed
1 Cup Almonds – toasted
½ Cup Sage Leaves – loosely packed
Pinch of Pepperoncini
1 Tbs Lemon Juice – freshly squeezed
Additional Extra Virgin Olive Oil –
    for topping

1 Cup Italian Parsley – loosely packed
½ Cup Grated cheese – your favorite
Zest from ½ Lemon
½ Cup Extra Virgin Olive Oil
Salt and Freshly Ground Black Pepper

With the food processor or blender running, add the garlic, parsley, almonds, grated cheese, sage, lemon zest, and pepperoncini. Process until all finely chopped, then gradually add the oil and lemon juice. Season to taste with salt and pepper. If too thick, add a little more olive oil.

Store in covered jar or bowl topped with extra virgin olive oil.

Salsa di Noci

20 Walnuts
1 Garlic Clove
1 Pint Heavy Cream

6 Tbs Parmigiano Cheese
3 Tbs Olive Oil

Place nuts in a blender, add garlic and oil, and blend for 5–8 seconds. Slowly add the cream, and keep blending until thickened. Pour into a small bowl and stir in the cheese. Use this sauce cold. It is delicious over cheese ravioli.

Sausage Paella

Paella con Salsiccia

½ Cup Olive Oil

2 Onions – chopped

2½–3 Lbs Italian Sausage Meat

1 tsp Saffron – soaked in 1 cup water

½ Cup White Wine – one you will
enjoy drinking while you cook

3 Garlic Cloves - minced

3 or 4 Peppers – yellow, red, orange, chopped

1 Cup Chopped Pancetta

2 Cups Arborio Rice

2 Cups Canned Crushed Tomatoes

Salt and Pepper to Taste

In a large sauté pan with a lid, heat the olive oil and garlic over medium heat. Add the onions and peppers, and sauté for about 5–7 minutes. Add the pancetta and mix in, and then add the sausage, breaking up any very large lumps. Sauté for 10 more minutes.

When the sausage has cooked for 10 minutes, add the rice, saffron, water, wine, and tomatoes. Mix all thoroughly, and slowly bring to a boil. Mix in a little salt and pepper, cover, and cook until the liquid is absorbed and the rice is cooked. If the rice is not ready and the liquid is absorbed, add a little more wine and/or water and continue to cook. Transfer to a low-rimmed bowl and serve. All the easier if you are cooking in a paella pan; then, it goes right to table.

Note: Rice dishes are common in Italy, and paella is very similar to risotto. You will find some of the most delicious paella in Venezia.

Sicilian Rice Timbale

A Very Impressive Dish

2 Cups Arborio Rice

Freshly Ground Black Pepper

½ Lb Penne Rigate

½ Cup Frozen Peas

4 Eggs – divided and lightly beaten

Salt – as needed

1½ Cups Grated Cheese – your favorite

2½ Cups Thick Tomato Sauce – your favorite

½ Cup Breadcrumbs – flavored or plain

Cook the rice in a large pot of salted, boiling water until al dente. Drain and rinse quickly with cold water to stop the cooking, and then transfer to strainer to drain and cool. When cool, pour into a bowl, stir in 3 eggs and 1 cup of grated cheese, cover, and place in refrigerator for 8 hours or overnight.

Preheat oven to 400°. Cook pasta until al dente in a large pot of salted, boiling water. Drain well and scoop into a large bowl, and toss well with 1 cup of sauce. (The sauce can be a meat sauce, like a Bolognese, or it can be meatless, but it must not be thin, or the timbale will not hold the mold. This is very important.)

Add the peas with a ½ cup of grated cheese and mix gently (do not mash) with a wooden spoon. Allow to cool.

Oil well a 2-quart ovenproof bowl and coat well with the breadcrumbs (I prefer to use seasoned crumbs). Wet your hands to prevent the rice from sticking to them, and line the bowl evenly and completely with the rice until it is about ½-inch thick. Reserve some rice for topping. Carefully pack the pasta into the bowl, spread the remaining rice over the top, and press it gently but firmly in place. Brush the remaining lightly beaten egg all over the top of the rice.

Bake until golden, about 1 hour. Allow to cool for 10 minutes, and then try to loosen the sides a little with a thin knife. Turn out onto a large platter. Give the bottom a few taps while doing this. Slice into pie-shaped wedges, and pass additional sauce and grated cheese.

Note: A bolognese ragu would be an excellent sauce to use with this recipe.

Spaetzle and More Spaetzle

My Favorite Spaetzle Recipe

Salt	3 Tbs Sparkling Seltzer Water
1¾ Cups Flour	3 Tbs Butter – softened
½ tsp Nutmeg – freshly grated, if possible	1 Tbs Chopped Parsley or Basil – your
4 Eggs	preference

Bring a large, deep pot of salted water to a boil over high heat. Meanwhile, combine the flour, ½ tsp salt, and nutmeg in a medium bowl. Beat eggs and water together in another bowl and add to the flour mixture, beating in with a wooden spoon until the batter is elastic and is forming small bubbles. This will take several minutes, possibly 5 to 6. Batter should be able to fall from spoon in long strands. If it can't, then whisk in 1 more Tbs of water at a time until you have the right consistency. Spray your spaetzle maker with a little vegetable spray. Fill it with a good amount of the batter, and holding it a few inches above the boiling water, slide the spaetzle cup slowly back and forth, letting it fall through the holes into the boiling water in 2-inch strands. The faster you slide the batter-filled cup, the shorter the strands will be. Continue until all the batter is used.

Cook, stirring often for about 2–3 minutes. If you don't stir, you will end up with one big ball.

Carefully remove the spaetzle with a large mesh strainer, shake out excess water, and transfer to a bowl. Toss with warm butter, taste for salt and pepper, and garnish with parsley or basil to serve.

Note: Sometimes it helps to have someone stir while you slide the cup back and forth and refill the cup with more batter. As soon as you are finished with the spaetzle maker, soak it in hot, soapy water to make it easier to clean. Otherwise, the batter will adhere like glue if it gets dry.

Spaghetti alla Checca

A Recipe from Rodolfo

1 Lb Spaghetti
6 Large Salad Tomatoes – not very ripe
2 tsps Dried Oregano
4–5 Oz Extra Virgin Olive Oil

1–2 Fresh Garlic Cloves
1 Bunch (20–30 Leaves) Fresh Basil
Salt and Ground Black Pepper
Parmesan or Romano Cheese – grated

Peel the tomatoes and cut into large chunks. Peel the garlic cloves. Detach leaves from basil stems. Combine diced tomatoes, garlic cloves, basil leaves, oregano, salt, and freshly ground black pepper with olive oil. Pulse all in blender for 3 seconds and set aside.

Cook spaghetti al dente in a pot of salted water. When spaghetti is cooked, drain and scoop into a large heated skillet. Pour the tomato sauce over the pasta and heat all ingredients together. Pass grated cheese when serving.

Spaghetti alla Puttanesca

1 Lb Spaghetti
1 Can (28 Oz) Italian Plum Tomatoes
1 Tbs Capers
½ Cup Extra Virgin Olive Oil
1 Onion – chopped

6 Anchovies – chopped
1–2 Garlic Cloves – chopped
1 Cup Black Olives
½ tsp Red Pepper Flakes

Put olive oil in a large sauté pan, and when it is hot, add the onions and cook until they start to get translucent and slightly brown. Pour the tomatoes into a blender and pulse for 3–4 seconds, and then add to the pan with the onions. Simmer for about 20 minutes. Add the remaining ingredients and let simmer.

Meanwhile, cook the spaghetti in 4 quarts of salted, boiling water until al dente. Taste the sauce and adjust the seasonings. Drain the pasta and pour into the pan with the sauce. Toss well. Serve with some grated cheese to sprinkle on top.

Spaghetti and Fresh Crabs

A Down-On-The-Farm Recipe

⅓ Cup Olive Oil
4 Garlic Cloves – chopped
1 Large Onion – chopped
1 Tbs Red Pepper Flakes
1 Tbs Oregano
2 (28 Oz) Cans San Marzano Tomatoes

Salt and Pepper to Taste
6 Leaves Fresh Basil – whole or torn
8 Fresh Crabs – rinsed
½ Cup White Wine
1 Lb Spaghetti
Freshly Grated Cheese

Heat oil in a large pot over medium heat. Add the garlic, onion, red pepper flakes, and oregano. Sauté for a few minutes until the onion is just translucent. Add the tomatoes. Now, you can pulse them a few times in a processor, or do as I do and crush the tomatoes by hand as I pour them into the pot. Simmer for a few minutes. Taste for salt, pepper, and possibly more red pepper flakes, and add the basil. Bring the sauce to a slow boil and add the rinsed crabs. Stir gently, tossing the crabs around in the hot sauce. Adjust heat to medium-high and add the white wine. Let it come to a soft boil again, and taste again for seasonings. Cover and simmer for about 1 hour.

Meanwhile, when the sauce is almost ready, cook the pasta. Drain the pasta and add back to the pot it was cooking in. Toss with some sauce and stir until all coated. Pour into a large serving plate that is not flat. Spread crabs on top. Pass the remaining sauce when serving (and the cheese!).

Needless to say, rinsing the crabs is the tricky part, so my Grandmother would pull the claws off of the live crabs so that they would not run all over the counter or escape from the pot. Occasionally, one would get away, and we would chase it down on the kitchen floor. We didn't buy the crabs, but went crabbing in a local river. We would walk up the long road to the main road, which was Old Hwy 17, and hitch a ride to the river. Usually, we were picked up by a local farmer who knew my Grandmother. We would pile in the back of his truck, usually about 8 of us, enjoying the breeze as we rode along. Then, we would do the same thing to get back home with our basket of crabs.

Spaghetti con Acciughe

2 Tbs Olive Oil	**2 Cups Tomato Sauce**
½ Cup Olive Oil	**Salt and Freshly Ground Pepper to Taste**
1 Cup Breadcrumbs – dried	**Pinch of Red Pepper Flakes – optional**
12 Anchovy Fillets – finely chopped	**1 Lb Spaghetti**

Heat 2 Tbs of olive oil in a large pan. Add the breadcrumbs and cook over low-to-medium heat until the breadcrumbs are toasted, stirring constantly. Pour out onto a plate to cool. Heat the remaining ½ cup of olive oil in a large saucepan with the anchovies, and cook gently just to infuse the flavor of the anchovies. Add the tomato sauce, salt and pepper, and red pepper flakes, if desired. Meanwhile, cook pasta in salted, boiling water until al dente. Drain, reserving about a cup of water. Transfer pasta to a bowl, top with the sauce, and toss. If too thick, add a little of the hot water. Plate the pasta and sprinkle with the breadcrumbs. No grated cheese this time . . . except possibly in our house!

Spaghetti with Gorgonzola and Walnuts

1 Lb Spaghetti – your favorite	**2–3 Tbs Butter**
2 Garlic Cloves	**½ Cup Walnuts – roughly chopped**
1 Cup Heavy Cream	**6 Oz Gorgonzola – crumbled**

Cook spaghetti according to package directions in a large pot of lightly salted, boiling water.

Meanwhile, in a large skillet, melt the butter over medium heat. Add the garlic cloves and walnuts. Run the garlic around the skillet to flavor the oil. Remove the garlic when they have turned golden, making sure they do not burn. Add the cream, a pinch of salt, and the gorgonzola. As soon as the sauce begins to thicken, add the cooked, drained spaghetti directly to the skillet.

Cook all together, tossing well for about 1 minute. Serve immediately.

Note: Using tongs, I just grab the spaghetti out of the water, give a little shake to release extra water, and add directly to the skillet. This recipe calls for spaghetti, but if I have a recipe that calls for short pasta, I use a kitchen spider to do the same.

Spaghetti with Tuna and Lemon

1 Lb Spaghetti – your favorite
2–3 Garlic Cloves – finely chopped
1 Cup Italian Tuna – packed in oil with oil
½ Cup Fresh Parsley Leaves
½ Cup Fresh Basil Leaves
½ tsp Dried Chili Flakes
Kosher Salt to Taste

3 Tbs Olive Oil
¾ Cup Breadcrumbs
3 Tbs Capers – drained
2 Garlic Cloves
Grated Zest of 1 Lemon
Additional Olive Oil

Cook spaghetti according to package directions in a large pot of lightly salted, boiling water.

Meanwhile, in a large skillet, combine oil and garlic, and cook for about 4–5 minutes. Add the breadcrumbs and cook until toasted, but not too dark. Remove from heat and set aside. In a food processor, combine remaining ingredients (except additional olive oil), and process into a paste.

When the pasta is cooked, toss with the tuna mixture and breadcrumbs. Serve immediately with an extra drizzle of olive oil.

Note: Occasionally, we will halve a few cherry tomatoes and toss them into the drained hot pasta just before tossing with the tuna mixture and breadcrumbs. We top with grated cheese. A good Friday night dinner during Lent in our house!

Sticky Rice

2 Cups Long-Grain Rice   **3 Cups Water**

Rinse rice several times until the water runs clear. Drain thoroughly.

Bring rice and water to a boil over medium-high heat. Cook uncovered, and do not stir until water level drops just below the surface of the rice and small holes start to form, about 5–6 minutes.

Reduce heat to low, cover, and cook until water is absorbed, about 12–15 minutes. Fluff and serve.

Note: There are a few Asian dishes that we enjoy, and this is the best rice recipe to use. Sticky rice is also good when used for stuffing things, like peppers.

Tortino di Riso

2 Cups Whole Milk   **Salt – to taste**
1½ Cups Arborio Rice   **2 Tbs butter - unsalted**
5 Tbs Parmesan Cheese – freshly grated   **4 Large Eggs - separated**
Black Pepper – freshly ground to taste

Place the milk and salt in a large pot with a lid, and over high heat, bring to a boil. Add the rice, stir, cover, and then reduce heat to low. Let rice cook for about 15 minutes, stirring occasionally, until the liquid has been absorbed. The rice should be al dente.

Remove the rice from the heat and stir in 1 Tbs of the butter, along with the parmesan cheese and the egg yolks. Stir gently to combine everything, but do not mash the rice. Season with salt and pepper. Taste to see if more is needed.

Preheat the oven to 350°. Coat the inside of a 1½-quart baking dish with the remaining butter. Beat the egg whites with an electric mixer until the whites are stiff, but not dry. Fold the beaten egg whites into the prepared dish. Place the dish in the oven and bake 30 minutes, or until the top is golden brown. Remove from the oven, loosen the edges of the cake with a knife, and invert onto a platter. Serve almost immediately.

Tuna-Stuffed Canneloni

1 Lb Cannelloni
2–3 Tbs Flavored Breadcrumbs – for topping
3 (6 Oz) Cans Italian Tuna (packed in oil) – drain and reserve the oil
2–3 Cups Romano or Parmesan Cheese – freshly grated

½ Cup Grated Cheese – your favorite for topping
3 Lbs Whole-Milk Ricotta – drained
3 Egg Yolks
½ Lb Fresh Mozzarella – shredded
6–7 Large, Fresh Basil Leaves – torn

Cook the pasta in salted, boiling water until very al dente. If too cooked, the cannelloni will be difficult to fill and will fall apart during baking. Scoop into cold water to stop cooking process. Drain and spread out on a kitchen towel.

Make your favorite quick tomato sauce or use store-bought. Add a little of the reserved tuna oil for flavor.

Combine the ricotta, tuna, grated cheese, shredded mozzarella, basil, and egg yolks in a bowl, and mix well. You can also do this in your food processor. Spoon the filling into a pastry bag (or you can fill a plastic bag and snip off one corner). Carefully fill each shell with the mixture. Place the filled shells in a large baking dish, spread out over a thin layer of sauce. Spoon remaining sauce over the shells, and top with grated cheese and a few tablespoons of flavored breadcrumbs. If desired, also top with a little extra shredded mozzarella. Bake at 350° for 35–44 minutes, or just until you know the filling is heated through.

Note: Do not layer the filled shells, or the weight will squeeze the filling out. If necessary, use two baking pans.

Chicken

Aunt Elly's Favorite Easy Chicken Recipe

Preheat oven to 425°. Blend contents of 1 packet Good Seasons Italian Dressing Mix with ½ cup melted butter and 1 tsp freshly squeezed lemon juice. Brush this generously over 3 lbs of frying chicken pieces (your favorite parts).

Roll chicken in 1 cup of breadcrumbs, and then let rest for 15 minutes. Put into a casserole or baking dish, and bake at 425° for 15 minutes. Then, turn chicken and bake 15–25 minutes longer, until golden brown and the chicken is cooked all the way through.

Note: This is how the recipe was written for me years ago. A very easy and quick meal if served with Rice-A-Roni or Minute Rice and a salad.

Butter Chicken

8 Chicken Thighs	**Juice of 1 Lemon**
Kosher Salt and Ground Black Pepper	**1 Tbs Smoked Paprika**
3 Tbs Butter – divided	**2 Cups Spinach**
3 Garlic Cloves – minced	**1 Cup Chicken Broth**
½ Cup Cream	**¼ Cup Parmesan Cheese – grated**

Preheat oven to 400°. Season chicken with paprika, salt, and pepper. Melt 2 Tbs of butter in ovenproof pan over high heat. Add chicken (skin side down) and sear both sides until golden brown, about 3–4 minutes per side. Remove chicken to a plate and tent it to keep warm. Drain off most of the excess fat.

Melt remaining butter in the pan. Add garlic and cook for a few minutes. Stir in the chicken broth, cream, cheese, lemon juice, and then bring to a slow boil. Reduce heat and cook until sauce is thick, about 3–5 minutes. Return chicken and any accumulated juices to the pan, and place pan in oven. Cook for about 20–25 minutes until the chicken is completely cooked. Serve with its gravy over rice, farro, or mashed potatoes.

Breast of Chicken in Egg Sauce

Petto di Pollo con Salsa di Uovo

2 Chicken Breasts
Salt and Freshly Ground Pepper
3 Tbs Butter – unsalted
2 Tbs Flour

1 Cup Chicken Stock
½ Cup Light Cream
Pinch of Nutmeg
1 Egg Yolk – lightly beaten

Wash chicken, dry, and remove backbone. Sprinkle with salt and pepper, and sauté in butter over a medium flame until golden brown on all sides. In about 20 minutes, the chicken should be cooked through. Transfer to a serving dish and keep hot.

Combine flour, chicken stock, and cream, and add to the pan where the chicken was just fried. Cook over a low flame, stirring constantly until the sauce is thick and smooth. Adjust seasonings. Remove from the heat, mix in the slightly beaten egg yolk, and return to the stove. Cook over very low heat for another minute or two longer, stirring until all has thickened. If the sauce looks lumpy, strain if you want it smooth. Otherwise, pour over the chicken and serve with a side of rice.

Chicken Breast Involtini with Potatoes

1¼ Lbs Chicken Breasts – skinless, sliced thin
4 Yukon Gold Potatoes
1 tsp Fresh Rosemary – minced
2 Garlic Cloves – chopped
Salt and Pepper to Taste

¼ Lb Mortadella – sliced thin
4 Large Sage Leaves – shredded
Pinch of Oregano
Extra Virgin Olive Oil
⅓ Cup Chicken Broth – optional

Preheat oven to 375°. Sprinkle each chicken breast with a pinch of salt and pepper, and cover with a slice of mortadella. Roll each breast up and secure with kitchen twine or toothpicks. Set aside. Peel and dice the potatoes. Put them in an ovenproof dish that can also go on the burner. (I use a Le Creuset pan for this, but a similar pan will work just as well.) Sprinkle a little olive oil on the bottom of the utensil you are using before placing the potatoes in. Once the potatoes are in, sprinkle them with more olive oil and dust them with the sage, rosemary, and a little salt and pepper. Mix them up so that all are combined well. Cover and cook over a medium flame for about 10 minutes. Carefully add the chicken breasts and continue cooking, turning them over to brown on all sides. Check for seasonings, and then finish cooking in the oven for about ½ hour. If the pan seems to be getting dry, add some chicken broth. Serves 4.

Chicken Bombolina

1 Lb Rigatoni Pasta
1 Cup Mushrooms – sliced
½ Cup Parsley – chopped
2 Cups Fresh Mozzarella – divided
6 Boneless Chicken Breast Halves
½ Cup Freshly Grated Cheese – for
    garnishing

3 Cups Tomatoes – peeled and diced
2–3 Garlic Cloves – chopped
Salt and Pepper – to taste
1 Tbs Olive Oil
2 Cups Pasta Sauce
Fresh Basil Leaves – torn in little pieces for
    garnishing

Preheat oven to 350°. Butter a 13" x 9" ovenproof casserole dish.

Bring a large pot of salted water to a boil. Add the pasta and bring the water back to boiling. Stir a bit so that the pasta does not stick together and clump. Boil just until al dente. Drain and toss in a bowl together with the tomatoes, mushrooms, garlic, parsley, salt, and pepper. Add 1½ cups of mozzarella that has been shredded. Stir well to combine all, and place in prepared baking dish.

Heat oil over high heat in a skillet large enough to hold the chicken comfortably. Brown the chicken on both sides. Remove the chicken with tongs and place on top of the rigatoni. Pour your favorite pasta sauce over the chicken and top with the remining ½ cup of shredded mozzarella. Cover the baking dish with foil and bake for 35-40 minutes. Remove foil for the last few minutes.

To serve, place some pasta on a plate and top with a chicken breast. Pour some of the sauce and cheese on top. Sprinkle with some basil and grated cheese.

Chicken Cacciatore

3 Tbs Olive Oil
1 Chicken (2–2½ Lbs) – cut in pieces
1 Garlic Clove – minced
1 Carrot – finely diced
⅔ Cup Red or White Wine
Sea Salt and Ground Black Pepper

2 Tbs Butter
1 Large Onion – roughly chopped
6 Fresh Tomatoes – ripe and slightly soft
1 Celery Stalk – finely diced
4 Tbs Italian Parsley – finely chopped
Garlic Powder – optional

Season the chicken pieces with a little salt and freshly ground pepper and garlic powder. In a large skillet with a cover, heat the oil and butter. Add the chicken pieces (skin side down) and the onions. Sauté for 10 or 12 minutes. Add the minced garlic and stir. Continue cooking until the chicken is browned on both sides.

Add the tomatoes that have been peeled, seeded, and chopped. (If you prefer, you can use 6–8 chopped, canned plum tomatoes with a little of their juice.) Add the carrot, celery, and the wine of your choice. Cover and simmer until the chicken is cooked through and is tender. Remove the cover, add the parsley, and sprinkle with salt and freshly ground black pepper.

Chicken Carbonara with Pasta

1 Tbs Olive Oil
2½ Cups Heavy Cream
8 Large Egg Yolks
¼ Cup Italian Parsley – chopped
4 Cups Cooked Chicken – shredded
½ Cup Walnuts – toasted and chopped

4 Oz Pancetta – thinly sliced
1 Cup Freshly Grated Parmesan Cheese
¼ Cup Fresh Basil – chopped
2 tsps Minced Garlic
1 Lb Spaghetti – your favorite
1 Tbs Freshly Grated Lemon Zest

Heat oil in a large heavy-duty frying pan over medium heat. Add pancetta and sauté until it is brown and slightly crisp. Let cool slightly. Whisk in the cream, cheese, yolks, basil, parsley, and garlic. Stir in the chicken.

Meanwhile, bring a large pot of salted water to a boil. Add the pasta and cook al dente. Drain.

Add the spaghetti to the cream mixture and toss well over medium-low heat until the chicken is heated through and the sauce coats the pasta with a thick coating. Do not let the sauce boil.

Season with salt and freshly ground black pepper. Pour into a large serving bowl and sprinkle with walnuts and lemon zest.

Note: This is a good way to use up leftover roasted or rotisserie chicken.

Chicken Francese

½ Lb Chicken Breasts – cut into cutlets
Freshly Ground Black Pepper to Taste
¼ Cup Flour
⅛ Cup Olive Oil

Salt to Taste
½ tsp Garlic Powder
1 Egg
Lemon Butter Sauce

Place flour in a shallow dish. In a separate dish, add one beaten egg. Season the chicken cutlets with salt, pepper, and garlic powder. Dredge with flour and dip into beaten egg. If you like a thicker coating, repeat those steps again.

Heat olive oil in a heavy-duty pan. Add chicken cutlets, and cook on low heat until golden and cooked through. Remove the chicken from the pan.

Lemon Butter Sauce:

½ Cup Chicken Broth
Juice from ¼ Lemon – or to taste
1 Tbs Butter
½ tsp Fresh Parsley or Basil

¼ Lemon – cut into rings
¼ Cup White Wine
½ tsp Cornstarch
Salt to Taste

After removing chicken cutlets from pan, place them on a dish, and tent to keep warm. Add lemon rings to the pan and fry quickly. Add lemon juice, a pinch of salt, chicken broth, and white wine, and cook for a few minutes. Add butter mixed with cornstarch and slowly let it melt into the sauce. Return the chicken to the pan with all the accumulated juices and cook until thoroughly heated through.

Serve immediately with a side of pasta, rice, or spaetzle.

Chicken Piccata with Ziti

3 Chicken Breast Halves – skinned and boned
¼ tsp Freshly Ground Pepper
⅛ tsp Paprika
1 Tbs Butter
4 Tbs Dry Madeira Wine
¾ Lb Ziti – cooked according to package directions

½ Cup Flour
½ tsp Garlic Powder
¼ Cup Olive Oil
Salt and Pepper – to taste
3 Tbs Fresh Lemon Juice
Capers and Lemon Slices – for garnish

Place chicken breast halves between two sheets of wax paper or plastic wrap and pound evenly until thin. Combine flour, pepper, garlic powder, and paprika in a plastic bag. Add the chicken and coat. Shake off excess.

In a large skillet, heat olive oil and butter. Sauté chicken breasts for about 3 minutes on each side, lightly salting each piece before frying. Remove from skillet. Place on a plate lined with a paper towel and cover with foil to keep warm. Drain fat from the pan, reserving about 3-4 Tbs. If desired, add 1 additional tablespoon of butter. Add madeira wine to the pan and deglaze, scraping up all the little bits stuck to the bottom. Add lemon juice and heat through.

Return chicken breasts to skillet with lemon slices and cook until sauce thickens. Arrange ziti on serving platter. Place chicken breasts, with sauce, over well-drained ziti, and sprinkle with minced parsley and capers.

Note: This is really an easy dish. The trick is to time the pasta to finish cooking at about the time you add the chicken breasts back into the skillet.

Chicken Pomodoro

4 Chicken Cutlets
2 Tbs Vegetable Oil
¼ Cup White Wine or Vodka
½ Cup Tomatoes – chopped
2 Tbs Fresh Parsley or Basil – chopped

½ Cup Chicken Broth
2 Tbs Freshly Squeezed Lemon Juice
⅓ Cup Scallions
2 Tbs Heavy Cream

Heat a large frying pan with 2 Tbs of olive oil. You do not want to put the cutlets into the pan if the oil is not hot, or they will not fry and crisp, but just absorb the oil.

Put the cutlets between two pieces of plastic wrap or into a plastic bag large enough to hold them flat. Pound them lightly. Season them with salt and pepper (I am a garlic fan, so I also sprinkle them with a little bit of garlic powder). Lightly dust the cutlets with flour and sauté them in the oil until golden brown. Turn each one with kitchen tongs over and repeat on the second side. Transfer the cutlets to a platter and pour off a little of the fat from the pan.

Deglaze carefully (if a novice at this, do off heat) the pan with the vodka or white wine, and cook until the aroma is gone, all the while stirring up the browned bits on the bottom of the pan with a wooden spoon. Add the broth and lemon juice, and stir to get all incorporated.

Return the cutlets to the pan and cook, turning on each side for a few minutes, and transfer again to a warm plate.

Finish the dish by adding the tomatoes and cream to the pan and stir until all is hot and heated through. Pour over the cutlets and top with the scallions and parsley (or basil).

Chicken, Porchetta Style

A Recipe from Tuscany

2 (1½ Lb) Boneless Chicken Breasts – skin on	1 Cup Dry White Wine
½ Cup Olive Oil	⅓ Cup Honey
3 Tbs Sea Salt – or to taste	2 Tbs Minced Rosemary
¼ Cup Rosemary Leaves – or to taste	Freshly Ground Black Pepper to Taste
3 Lbs Yukon Gold Potatoes	12 Garlic Cloves – peeled and divided
1 Tbs Fennel Powder	3–4 Oz Pancetta – thinly sliced

Peel the potatoes, dice, and set aside. Using the flat side of a mallet, pound the chicken until it is about ¼-inch thick and set aside. Whisk together wine, ⅓ cup olive oil, honey, 3 Tbs salt, minced rosemary, and a grinding of black pepper in a bowl. When well blended, add the chicken and toss to coat all over. Cover with plastic wrap and chill for about 1 hour.

Preheat oven to 400°. Toss the remaining oil, all the rosemary leaves, diced potatoes, salt, and a little ground pepper on a baking sheet. Smash six of the garlic cloves and mix in. Roast, stirring occasionally, until slightly golden and a little tender, about 30 minutes. Set aside and keep warm.

Meanwhile, heat your grill, adjusting the flame so that the heat is at medium-high. If you prefer, you can use a heavy-duty grill pan heated on your stove top over a medium-high flame. Mince the remaining garlic cloves with a tiny bit of oil to make a paste. Remove the chicken from the marinade and pat a little dry. Place chicken on a work surface, skin side down, and rub with half of the garlic paste, fennel (Fiore di Finocchio), and some salt and pepper. Lay half the pancetta, overlapping slightly, on top. If you prefer or find it easier, you can give the pancetta a coarse chop and spread it on the garlic paste. Working from the long side, roll the chicken into a tight roll and secure using the butcher's string. Repeat with the second breast. Season the outside of the chicken with a little salt and pepper (I also like to add a little garlic powder, as I am a big fan of garlic).

Grill the rolls, turning occasionally and several times, until the skin is slightly charred and crisp, about 10 minutes. Place the chicken on the potato mixture and roast until the potatoes are very tender and you know the chicken is cooked all the way through, about 30–40 minutes.

If checking with a thermometer inserted into the thickest part of the roll, it should read 165°. Let rest a few minutes to retain all the juices, and then remove string and slice. Place the slices over the potatoes and serve.

Note: You will need some butcher's string for tying.

Chicken Savoy

3–4 Lbs Chicken – cut in 8 pieces	Kosher Salt and Ground Black Pepper
4 Garlic Cloves – minced	1 Tbs Dried Oregano
1 tsp Dried Thyme	⅓ Cup Romano Cheese – grated
3 Tbs Olive Oil	1 Cup Red Wine Vinegar

Salt and pepper the chicken pieces and sauté in the oil in a large ovenproof skillet until the skin is golden brown. Using a mortar and pestle or a small food processor, make a paste with everything but the red wine vinegar and spread the paste evenly over the skin of the chicken. Transfer skillet to a 500° preheated oven and bake for 20–30 minutes until chicken is done. Remove from oven, pour off the fat, and add 1 cup red wine vinegar to the pan. Spoon sauce over the chicken, and serve chicken with the remainder of the vinegar sauce on the side.

Note: This is a very popular recipe created by "Stretch" in the Belmont Tavern in Bloomfield, New Jersey. I read about it in one of the many food magazines we get.

Chicken Scarpiello

The Shoemaker's Chicken

2½–3 Lbs Chicken Parts – your favorite	Sea Salt and Ground Black Pepper
Garlic Powder to Taste	4 Tbs Olive Oil – divided
1 tsp Garlic – chopped	8 Italian Sausage Links – sliced
½ Cup Shallots – sliced	¼ Cup Dolce Piquant Peppers
2 Tbs Red Wine Vinegar	Pinch of Fresh Oregano
8 Tbs Chicken Stock	Salt and Ground Pepper to Taste

Season the chicken with sea salt, freshly ground black pepper, and garlic powder. Drizzle 2 Tbs of oil over the chicken and rub in. Roast uncovered for about 30–45 minutes, or until almost cooked through.

Add the remaining tablespoons of olive oil to a cast-iron pan or other heavy-duty pan over medium heat. Add the garlic, sausage, shallots, and peppers, and brown everything (about 5 minutes). Deglaze the pan with the red wine vinegar. Reduce the heat to low and let sauce cook until it is reduced by half, about 3 or 4 minutes. Add the white wine, salt, pepper, and oregano. Increase the heat to high, and add the chicken pieces and chicken stock, basting with the white wine sauce while it cooks all together for a few minutes and the chicken is now thoroughly cooked. Place the entire pan under the broiler for 3 minutes to crisp the top a little.

Transfer the chicken pieces to a serving platter, and pour the sauce and peppers over the chicken. Serve at once.

Chicken Vesuvio

A Garlicky Chicken Dish

1 Cup Olive Oil
10 Garlic Cloves
4 Russet Potatoes – large, peeled, and
    quartered
6–8 Lbs Chicken Parts – your favorite

1½–2 Cups Chicken Stock
1½ Cups Good White Wine
⅓ Cup Parsley – chopped
1 Tbs Dried Oregano
Salt and Freshly Ground Black Pepper

Heat oven to 375°. Heat oil in a roasting pan set over two burners on medium heat. Add garlic and potatoes, and cook, turning until the potatoes are golden brown (approximately 45 minutes).

Transfer potatoes and garlic to a plate. Add chicken pieces to pan and cook until golden brown, turning once (approximately 20 minutes). Add wine and cook until reduced by half (approximately 5 minutes). Return potatoes and garlic to the pan. Sprinkle with parsley, oregano, salt, and pepper. Add the stock and transfer the pan to the oven. Bake until everything is thoroughly cooked (approximately 45 minutes).

Note: Serve this with a small side dish of spaghetti. There should be enough liquid in the pan to stir into the pasta. Or, just serve a nice tossed salad. Although this is how my grandmother did it, I do find it easier to cook the chicken, etc., in two parts in a large frying pan, and then transfer everything to the roasting pan.

Continental Chicken Meatballs

1 Lb Ground Chicken
¼ Cup Breadcrumbs
1 Egg – beaten
1 tsp Kosher Salt
2 Tbs Olive Oil – to grease baking sheet

½ Cup Gruyere – shredded
2 Tbs Fresh Parsley – chopped
2 Cloves Garlic – minced
Black Pepper – freshly ground

Meatballs:

Preheat oven to 425° and line a large baking pan with foil rubbed with olive oil.

In a large bowl, combine the chicken, gruyere, breadcrumbs, parsley, egg, and garlic. Season with salt and pepper, and form into 16–18 meatballs. Place the meatballs on the baking sheet, and bake until golden and cooked through. This will take about 20 minutes. You don't want them too well done.

4 Tbs Butter – unsalted	2 Good Sized Onions – very thinly sliced
3 Garlic Cloves – minced	2 Cups Beef Broth
2 tsps Fresh Thyme – chopped, plus extra	Kosher Salt
1½ Cups Gruyere – shredded	Freshly Ground Black Pepper

Sauce:

In a large skillet, melt the butter on medium heat. Add the onions, and cook until softened and golden, stirring often to not let burn, since they are thin. Add the garlic, and cook until soft and fragrant. Add the broth and thyme, and season with salt and pepper. Bring slowly to a boil and then reduce the heat to let it simmer until it gets slightly thicker. Add the meatballs to the skillet and sprinkle with the shredded gruyere. Cover and cook until the meatballs are warmed through and the cheese has melted.

Note: I like to serve this dish with spaetzle and a nice plain salad. However, rice or mashed potatoes would be good, too.

Honey Fried Chicken

Chicken – 10 pieces of your favorite parts	4 Cups Buttermilk
1¾ Tbs Kosher or Sea Salt	½ Tbs Ground Black Pepper
1½ Tbs Paprika	8 Cups Canola Oil
4 Cups Flour	2 Tbs Garlic Powder
2 Tbs Onion Powder	1¼ Cups Honey – your favorite

Place the chicken pieces (I only use thighs) in a large bowl. To the 4 cups of buttermilk, add the salt, 1 tsp pepper, and 1 tsp paprika. Mix well to combine and pour all over the chicken, tossing the chicken to make sure it is well covered. Marinate in the refrigerator for 1 to 6 hours.

In a large, deep pot, pour enough oil to fill the pot up to about four inches. Heat over medium-high heat until a deep-fry thermometer inserted in the oil reaches 350°. Set a cooling rack over a baking sheet lined with newspaper or paper towels.

In a large bowl, whisk to combine the flour, garlic powder, onion powder, and the remaining salt, pepper, and paprika. Whisk well, as you want the dredge to be well incorporated.

Lift the chicken out of the buttermilk, then coat the pieces completely in the flour. Transfer the chicken to a separate baking sheet or a large platter. Working in batches, add the chicken parts to the hot oil and cook, turning and monitoring the oil temperature. Do not overcrowd the chicken, or it will not crisp. Also, do not let the oil get cool, or the chicken will not cook and crisp. Cook about 5–6 minutes per side. Transfer the chicken to the rack. When all the chicken is cooked to a deep golden brown, drizzle with the honey and serve.

Honey Fried Chicken reminds me of some happy times with good friends during the late '60s and into the '70s. Charlie worked for Erie Tech, and they had a plant in State College. We would all meet in State College to cheer on the Nittany Lions at a Penn State Game. We'd make a weekend of it, and one night was dinner at the Corner Room near Toftrees Resort, where we stayed. The Corner Room had a dinner buffet, and the Honey Chicken was my favorite. We still keep in touch with Lee and Marlene, and her sangria is something I still talk about and make. But, those happy days and the laughs were the very best.

Lemon Chicken Thighs

8 Chicken Thighs – skin trimmed, bone in	¼ Cup Extra Virgin Olive Oil
2 tsps Kosher Salt	Ground Black Pepper to Taste
1 tsp Paprika	1 tsp Dried Oregano
Garlic Powder to Taste	10 Sprigs Fresh Thyme
1 tsp Lemon Zest – freshly grated	2 Tbs Chopped Fresh Parsley

Season chicken with a little oil, salt, pepper, garlic powder, paprika, and oregano, and rub into the chicken skin until well coated. Pour extra virgin olive oil into the bottom of a heavy-duty pan that can go into the oven. Nestle thyme sprigs on top of the chicken and top with lemon juice. Cover well and cook in a preheated oven for 1 hour at 375°. The time varies depending on the thickness and weight of the chicken. When the chicken tests done, discard thyme sprigs and move chicken to a platter. Tent to keep warm.

Stir parsley and lemon zest into the sauce in the pan. Mix well and then spoon over the chicken thighs. Serve with a nice, fluffy, buttered white rice.

Pollo alla Milanese

2 Chicken Breasts – halved and lightly
   pounded
6 Tbs Breadcrumbs
2 Garlic Cloves
1 Lemon – quartered

Salt and Pepper – to taste
4 Tbs Flour
1 Sprig of Fresh Rosemary
2 Eggs – well beaten
4 Tbs Butter

Flour the chicken. Dip into beaten eggs and then into breadcrumbs. Melt butter in a large skillet with the garlic and rosemary. Add the chicken and cook on medium-high heat until the chicken is golden brown on both sides. Serve with lemon wedges.

Note: Serve with a side of pasta, a few sautéed vegetables, or a garden salad.

Pollo alla Romana

2 Whole Boneless Chicken Breasts
1 Large Onion – sliced
½ Cup White Wine
4 Plum Tomatoes – crushed
Pinch of Salt – or more to taste

1 Each Green, Red, Yellow Pepper
1 Rosemary Sprig
2 Garlic Cloves
¼ Cup Olive Oil
Freshly Ground Black Pepper

Cut the chicken breasts into pieces. Remove the seeds from the peppers and slice each into 8 pieces. Sauté the chicken in the olive oil in a large skillet, together with the garlic and rosemary. Cook for about 3–5 minutes. Add the wine and simmer until it has almost evaporated. Add the onions and peppers, and cook for 6–7 minutes more on medium-high heat. Taste for salt and pepper, and adjust. Add the tomatoes and continue cooking for a few more minutes until the tomatoes are soft and have released their juice.

Pollo alla Trasteverina

Official Roman Dish for Festa de Noiantri

8 Chicken Thighs – skin on, bone in
1 Vidalia Onion – chopped
3 Red Bell Pepper – roasted, seeded, skinned
1 Tbs Olive Oil
1 (28 Oz) Can San Marzano Tomatoes – drained and chopped
5–6 Sprigs Fresh Marjoram Leaves – chopped
¼" Thick Slice Panetta – chopped

1 Pepperoncino – seeds removed, chopped
½ Cup Dry White Wine – Frascati would work well
½ Cup Chicken Broth
2 Garlic Cloves – sliced thin
Salt and Pepper to Taste

Set a large heavy-duty pan with a lid over medium heat and add 1 Tbs olive oil. Slice the seeded bell peppers into thick strips. When the oil is hot, add the chicken (skin side down), season all over with salt and pepper, and brown it well. The skin is crisp when it will turn over easily. Turn the chicken over and brown the other side, about 5 minutes on this side. Remove the chicken from the pot and let rest, covered, on a plate.

Pour off any excessive fat. Add the pancetta and let it start to crisp, about 4–5 minutes. Add the onion and cook until softened. Add the garlic, pepperoncino, and sliced red peppers. Sauté all until everything is fragrant and tender.

Return the chicken and any accumulated juices back to the pan. Add the white wine and let it all simmer for a few minutes. Add the tomatoes and chicken broth, and bring to a slow boil. Turn the heat to low, cover the skillet, and simmer until the chicken is tender and cooked through, about 30 minutes. Add the marjoram, and taste for salt and pepper. Drizzle with a little extra virgin olive oil. This dish needs a good crusty Italian bread to soak up the sauce. Would be great also with a side of pasta.

Note: Festa de Noiantri is a celebration of the local Madonna held in mid-July in Rome's Trastevere section.

Pollo Villa D'este

2 Large Chicken Breasts – split in half
1 Pkg (12 Oz) Mushrooms – your favorite
4 Thick Slices Mozzarella
Salt to Taste

1 Garlic Clove – chopped
8 Tbs Olive Oil
½ Pint Heavy Cream
Freshly Ground Black Pepper

Sauté the mushrooms and garlic in 4 Tbs of olive oil. Add the cream and simmer about ½ hour until thickened.

Meanwhile, sauté the chicken in the remaining oil in a skillet on medium-low heat for about 8–10 minutes on each side. Place chicken on a cookie sheet. Pour the cream sauce over each piece of chicken and top with a slice of mozzarella. Bake at 350° until the cheese melts.

The Boss's Chicken

Pollo del Padrone, Charlie's Version

½ Oz Dried Italian Mushrooms
½ Cup Warm Water
2 Tbs Tomato Paste
3 Oz Salt Pork – diced
¼ Cup Olive Oil
2½ Lbs Chicken Pieces – your favorite
** chicken parts**
2 Cups Canned Plum Tomatoes – chopped

¼ Cup Butter
¾ Lb Onions – peeled and diced
3 Garlic Cloves – finely chopped
Pinch of Fresh Rosemary
Salt and Freshly Ground Black Pepper
¾ Cup White Wine – preferably dry
** and one you would enjoy drinking**
** while you cook**

Soak the dried mushrooms in warm water for about 20–30 minutes. Drain, saving the water, and chop the mushrooms. Set the mushrooms aside. Stir the tomato paste into the mushroom water.

Wash and dry the chicken pieces and set aside.

Place olive oil, butter, and salt pork in a large skillet. Sauté for a few minutes. Add the onions and cook until medium brown. Add the chicken (skin side down), but allow plenty of room. Do not crowd the chicken, or it will not brown. Cook chicken for about 10 minutes until nicely browned, but do not burn. Add garlic, rosemary (you can chop these together), and a tiny pinch of salt and pepper. Stir and cook for about 5–10 minutes. Add wine, cover, and simmer slowly for another 5 or 10 minutes. Add tomatoes, mushrooms, and the mushroom water with the tomato paste. Cook uncovered for about 30 minutes. Taste for salt (remember, you had sautéed using salt pork, so more salt may not be needed). Serve with your favorite pasta or gnocchi, spooning the sauce on top of your choice.

This was a very favorite Sunday night dish that Charlie would cook, and the Children thought the name came from the fact that Charlie had prepared it. Because we prepared it so often for friends, it ultimately became to be called "Charlie's Chicken," and that is what we call it to this day.

Tuscan Chicken White Bean Stew

3–4 Slices Pancetta – chopped
Olive Oil
8 Chicken Thighs – with skin and bones
All-Purpose Flour
2 (28 Oz) Cans Italian Tomatoes
1½ Cups Chicken Broth

1 Cup White Wine – not too dry, a little fruity
½ Cup Basil – freshly chopped
2 (15 Oz) Cans Cannellini Beans – drained
½ tsp Sugar
Salt and Pepper to Taste

Put olive oil in a large heavy-duty, ovenproof pot and add pancetta, cooking until slightly translucent. Add onions and cook until limp. Remove all to small bowl and save. Meanwhile, coat chicken with flour, salt, and pepper. Shake off extra and add to pot a few at a time, turning until slightly brown. Add a little more olive oil if needed to keep chicken from burning. Using a slotted spoon, remove cooked chicken and put into a dish to keep for a while. Put onions and pancetta back into the pot. Add the garlic and cook for about 5 minutes over a low flame. Add white wine, stirring to scrape any bits that have stuck to the bottom or sides of the pot. Add chicken broth, tomatoes, basil, and sugar, and simmer for a few minutes. Return chicken and any juices that have accumulated back to the pot. Add drained beans, and after a few minutes, taste for salt and pepper. Heat oven to 325°. Cover and put in oven for 2–3 hours.

To coat chicken, I put the flour in a plastic bag, sprinkle the chicken with salt and pepper (rubbed in well), and put a few pieces in the bag at a time and just shake until coated.

Note: This is a meal in itself, served with crusty Italian bread and a salad. Any leftovers can be saved for a second night's supper and served over pasta. Sometimes I add a few small potatoes to the sauce on either night. They need about ½ hour to cook through.

White Chicken Chili

1½–2 Lbs Precooked Chicken – (like rotisserie-style or boiled breasts) shredded

4 Cups Chicken Broth

1 Small Can Diced Green Chiles

2 tsps Chili Powder – or to taste

24 Oz Monterey Jack – shredded

4 Cans Northern White Beans – undrained

1 Medium Onion – chopped

3 Garlic Cloves – minced

½ tsp Hot Pepper Flakes

Pinch of Paprika

In a large soup pot, add a little olive oil and lightly sauté the onion and garlic. When the onion has softened, add the broth and cook until getting hot over a low flame. Add in all the ingredients (except for the cheese), draining the chilies, and slowly bring back to a boil. After a few minutes, lower to simmer and cook for about 20 minutes to allow all the flavors to blend. When the soup is very hot and has cooked for a while, start adding the shredded cheese a little at a time, stirring constantly, or the cheese will fall to the bottom and stick to the bottom of the pot. Taste for salt and pepper. Great served with corn muffins.

Meat

Osso Buco Beer-Braised

4 Tbs Extra Virgin Olive Oil
2 Large Onions – sliced
½ Cup Chicken Stock
1 Garlic Clove – sliced

1 Veal Shank – about 1½ lbs
1 (12 Oz) Bottle German Beer – divided
Salt and Ground Black Pepper
Flour – for dredging

Preheat oven to 275°. Heat the oil in a deep, ovenproof pan over medium-high heat. Season the veal shank with salt, pepper, and a sprinkle of garlic powder (optional). Dredge in the flour, shake off any excess, and carefully put it in the hot pan and sear for about 5 minutes on each side. Lower the heat to medium after you are sure you have gotten a good crust on both sides of the shank. Remove the shank from the pot and set aside.

Add the onions and garlic and cook, stirring until soft and golden (about 15 minutes). Add half of the beer, and then continue cooking until the beer has almost evaporated. Add the veal back to the pot, add the rest of the beer and the chicken stock, cover with a tight-fitting lid or foil, and put into the hot oven. Let it braise for about 3 hours or until the meat is very tender. Serve with a side of mashed potatoes or spaetzle.

Beef Stew with Beer

2 Lbs Stew Beef – not too lean,
  cut in 1-inch cubes
1 tsp Salt
¼ tsp Dried Leaf Thyme
¼ tsp Dried Leaf Tarragon
1 Bay Leaf
12 Oz Beer – your favorite
4 Large Potatoes – cut in 1-inch cubes
Salt to Taste
¼ Cup Cold Water

2 Tbs Oil or Part Bacon Drippings
½ tsp Black Pepper
¼ tsp Dried Ground Marjoram
¼ tsp Dried Basil
1 Container (10 Oz) Beef Broth
4 Carrots – cut in 1-inch pieces
6 Small Onions – peeled and cut in
  quarters
¼ Cup Flour

In a skillet, brown the meat in the hot oil. Add the herbs and seasonings, beef broth, and beer. Cover and simmer for 1½ hours.

Add the vegetables and continue cooking for 30 minutes or longer, until vegetables are tender. Taste and add salt to taste.

In a small bowl or cup, mix the flour and water until smooth; stir into the stew until hot and thickened. Serves 6.

Note: This is a great recipe for a cold day.

Bis Nonna's Meat Loaf

This little saltshaker was never out of my mother's reach and is over seventy-five years old

2½–3 Lbs Ground Chuck
2 Cups Seasoned Breadcrumbs
1 Cup Heinz Ketchup
1 Cup Onion – chopped
1½ tsps Garlic Powder
2 Tbs Parsley – fresh and chopped
3–4 Eggs – large
Salt and Pepper to Taste
2 Eggs – hard-boiled, optional

Mix meat with ketchup, breadcrumbs, onions, and all seasonings. Shape into easy-to-handle loaves and place in lightly greased casserole dish and brown in 350° oven, turning once. When finished browning, pour off some of the liquid on the bottom of the casserole dish. Now, pour the sauce over and continue baking. As a surprise, I sometimes would add 1 or 2 hardboiled eggs in the middle of the meatloaf.

Meat Loaf Sauce:

4 Cups Water
4 Beef Bouillon Cubes
½ Can Tomato Paste

2–3 Tbs Ketchup to Taste
2 Garlic Cloves – peeled and sliced
Cornstarch – as needed

Bring water to a boil and add beef cubes. Stir to dissolve, and then add the tomato paste, ketchup, and garlic cloves. Stir until all is well incorporated and hot. Carefully pour over the browned meat loaves in the casserole dish. Cover with aluminum foil and cook for one hour, basting frequently. Cover and cook for ½ hour more. Just before serving, you can thicken sauce with little cornstarch if you prefer it a little more thickened.

Note: Goes well with rice. Cook rice in lightly salted water as directed. Drain and add a few pats of butter. Beat two eggs in a small bowl and add to rice, mixing quickly. Be careful not to mash down the rice. Enjoy. My Mother was not a cook, but this she did well so we had it often.

Sometimes with rice, sometimes with mashed potatoes and sometimes with polenta. My Mother was addicted to salt and her version would have had a lot more salt in it. This little saltshaker pictured on this page was one that always sat on the table and very close to my Mother.

Bistecca alla Fiorentina

Extra Virgin Olive Oil
Salt and Freshly Ground Black Pepper
Lemon Wedges

Steak from the Rib – bone left on, 2–3 inches thick

Rub the steak on both sides with olive oil and sprinkle only with pepper. Cook over a very hot grill until it is rare but no more than medium-rare. Add the salt after the meat has cooked so that the salt does not draw out all the juices from the meat. Slice and serve with lemon wedges. Figure on ½ pound per person.

Note: Tuscany has a very special kind of beef cattle called Chianina, and this is where you will have the most delicious beef steak. (Chianini cattle have ancient origins: large white cattle were known as early as Roman times and the Romans revered them for their beauty and strength rather than for gastronomic reasons, as they are today.) This dish was a special Father's Day dinner for Charlie and the family one Father's Day. We also indulged again in Italy with the true Chianina beef when we were in Tuscany.

Braciole in Tomato Sauce

2 Lbs Top Round Steak – ¼ inch thick
2 Cups Fresh Italian Parsley – chopped
1 Cup Fresh Basil – chopped
1 Cup Italian Seasoned Breadcrumbs
3 Tbs Garlic – minced
1 Cup Parmigiano Reggiano Cheese – grated

Salt and Freshly Ground Black Pepper
  to Taste
½ Cup Olive Oil
2 Cups Tomato Sauce – your favorite,
  and more as necessary

Cut the meat into 4" x 6" slices and pound thin. Avoid tearing or making holes. Blend the parsley, garlic, and basil and spread over each meat slice. Mix the breadcrumbs and the cheese and sprinkle over the meat. Sprinkle each with a little salt and pepper. Roll the meat, tuck in the ends, and tie with twine. Sprinkle each bundle with a little more salt and pepper. Brown the meat in the olive oil over a low-medium heat, turning gently until evenly browned. Remove the meat from the pan when done and add to your favorite tomato sauce. Simmer for about 45 minutes and just until the meat is tender, but not overcooked. When ready to serve, remove from the sauce, remove the twine, and slice and arrange on a platter. Or you can make smaller ones and serve each individually.

Braciole

Easy and Delicious

2 Slices of Flank Steak – pounded thin
2 Garlic Cloves – minced or mashed
1 tsp Raisins – chopped
Salt and Freshly Ground Black Pepper
½ Cup Chopped Onions
3 Cups San Marzano Tomatoes – puréed in
  a blender

1 tsp Fresh Parsley – chopped
1 Tbs Pine Nuts
1 tsp Grated Cheese – your favorite
4 Tbs Extra Virgin Olive Oil
¼ Cup White Wine – your favorite to
  drink
A Few Basil Leaves – torn

Pound the steak slices until they are thin enough to roll. Spread the parsley, garlic, pine nuts, raisins, grated cheese, salt, and pepper evenly onto the steaks. Roll up the meat, and then tie each one with string, making sure to secure the ends so that the stuffing does not fall out while cooking.

In a pan large enough to hold the Braciole, brown the onions in the olive oil until soft. Then add the meat, browning all over. When browned, add the wine and cook until the aroma is gone. Add the tomatoes and basil and cook slowly on low heat for at least two hours while occasionally spooning sauce over.

Note: This is a good standalone dish with a salad. I usually make several and put them in the sauce with my meatballs, etc. My Nonna, Giovanna, who ran the Pensione/Restaurant, sometimes made these with pig skins, and they were so delicious. I'm fairly certain that my Mother-in-Law did the same.

Steak Diane

Charlie's Version

4 (6–7 Oz) ¾" New York Steaks – trimmed and pounded lightly	1 Tbs Kosher Salt
	Black Pepper to taste
2 Large Shallots – chopped	2 Tbs Olive Oil
4 Large White Mushrooms – sliced	2 Large Garlic Cloves
1 Cup Dry Young Red Wine	1 Cup Beef Stock
1 Tbs Worcestershire Sauce	1 Tbs Dijon Mustard
½ tsp Potato Starch or Arrowroot	2–4 Tbs Heavy Cream – optional
1 Tbs Fresh Parsley – chopped	1 Tbs Butter – unsalted

Season steaks with salt only a minimum of 1–4 hours prior to placing in the skillet.

In skillet, heat oil until hot but not smoking. Sauté each side of the steak for approximately 2 minutes or until rare or medium-rare. Set aside, covered.

Over medium heat, add shallots to skillet and cook for 20–30 seconds. Add mushrooms to skillet and cook, stirring, until mushrooms start to sweat, about 2–4 minutes. Add garlic cloves and cook to blend for about 2 minutes. Add wine (such as Dolcetto di Alba or Nebbiolo) to skillet and cook until reduced by half.

Add beef stock, Worcestershire sauce, and stir in. Mix potato starch or arrowroot with 2 tsps cold water and stir to dissolve and then add to sauce and bring to a boil. Add heavy cream, unsalted butter, and blend in.

Slice warm, rested steaks, place on individual dishes, and spoon sauce around and over the steak and garnish with parsley.

Cotechino con Lenticchie

Sausage with Lentils

2–3 Lbs Cotechino
½ Cup Onions – finely chopped
1 Celery Stalk – finely chopped
1½ Cups Small Lentils – rinsed and drained
Mustard for Serving

3 Tbs Olive Oil
1 carrot – finely chopped
1–2 Garlic Cloves – peeled
Salt and Pepper to Taste

If Cotechino is uncooked, drain it and put in large pot of cold water. Water should completely cover Cotechino. Bring slowly to a boil and then reduce heat to simmer and cook for about 3 hours. For packaged (precooked) Cotechino, just simmer for 1 hour.

When Cotechino is almost cooked, heat the oil in a medium heavy-bottomed pot and add the onion, carrot, and celery and cook until just getting soft. Add garlic and cook for a few more minutes until garlic is flavorful, making sure not to brown or burn. Add lentils and stir well until all is incorporated. Add enough cold water, or Cotechino water, to cover lentils by about 1 inch.

Cook for 30–45 minutes over medium heat, covered, until lentils are soft. Stir once in a while and add Cotechino water if getting too dry. This will also add extra flavor. When lentils are tender, remove from heat, drain of any extra water, and season to taste with salt and pepper. Spoon lentils into serving bowl. Slice Cotechino into slices thick enough not to fall apart and arrange on a platter. Serve warm and accompany by mustard.

Cotechino is a rich and wonderfully spiced sausage and makes for a hearty winter dish. However, for Italians, it is a New Year's Day traditional meal because it combines the two symbols of good luck—the lentil (which, being coin-shaped, represents a promise of wealth in the year to come) and the pig (which is believed to be an animal that eats while moving forward)—and symbolizes a year of hope and promise and good fortune. In our house, we eat Cotechino several times during the cold months. If you can find Castelluccio lentils from Umbria, you are in for a treat.

Note: I have turned this into a hearty meal by adding peeled potatoes and cabbage wedges to the Cotechino pot one hour before the sausage should be ready. Just adjust the amounts of cabbage wedges and potatoes according to the number of people you will be serving. Everyone takes a whole potato and mashes their own with butter or olive oil. I also add small, peeled onions. Also, one each per person. Cotechino is a rich and wonderfully seasoned sausage that makes for a hearty winter dish. For Italians, it is a New Year's Day tradition. Some believe it should be eaten on the Eve, while others will serve it on New Year's Day. In our house, we do it either way, depending on schedules. And we have it several times during the year, too.

Lamb Chops with Arugula Chimichurri

2 Cups Arugula
1 Large Garlic Clove – minced
⅓ Cup Red Wine Vinegar
12 Thick Rib Lamb Chops

1 Cup Fresh Parsley
½ Cup Extra Virgin Olive Oil
1 Tbs Ground Cumin
2 Tbs Salt and Freshly Ground Black Pepper

Chimichurri Sauce:

In a food processor, combine arugula, parsley, and garlic. Pulse to combine, slowly adding the olive oil. Pour into a small serving bowl, drizzle in the vinegar and cumin, stir very well, and set aside.

Lamb Chops:

Season the lamb chops by spreading a little olive oil on each chop and then sprinkling with salt, pepper, and garlic powder. Massage this well into the chops and set aside to rest. Broil or grill, as you desire, until the chops are medium-rare, put on a platter to rest for a minute or two to retain their juices, and then top with the chimichurri just before serving.

This is a big hit in our family and subsequently was a Father's Day dinner on more than one occasion, inspired in part by Bistecca alla Fiorentina.

Note: Arugula is also known as rucola or rocket.

Marsala Meatballs with Sage

1½ Lbs Ground Veal or Pork
3–4 Tbs Freshly Grated Cheese
3 Tbs Butter – unsalted
½ Cup Chicken Broth

¼ Cup Soft Breadcrumbs – moistened with milk
8 Fresh Sage Leaves
¾ Cup Good Dry Marsala Wine
⅓ Cup Heavy Cream

It is not always easy to get veal, so a good alternative is pork. Mix together the veal or pork, moistened breadcrumbs, cheese (your favorite), and a few pinches of sea salt and freshly ground black pepper. Mince half of the sage leaves and mix these in, too.

Grab bits of meat and form into little balls a little larger than a walnut. Fry them in butter in a hot skillet until they are golden and crisp; remove to a platter to rest. Add the wine to the skillet and scrape up any bits on the bottom of the pan with a wooden spoon. Be sure to use a good wine that you would enjoy sipping and not a cooking marsala. When the aroma of the wine has dissipated, add the broth and cook until the liquid is reduced by half.

Chop the remaining sage leaves and add these to the sauce. Let simmer for a few minutes and then taste for salt and pepper. Simmer for a few more minutes and add the cream, stirring until well incorporated. Add the meatballs back to the skillet along with any accumulated juices and cook until the meatballs are warmed all the way through, and the sauce has thickened. Serve this dish with the sauce spooned over the meatballs and with a side of spaetzle or rice and a nice salad. Don't forget some crusty Italian bread to soak up any liquid.

Meatballs, Etc.

3 Lbs Ground Meat – 2 Lbs Chuck and 1 Lb
   Ground Pork
2–3 Cups Italian Seasoned Breadcrumbs
1½ Cup Onions – chopped fine
½ tsp Salt – or to taste
½–¾ tsp Garlic Powder – or to taste

3–4 Large Basil Leaves – chopped
⅓ Cup Grated Romano Cheese
1–1½ Cups Water
2 Pieces Stale Italian Bread – soaked in milk
   and slightly squeezed dry
4 Large Eggs – slightly beaten

Mix meat, onions, salt, garlic, basil, and cheese together in a large bowl. Add soaked bread and mix in. Add breadcrumbs and eggs, mix well, and then add water a little at a time. Mix until all incorporated, but do not overwork the meat and make it mushy. If the meat seems little dry, add a little more water. **IF** it seems too wet or soft, add a little more breadcrumbs. They should be just a little "squishy." Roll into balls, whatever size you prefer, but making sure they are all about the same size. Brown in 375° oven on a Pam-sprayed roasting pan until evenly browned all over. If you prefer, fry them in a little olive oil in a large skillet. Save some of the pan juices to add to your sauce because that's where the flavor is.

Note: If adding sausage and other meats like country-style spareribs, cook until nicely browned but not crispy, and add to your sauce with some of the juices. Sausage cuts better when cooked. I add sausage to the sauce raw, semi-cook, and then cut on the diagonal and quickly add back to the sauce before all the juice flows out. I don't think our Grandson Vince has ever come to visit when meatballs were not on the stove waiting for him. And if served with rigatoni, Nick and Carson are very happy.

Let me add something about meatballs here while I think about it. This recipe will make about 36 meatballs. If I am making sauce for a holiday or celebration where I would have the entire family of 21+, I would be making more than 60 meatballs. So, the question I am always asked is whether I fry or bake or put into the sauce raw. First off, I never put the meatballs into the sauce raw. Tried it once with a few meatballs and the reaction was not at all positive, and my Grandchildren are true meatball aficionados. So, if I am only making a dozen or so, I will fry them. Any number more than that, I place on a parchment paper–lined baking pan and set my oven on roast around 375°. I add them immediately, with all the accumulated juices, to the pot of sauce cooking on the stove.

Wouldn't be Sunday family dinner without them

Osso Buco Milanese

4 Veal Shanks	1 Cup Beef Broth
1 Can (35 Oz) Plum Tomatoes	1½ Cups White Wine
1 Carrot – roughly chopped	2 Garlic Cloves – thickly sliced
1 Medium Onion – roughly chopped	1 Cup Flour – or as needed
1 Celery Stalk – roughly chopped	1 Sprig Fresh Rosemary
¾ Cup Extra Virgin Olive Oil	Salt and Ground Pepper to Taste

Pour ¼ cup olive oil, tomatoes (that have been pulse-blended for 3–5 seconds), and garlic in a saucepan over medium heat. Bring almost to a boil and reduce the heat. Flour each veal shank and sprinkle with a little salt and pepper. In a sauté pan, heat ¼ cup of olive oil and when heated, add the rosemary and veal shanks. Cook until evenly browned on all sides. Place the veal shanks in a baking pan, add the broth and white wine, and bake at 350° for 30–45 minutes. In the sauté pan, heat the remaining ¼ cup of olive oil and sauté the vegetables, add the tomato sauce, bring to a slow boil, and pour over the veal shanks. Continue baking for another 1½ hours or until the meat starts to fall away from the bone.

Note: I have also made this using thick pork shanks, and they were delicious. Both are a perfect match when served with Risotto Milanese.

Piedmont Pot Roast

Manzo alla Piemontese

1 Rib Roast (3½ Lbs)	1 Celery Stalk – chopped
6 Slices Prosciutto or Pancetta	2 Tbs Fresh Parsley – minced
2 Slices Prosciutto – chopped	1 Onion – chopped
2 Tbs Butter	1–2 Tbs Tomato Paste
1 Carrot – diced	½ Cup Sweet Vermouth
2 Cups Beef Stock	Salt and Pepper to Taste
2–3 Garlic Cloves	

Remove the bone from the roast and cover the meat with the prosciutto or pancetta. In a heavy pan, brown the meat in butter, add the chopped prosciutto (or you can use pancetta here too), garlic, carrot, celery, parsley, and onion. Add the tomato paste (more or less as you prefer) to the stock and stir to incorporate. Pour over the meat in the pan and add the wine and seasonings.

Cover and cook over a low flame until tender for about 2½–3 hours.

Note: In Piedmont, this dish might have 1 sliced truffle inserted into the meat and then rolled and tied to keep it secure while cooking. Truffles are an acquired taste and quite delicious. In the absence of a truffle, you can use truffle oil and sprinkle a little over the top of the meat before serving. This is good dish to serve with mashed potatoes, rice, or pappardelle.

Piedmontese Boiled Beef

Insalate de Manzo Bollito

In the northern regions of Italy where my maternal ancestors are from and where my Mother was born, this dish is a favorite. Boiled beef is the basis of a common dish called Bollito Misto, in which you could find capon, tongue, veal head, cotechino, and beef. Making this dish can be a complicated procedure if done in the traditional way. But here is a recipe for boiled beef that is delicious and easy. You first boil the beef, which is what gives you a great pot of stock in the process.

This poaching liquid can be strained and served as a soup with small pasta and freshly grated cheese.

4 Carrots – peeled and cut into thick slices	1 Onion – cut into large chunks
3 Celery Stalks – cut into large chunks	6 Tbs Fresh Italian Parsley – finely chopped, divided
2 Lbs Boneless Beef Top Chuck	
1 tsp Kosher Salt	1 Cup Cornichons
1 Medium Red Onion – halved, sliced thin	3–4 Tbs Red Wine Vinegar
1 Tbs Dijon Mustard	⅓ Cup Extra Virgin Olive Oil

In a large pot, combine 8 quarts water, carrots, onion, celery, 2 Tbs parsley, and the beef. Slowly bring to a simmer and continue cooking until the beef is very tender (about 1¾–2 hours). Let cool. Remove the beef, carrots, and some of the onion.

Strain the stock or serve intact for another use. Chop the carrots and onions and put in a large bowl. Cut the beef in small cubes or sliced extremely thin and add it to the bowl. Season all with some salt and freshly ground pepper. Add the cornichons and red onion.

In a small bowl, whisk together the vinegar, mustard, and remaining salt. Whisk in the olive oil until smooth and it becomes very creamy. Drizzle this dressing over the beef, add the parsley, toss well, and serve.

Pork and Cabbage Packets

Farcellets de Col alla Catalan

16 Large Savoy Cabbage Leaves   Salt and Freshly Ground Black Pepper

Trim the tough ends of the cabbage leaves. Boil in lightly salted water just until pliable enough to fold when filled. Cool.

Sofregit:

⅓ Cup Olive Oil   2 Yellow Onions – finely chopped
1 Carrot – peeled, finely chopped   6 Garlic Cloves – finely chopped

Warm the oil in a frying pan over medium heat and warm the olive oil. Add the onions, carrot, and garlic and sauté until the onions are soft, being careful not to burn the garlic. Spread half of this mixture in the bottom of a baking dish.

Filling:

10 Oz Lean Ground Pork – minced   10 Oz Ground Beef – minced
Salt and Freshly Ground Black Pepper   1 Egg – lightly beaten

Add the pork and beef to the pan that has the remaining sofregit and cook all together until the meat is lightly browned (about 8–10 minutes). Transfer to a bowl, season well with salt and pepper, and stir in the beaten egg.

Assemble:

Place a heaping tablespoonful of the filling in the center of each cabbage leaf and fold the sides over the filling. Roll into a neat little packet, about the size of a lemon. Seal each packet with a toothpick.

Dust the farcellets with flour. In a wide, heavy-bottomed sauté pan, over medium-high heat, warm the olive oil. In batches, add the packets and fry, turning, until both sides are golden brown. As they finish frying, place them in the casserole dish on top of the sofregit. When you have finished frying all the packets, deglaze the pan with wine, scraping up all the little bits stuck to the bottom of the pan. Stir in the stock, cook for a minute or two, and then pour all over the farcellets.

Cover the baking dish and bake until cooked through, about 25–30 minutes. Let rest for a few minutes and then serve.

Note: Sofrgit, sofrito, or soffrito is a sauce used as a base in Spanish, Italian, and many other Latin American recipes. Ingredients will vary a little, but it typically consists of sautéing minced onion, garlic, celery, and carrots sprinkled with a little salt and pepper in a very good olive oil. This is what adds much flavor to many dishes.

Pork Chops with
Cherry Peppers and Potatoes

2 Center Cut Pork Chops – not too thin
1 Red Bell Pepper – seeded and diced
1 Garlic Clove – chopped
1–2 Tbs Red Wine Vinegar – or to taste
2 Tbs Extra Virgin Olive Oil
1–2 Yukon Gold Potatoes – parboiled

½ Onion – thickly sliced
4 Small Vinegar Cherry Peppers – seeded and diced – reserving some juice
1 Cup Dry White Wine
Sea Salt and Freshly Ground Black Pepper

Cut the potatoes into 1-inch slices. Liberally sprinkle both sides of the chops with sea salt and freshly ground black pepper. Put a large cast-iron pan on the stove over medium-high heat and add the olive oil. When the oil is hot enough, put the potatoes in the pan in a single layer and sprinkle with a little sea salt and some pepper. Brown the potatoes on both sides, turning carefully and then set aside.

Add the chops to the pan giving them some space in between so that they brown nicely. Leave the chops alone until you have a nice crust on both sides. **Do not overcook or they will be too dry.** They should be a little pink inside. Remove the chops from the pan and keep warm.

If the pan seems too dry, add a little olive oil; otherwise add the onions and sauté until they are slightly limp and the bell pepper is a little soft. Add the cherry peppers with some of their juice and garlic, mix everything together, and cook for a few more minutes. Add the vinegar and mix well.

Remove everything from the pan, raise the heat to high, and add the white wine, scraping up all the bits on the bottom of the pan, and let the wine simmer until it is reduced by about one-third.

Put the chops, vegetables, and all juices back into the pan just to reheat. Place the chops on serving plates, surrounded by the potatoes, onions, and cherry peppers. Pour over all any sauce that is left in the pan. Serve immediately and pass some crusty Italian bread.

Pork Chops with Marsala

Marsala Cotolette di Maiale

4 Loin Pork Chops
6 Tbs Romano Cheese – freshly grated
Salt and Pepper to Taste
1 Tbs Fresh Parsley – chopped
½ Cup Marsala

2 Eggs – slightly beaten
1 Cup Breadcrumbs
1 Cup Celery – diced
2 Small Onions – sliced

Combine crumbs, cheese, seasonings, and parsley. Dip the pork chops in the slightly beaten egg and then coat well on both sides in the crumb mixture. Fry the chops in a small amount of oil until well browned on both sides. Drain the fat from the pan, arrange the pork chops in the pan, and spread the diced celery and sliced onions on top of them. Sprinkle lightly with salt and pepper and add the marsala. Cover the pan and cook over a low flame until the meat is tender but not overdone. Serve hot with the accumulated gravy.

Pork Meatballs

From the Emilia-Romagna Area

4 Slices White Bread – crusts removed
1 Cup Whole Milk
1 Lb Lean Ground Pork
6 Oz Mortadella – roughly chopped
1 Cup Romano or Parmesan Cheese –
    freshly grated

Pinch of Freshly Grated Nutmeg – or to taste
Salt and Freshly Ground Black Pepper
Olive Oil – for frying
Extra Grated Cheese – for topping
6–8 Cups Tomato Sauce – your favorite
2 Large Eggs – lightly beaten

In a small bowl, soak the bread in the milk. In larger bowl, add the ground pork and the chopped mortadella. Mix to combine. Remove the bread from the milk and discard any milk left in the bowl. Add the bread to the meat along with the beaten eggs, cheese, salt, pepper, and nutmeg. Mix well until all incorporated but try not to mash. Cover and chill for an hour or two. When ready to cook, form the meat into small balls. You should yield 12–14. Heat a large sauté pan with the oil and when hot enough, add the meatballs. Give them enough room as they do swell up a little. Turn the meatballs as they are cooking so that they brown on all sides. When all are cooked, pour your tomato sauce over all and continue cooking on medium-low heat for an additional 30 minutes. Top with grated cheese and serve.

Pot Roast

A Great Dish for a Dreary Day

1 Beef Chuck Pot Roast – 3 Lbs
10 Red-Skinned Potatoes – small and halved
A Few Carrots – sliced on diagonal
1 Large Onion – quartered
1 tsp Dried Oregano
Salt and Ground Pepper to Taste
¾–1 Cup Beef Broth

1–2 Tbs Olive Oil – plus extra
1 Onion – large, halved and sliced

A Few Parsnips – sliced on diagonal
3 Tbs Cornstarch – dissolved in 3 Tbs water or beef broth
Garlic Powder to Taste
Lemon Zest – Optional

Wipe meat with paper towel and then rub with a little olive oil. Massage salt, pepper, and garlic powder into the meat. Heat olive oil in large pot that can go into the oven. Brown onions and remove to a dish. Add pot roast and brown over medium-high heat. Turn carefully to brown all over. Add beef broth or water and bring to a boil. Return onions to the pot and spread over the meat.

At this point you can cover tightly and cook on the stove; simmer for about 2 hours, checking occasionally to make sure liquid doesn't dry up. Or, you can cook in the oven at 275° –300°, where it needs very little watching. After 2 hours, add the vegetables that have been rubbed with oil and seasoned with salt, pepper, and garlic powder and cook until vegetables are tender but not falling apart.

Remove meat and vegetables from pot and place on dish, covered to keep warm. Skim fat from pot and then stir in cornstarch mixture. Cook while stirring until thickened (about 2 minutes).

Carve roast and serve on a warmed lipped plate with vegetables and sauce poured over all or served on the side.

Note: We like lemon, so I sometimes top all with a little lemon zest. On a cold day, your kitchen will be warm and the aroma will be comforting!

Ricotta-and-Bread Meatballs

1 Lb Ground Pork
1 Lb Italian Sweet Sausage – casing removed
6 Cups White Bread – crusts removed and cubed
½ Cup Italian Parsley
Pinch of Oregano – optional
Sprinkle of Garlic Powder to Taste
½ Cup Onion – finely chopped

Pinch of Red Pepper Flakes to Taste
Salt and Freshly Ground Black Pepper
1 Cup Whole Milk Ricotta – drained
Pinch of Salt
4 Eggs – lightly beaten
Olive Oil – for coating the pan
3–4 Cups of Your Favorite Spaghetti Sauce
1 tsp Fennel Seeds

Preheat oven to 425°. In a large bowl, add pork, Italian sausage, bread cubes, parsley, oregano, fennel, onion, red pepper flakes, garlic powder, salt, and pepper. Mix all together until everything is well combined. Try not to overwork and mash the meat and do not use a mixer. In a separate bowl, whisk the eggs and the ricotta together with a pinch of salt until smooth and not lumpy. Add this to the meat mixture and gently mix until all incorporated. Put enough olive oil in the bottom of a roasting pan to coat well. Form small-to-medium-sized meatballs and arrange in the pan, leaving enough space between them so that they are not crowded and will bake and brown. Total roasting time is about 30 minutes, but halfway through the baking time turn the meatballs over to brown evenly. Remove from the pan and add to your favorite sauce with some of the pan juices (that is where a lot of flavor is). Continue cooking over low heat until sauce is hot and meatballs are cooked all the way through.

Note: I like to heat the roasting pan with oil in the oven for a few minutes before adding the meatballs, just enough to get the oil hot. Be careful when adding the meatballs this way because the oil will splatter.

Roast Pork, Tuscany Style

Arrosto di Maiale Stile Toscano

4–5 Lbs Pork Loin
2–3 Garlic Cloves – sliced
1 Tbs Extra Virgin Olive Oil

2 Sprigs Fresh Rosemary
Salt and Black Pepper – freshly ground

Preheat oven to 450°. Make a few incisions in the roast with a sharp knife and insert the garlic slices into them. Rub the meat all over with the olive oil, and then rub in the garlic and rosemary and sprinkle all with salt and black pepper.

Put the roast in an uncovered roasting pan and roast for 10–15 minutes at the high heat. Reduce the heat to 350° and roast for 1½–1¾ hours, basting frequently with the drippings in the pan. Before removing from the oven, check to make sure that the roast is done and the juice is not pink.

Remove from the oven, let rest for a bit, and then slice and serve. Serve with an assortment of roasted vegetables or mashed potatoes.

Saltimbocca alla Romana

2 Large Veal Scaloppini – well pounded, 2
   per person
1 Fresh Sage Leaf – per each scaloppini
2 Garlic Cloves
½ Cup Dry White Wine

1 Thin Slice of Prosciutto – for each
   scaloppini
½ Stick of Butter
4 Tbs Flour

Make a sandwich with one scaloppini and one slice of prosciutto, putting a sage leaf in between. Flour them on the meat side only. In a frying pan, melt the butter and add the garlic. Sauté the scaloppini first on the prosciutto side. After you have sautéed the scaloppini on the other side for about 1 minute, add the wine to the pan and let it thicken a bit and then serve.

Note: Spinach sautéed in a little olive oil and chopped garlic is the traditional side dish for Saltimbocca.

Sausage and Peppers

3 Tbs Olive Oil
2 Garlic Cloves – finely chopped
2 Lbs Italian Sausage – cut on diagonal
1 Lb Peppers – red, yellow, and green
    mixed – sliced in wide strips

1 Onion – thinly sliced
Salt, Pepper, and Garlic Powder to Taste
3–4 White or Yukon Gold Potatoes –
    see note

In a large skillet, combine the olive oil and garlic and cook on low heat for about 2–3 minutes. Do not let the garlic burn. Add sausage, peppers, and onion and season with salt, pepper, and, possibly, additional garlic powder. Cover and cook on low for about 1 hour, stirring occasionally to avoid sticking, until the sausage is fully cooked. Taste again for salt and pepper.

Note: Always serve this dish with some good crusty Italian bread. To make this a very hearty meal, peel 3 or 4 white potatoes, cut into thin wedges, toss with a little salt, pepper, and olive oil, and add to the pan when adding the sausage and peppers.

Steak Diane

Once Considered the Epitome of Continental Cuisine

1 (16 Oz) Boneless New York Strip or
    Sirloin Strip
2 Tbs (¼ Stick) Unsalted Butter
6 Tbs Cognac – divided
2 tsps Dijon Imported Mustard
½ Cup Beef Broth
2 Tbs Chives – finely chopped

Salt to Taste
Freshly Ground Black Pepper to Taste
3 Tbs Finely Minced Shallots
2 Tbs Dry White Wine or Dry Vermouth
2 Tbs A.1. Steak Sauce
2 Tbs Heavy Cream – optional

Trim away some of the outside fat from the steak. Cut in half horizontally creating 2 approx. 6–7 Oz steaks. Pound each one lightly to flatten them to ¾-inch thickness and season liberally on both sides with salt and pepper.

Heat a 12-inch skillet until a drop of water sizzles on the surface. Add 1 Tbs of the butter. As soon as the foam subsides, add the meat. Cook on each side for 1 minute. Remove to a plate.

Immediately adjust the heat to low. Add the second pat of butter and the shallots. Sauté for 1 minute.

Increase the heat to high. Add 3 Tbs of cognac and flambé, if desired. Add the wine and with a wooden spoon, scrape up any browned bits on the bottom of the pan while it is deglazing. Stir in the Dijon mustard and A.1. sauce. Cook for 1 minute or until the liquid has reduced to a syrup.

Add the broth and continue to boil for about another minute until it is reduced now to a few tablespoons, stirring well to incorporate. Boil a few seconds, taste for seasonings, and add a little more freshly ground pepper. Add the remaining cognac and ignite. When the flame dies down, stir in the chives and taste again for seasonings. If you are adding the heavy cream, add it now and cook for a few more minutes.

Now, add the steaks along with their juices to the simmering pan. Turn the steaks in the sauce a couple of times to let them absorb all the flavor. The sauce will reduce slightly more.

Place the steaks on plates and divide the sauce over.

Serve with good crusty Italian bread to mop up the sauce.

This is the recipe from the original Delmonico's in New York City. When our Children were growing up and still living at home, we had a tradition called "Family Dinner." This took place every Sunday evening. Charlie would cook something special, I'd have a dessert made, and while we were eating dessert, we'd sit around the table and the Children could bring up something they wanted to talk about. No topic was closed as long as they were respectful in their discussion or their argument. This turned out to be a good way to air gripes and settle problems. Steak Diane was one of the favorite dinners on Sunday nights. Our version did not use the heavy cream, but I've had it with the cream and it is good either way. Charlie's version, also in this book, does not use cognac, but I'm sure my Dad and my Uncle did use cognac.

Steak, Sicilian Style

Bistecca alla Siciliana

2 T-Bone or Sirloin Steaks	**3 Tbs Parmesan Cheese – freshly grated**
3 Garlic Cloves	**1 Cup Breadcrumbs**
1 Cup Olive Oil	**Salt and Freshly Ground Black Pepper**

Peel garlic, smash, and crush in a bowl. Add the oil and blend well. Dip steaks in the oil and garlic or use a brush to coat well. Combine cheese, breadcrumbs, and seasonings and roll the steaks in the crumbs. Grill or broil steaks until they have your desired degree of rareness.

Trippa alla Fiorentina

1¾ Lbs Precooked Tripe	5 Tbs Olive Oil
1 Clove Garlic	1 Celery Stalk – finely chopped
4 Fresh Basil Leaves – finely chopped	1 Cup Grated Parmesan Cheese
1¾ Cups Dry White Wine	Salt and Pepper
1 Lb Tomatoes – peeled, seeded, chopped	Lemon Strips from 1 Lemon

Bring a large pan of salted water to a boil and cook the tripe for 20 minutes, then drain and plunge into a bowl of cold water to stop the cooking process.

Meanwhile, heat the oil in a large saucepan. Add the garlic clove and cook over low heat for a few minutes until golden, then remove and discard. Add the celery, carrot, onion, and basil and cook over very low heat, stirring occasionally, for about 20 minutes more until slightly browned. Add the wine and cook until the alcohol has dissipated.

Drain the tripe thoroughly and cut into bite-sized strips and add to the saucepan. Sprinkle with half of the Parmesan cheese and mix well. Next, stir in the tomatoes, lemon peel strips, and season with salt. Simmer gently, adding a little hot water if the mixture seems to be getting too dry (about 30–45 minutes).

Remove the pan from the heat, transfer the tripe and sauce to a warmed serving bowl, remove the lemon strips, and serve immediately.

Note: In Italy, tripe is usually sold precooked, which means that it has also been cleaned. If the tripe you are buying has not been precooked, it will need a little bit of cleaning to get some of the fat off the back side. Also cooking time will need to be adjusted. Perfectly cooked tripe should always be tender, but also slightly chewy. This recipe is for precooked tripe because it was given to me by a relative in Italy.

Veal, Tuscan Style

Saltimbocca alla Toscano

2 Lbs Veal Cutlets
12 Slices Prosciutto – thinly sliced
12 Slices Fresh Mozzarella
½ Cup Marsala

½ tsp Sage – chopped
Salt and Freshly Ground Black Pepper
¼ Lb Butter

Flatten veal slices very thin and cut into 3-inch pieces. Put 1 slice of mozzarella and 1 slice of prosciutto and a pinch of sage on 1 piece of veal and cover, like a sandwich, with another piece. Sprinkle slightly with salt and pepper and skewer with a toothpick. Repeat until all the little sandwiches are made. Sauté in butter over a medium flame until golden brown on both sides (about 10 minutes). Remove from the pan and keep hot. Add wine to drippings in pan and heat, but do not boil. Pour sauce over the cutlets and serve immediately. Mashed potatoes is a good side dish.

Fish

Baccala Salad

A Christmas Eve Specialty

2 Lbs Salted Cod
2 Cups Jarred Sweet Peppers – roughly chopped
1 Cup Kalamata Olives – pitted and roughly chopped
1 Cup Parsley – roughly chopped
2 Celery Ribs – thinly sliced
¾ Cup Extra Virgin Olive Oil

6 Tbs Capers – rinsed and roughly chopped
Freshly Ground Black Pepper
½ tsp Red Pepper Flakes – or to taste
4 Garlic Cloves – finely chopped
Juice of 2 Lemons
Kosher Salt to Taste
1 Medium Head Escarole – cored and leaves separated

Place cod in a 2-quart saucepan and cover with cold water by 2 inches. Boil for about 20 minutes: Drain and return to the saucepan, repeating this process twice. Drain and cut into 1-inch chunks, and transfer to a bowl. Toss with the peppers, olives, parsley, oil, capers, black pepper, red pepper flakes, garlic, celery, and lemon juice, and stir. Taste for salt and stir again. Cover and chill for about 2 hours. Arrange escarole leaves on a serving plate and top with the cold cod salad.

Alternately, buy frozen baccala fillets and eliminate all the soaking; just rinse once and proceed.

Note: Traditionally, the baccala, or salt cod, was prepared from dried salt cod. It would be sold in large, dried flats that had to be submerged in water for days, changing the water several times a day. Then, the still-smelly fish had to be cleaned and the bones removed. Before the task was turned over to my Dad, this was the job of my Little Nonna, who soaked the fish in the cellar laundry tub. She would go down faithfully to change the water, but the odor still permeated throughout the two houses, because the cellar doors were never closed. Now, the process is easier, because it now is available as salt-cured fillets.

Cajun Shrimp Pasta

1 Lb Linguine – or your favorite long pasta
1 Tbs extra virgin olive oil
Freshly Ground Black Pepper
3 Tbs Butter

Kosher Salt
1 Lb Large Shrimp – peeled and deveined
2 Tbs Cajun Seasoning – or to taste
2–3 Tbs Flour

¾ Cup Heavy Cream   ½ Cup Parmesan Cheese – freshly grated
¼ Cup Fresh Parsley – chopped

In a large pot of salted, boiling water, cook pasta just until al dente. Drain, reserving 1 cup of pasta water, and return to pot to keep warm.

In the meantime, in a large skillet over medium heat, warm the olive oil. When hot, add the shrimp and season with salt, pepper, and Cajun seasoning. Cook just until pink, 2 minutes on each side, then remove to a plate and tent to keep warm.

Wipe the skillet and add butter. Once the butter is melted, stir in flour and whisk until golden.

Add heavy cream, and whisk until creamy and smooth. Add parmesan and ½ cup pasta water. Whisk again until creamy, smooth, and all combined. Adjust for more salt, pepper, and Cajun seasoning. Add the pasta and toss to make sure it is well combined and all coated. Add the shrimp and toss well.

Garnish with more cheese and the parsley. Ladle into bowls and serve.

Baked Fish with Tomatoes

A Quick-and-Easy Fish Dinner

3 Tbs Olive Oil   1 Large Tomato – seeded and chopped
2 (6–8 Oz) Fillets – sole, trout, grouper, or   1 Garlic Clove – chopped
    halibut (choose your favorite)   1 Tbs Fresh Parsley or Basil – chopped
Salt and Freshly Ground Pepper

Preheat oven to 400°. Brush small, shallow, ovenproof baking dish with a small amount of olive oil. Place fillets in a dish, and season with salt and pepper. Combine remaining olive oil with the tomato and garlic in a small bowl, and mix well. Spoon over fillets and bake until fish is cooked through, about 15–20 minutes depending on size and thickness. Sprinkle with basil or parsley, and serve.

Note: This is a great dish served on top of sautéed spinach.

Bis Nonno's Christmas Eve Dinner

Some Dishes Are so Tied to Tradition That It Wouldn't Be the Holiday without Them

3 Tbs Olive Oil – to coat bottom of large pot
1 Large Onion – roughly chopped
1 Medium Carrot – finely chopped
1 Celery Stalk – finely chopped
1 Bay Leaf
1 Large Lobster or 2 Chicken Lobsters – cut in pieces and shells cracked
½ Cup Sauterne
2 Cups Stock – 1 cup chicken, 1 cup beef
3–4 Tbs Tomato Paste
1 Lb Hearty White Fish – your favorite

½ Cup Sauterne
10 Sprigs Fresh Parsley – leaves only
2 tsps Bell's Seasoning
12 Little Neck Clams – scrubbed and rinsed
1 Can Oysters – drained through a cheesecloth or strainer
18–20 Medium Shrimp – peeled and deveined
1 Lb Squid – optional
1 Can (29 Oz) Scungilli – drained

Heat olive oil in a large pot. Sauté the onion slowly until caramelized. Add carrots and celery, and cook until starting to brown. Add the bay leaf and stir well. Add the lobster pieces. Cook just until shells are red, and remove to add again later. Add sauterne and cook down for a few minutes.

Add stock and tomato paste. (I'm sure when my Little Nonna prepared this for Christmas Eve, only fish stock was used.) Stir well and simmer, just until paste has dissolved. At this point, you can put this on hold until about 15 minutes before you are ready to serve. Best to do this early in the day.

Add the Fish:

Parsley
Garlic
Bell's Seasoning
Sauterne

Fish
Angel-Hair Pasta – amount depends on number of people serving

If the stock has cooled, reheat slowly before continuing. Chop parsley with garlic and add to stock. Add Bell's Seasoning, stir, and simmer for a few minutes. Add cut lobster and any juices that accumulated while it rested. Add clams and cook just until clams open, discarding any that do not. Add remainder of the fish and cook just until the white fish is cooked through. Taste for salt and pepper, and add more sauterne, if desired. (Optionally, you can use madeira.) Cook pasta al dente. Drain, pour into a large bowl, and add fish broth. Place fish in a large bowl to pass. Serve the pasta in bowls and top with some of the fish. You know I am going to say, "Pass the cheese," too.

This is one of those meals that is so tied to tradition that it wouldn't be a holiday without it. For as long as I can remember, my Dad prepared this for our Christmas Eve dinner. He started it early in the day, and the aroma was intoxicating and made dinner difficult to wait for, as if waiting for Christmas wasn't already hard enough for a Child. Fortunately, my Dad passed the recipe down to Charlie, and this has always been our much-anticipated Christmas Eve dinner. I believe it is everyone's favorite dinner for many reasons. While it is cooking, the aroma is inspiring, and the memories it brings back to me are a real Christmas present.

Boiled Crawfish for a Crowd

16 Lbs Crawfish – in shell
½ Lb Crab Boil or Creole Seasoning

12 Ears Corn – shucked
2–3 Dozen Small New Potatoes – scrubbed but not peeled

Rinse the crawfish. Bring a large pot (preferably a lobster pot or a pot with a drainer/strainer) of water to boil with the seasoning already well mixed in. Add the potatoes and boil for about 15 minutes until nearly tender. Add the corn and cook for another 6 to 8 minutes. (I like to cut the ears in half.) Add the crawfish and cook for another 5–8 minutes, just until the crawfish are cooked. Don't overcook. Carefully drain and transfer all to a large tray.

This gets messy, so it's fun to do this when you can eat outside where you can hose everything down afterward. We like to spread the crawfish out in a big tray, and put the corn and potatoes in a separate bowl.

If you don't have a lobster pot or a pot large enough to hold everything, just follow the same procedure, cook in batches, and keep warm.

Note: Figure on 2–3 lbs of crawfish per person, as they are small little creatures, and adjust the corn and potatoes accordingly. Oddly enough, we enjoy serving a drink that was introduced to us by an English couple we were neighbors with when we lived in Maryland, and it goes very well with this crawfish boil or steamed crabs. They called it a shandy, and it was cold beer mixed according to your taste with a lemon-flavored soda. If you can find Squirt, that's a perfect match. Try it; you'll like it! It is very refreshing.

Calamari Stew

3 Tbs Olive Oil
1 Small Onion – chopped
4 Garlic Cloves – peeled and sliced
2 Cups White Wine
4 Cups Spaghetti Sauce – homemade or jarred
1 Pinch Oregano

1 tsp Salt
1 tsp Black Pepper – freshly ground
2 Lbs Calamari Bodies – thinly sliced, whole tentacles included
Fresh Basil Leaves – torn for topping
2 Large Eggs – lightly beaten

Heat the olive oil over low heat in a medium pot. Add the garlic and onion, and cook, stirring frequently until fragrant and the onion is translucent. Do not let it burn. Slowly add the white wine and cook for another minute. Stir, and then add the tomato sauce, oregano, red pepper flakes, salt, and pepper. Bring the mixture to a simmer and cook for about 8 or 10 minutes. Do not overcook, or the calamari will be tough and rubbery. Taste for salt and pepper. Serve as a stew or over pasta. Top with some torn basil leaves. In our house, we also pass the cheese.

Traditional Italian Christmas Eve Dinner

1 Lb Pasta – angel hair, linguine, or your favorite
1 Medium Onion – chopped
1 Cup Fish Broth or Clam Juice
4–5 Basil Leaves – roughly torn
½ Lb Hearty White Fish
12 Shrimp – peeled and deveined
3 Tbs Olive Oil

2–3 Garlic Cloves – chopped
1 Cup Dry White Wine – your favorite
1 (35 Oz) Can San Marzano Tomatoes
Salt and Freshly Ground Black Pepper – to taste
3 Dozen Assorted Shellfish – scrubbed and rinsed

In a large, heavy pot, heat the olive oil over medium heat. Add the onion and sauté until soft. Add the garlic and cook until soft, but do not brown. Add the wine and cook until the aroma of the wine subsides, and then add the fish broth or clam juice. Crush the tomatoes with your hands while adding to the pot. Add the basil, salt, pepper, and simmer for about 15 minutes. Add the fish, cover, and cook until the shrimp is pink and the shellfish have opened. The white fish will be cooked by this time. Discard any shells that did not open. Ladle into large bowl.

Cook pasta according to package directions. Drain, pour into large bowl, and add some of the fish sauce to it, mixing well. Fill individual serving bowls and pass the fish sauce.

It is traditional that most Italian families celebrate Christmas Eve with a fish dinner. Sometimes this is referred to as the Feast of Seven Fishes. How that number originated, I do not know, and many stories abound. However, I do know that not every family adheres to seven fish; some have more, and some less. But, nonetheless, it is a fish dinner and consumed in countless ways.

In Italy, Christmas is anticipated with much excitement, but not just for the gifts. It's all about family, food, traditions, and church service. Christmas Eve marks the Feast of Seven Fishes, or La Virgilia, a celebration in which the entire meal is meatless. With so many courses, there is plenty of room for variety. Tradition holds that seven corresponds to the seven sacraments, or the last seven days of advent. Some households favor nine courses, because nine is a multiple of the Holy Trinity. And then, there are some who go all out for twelve for the twelve apostles. But, no matter how many courses or for what reasons, fish is still the central focus in many houses on Christmas Eve.

Cioppino

Soup or Stew—Your Choice

⅓ Cup Extra Virgin Olive Oil
6 Anchovies – mashed or chopped
4 Garlic Cloves
2 Bay Leaves – leave whole
1 Celery Stalk – diced
1 Large Onion – chopped
1 Cup Chianti
2 Tbs Red Wine Vinegar
5 Cups Good Fish Stock
8 Fresh Tomatoes – diced, but drained if using canned

1 Small Packet or Pinch of Saffron Threads
2 Tbs Worcestershire Sauce
½ Cup Italian Parsley – chopped
5 Tbs Lemon Juice – freshly squeezed
1 tsp Red Pepper Flakes – or more to taste
2 Tbs Oregano – fresh or dried
1 Rosemary Sprig – whole
Assortment of Seafood – your choice
6 Large Fresh Basil Leaves – torn

For the Seafood:

Use whatever is the freshest that day. Use about ¼ lb or more of each variety, such as shrimp, scallops, mussels, clams, and a firm fish cut into 1-inch pieces. For firm fish, you can use cod, halibut, scrod, or grouper. You can also add some calamari if you are adventurous.

Warm the olive oil in a large pot with the anchovies. Add the garlic and stir, making sure the garlic does not burn or brown. Add bay leaves, onions, celery, and fresh herbs. Stir. Add wine, vinegar, and Worcestershire sauce and let bubble lightly until reduced by almost half. Next, add the tomatoes and basil. Simmer for about 20 minutes. Slowly add the fish stock (you can use vegetable stock, but it will have a different flavor) and lemon juice and bring to a boil. Finally, toss in all the fish and the saffron and cook over medium heat for about 10 minutes. Ladle into large soup bowls and sprinkle with parsley. And our family passes the grated cheese!

Note: A good way to serve this is to ladle it into large soup bowls over a slice of grilled or toasted garlic bread, finished off with some grated cheese. This also is a great dish to serve over our favorite pasta. This recipe come from the Piedmont area where my Mother's side of the family hails from.

Cozze e Vongole Gratinate

Mussel and Clam Gratin

10 Mussels and 10 Clams
4 Tbs Parmigiano Cheese
2 Garlic Cloves – chopped
2 Cups Seasoned Breadcrumbs

1 Egg – whipped
4 Oz White Wine
Salt and Pepper to Taste

Preheat oven to 400°. Steam the shellfish in a stock pot with the white wine and garlic until the shells are open. Discard any that do not open. Let cool. Take the meat out of the shells and separate the mussels and the clams, put in two separate bowls, and chop each. Put into each bowl 1 cup of breadcrumbs, ½ of the whipped egg, 2 Tbs Parmigiano, salt and pepper. Add to each ½ of the juice from the pot that has been strained. Mix well. Fill each shell with its respective filling.

Place on a baking sheet, drizzle with a little olive oil, and bake for 15 minutes.

Crab Puppies

1 Lb Crabmeat – picked over
1 Cup Ritz Crackers – crushed
2 Tbs Fresh Lemon Juice
1 tsp Old Bay Seasoning

1 Egg – beaten
1 tsp Yellow Mustard
2 Tbs Fresh Parsley – chopped
1 Tbs Worcestershire Sauce

Place crabmeat in a mixing bowl. And pick over for any loose shells. Add crushed crackers, Old Bay Seasoning, and parsley, and mix well.

In a separate bowl, combine egg, mustard, lemon juice, and Worcestershire sauce, and whip with a whisk until smooth and a bit frothy. Pour over the crabmeat and crackers and mix gently to not break up the crabmeat too much.

Mold into golf-ball size and place on a cookie sheet. If time allows, cool in refrigerator for about 20 minutes to set. Bake in an oven preheated to 350° for about 30 minutes. Drizzle with melted butter and cool slightly.

These are great served plain or with a sauce made of ketchup and horseradish.

Insalata di Calamari

Squid Salad

4 Pieces Squid Tubes
½ Lemon – juiced
½ tsp Fresh Basil – chopped
4 Tbs Extra Virgin Olive Oil

1 tsp Italian Parsley – chopped
½ tsp Red Pepper Flakes – or to taste
Salt and Ground Black Pepper

Cut squid tubes (best to not use tentacles) into small rings. Place in a pot of water and bring to a boil. Turn the heat off and let cool. Drain and place the squid in a salad bowl. Add the remaining ingredients, toss well, and taste for salt and pepper. Toss again and serve.

Lowcountry Shrimp and Grits

1 Lb Medium Shrimp
1 Cup Whipping Cream
1 tsp Salt
1 Cup (4 Oz) Cheddar Cheese
Dash of Hot Sauce – optional

3 Cups Water
¼ Cup Butter
1 Cup Quick Grits
2 Garlic Cloves – minced
Chopped Fresh Chives – optional

Peel shrimp and devein (optional, not necessary). Bring 3 cups water, cream, butter, and salt to a boil in a large saucepan. Reduce heat to medium and whisk in the quick-cooking grits. Cook, whisking constantly, for about 8 minutes, or until the mixture is smooth. Stir in the shrimp, cheese, and garlic, and cook until the shrimp is pink and cooked through, and the cheese is melted and well-combined. Add a sprinkle of hot sauce, if desired. Garnish with chopped chives (optional). Additionally, you can cook the shrimp in bacon fat for a little different flavor.

Note: Legend has it that shrimp and grits started as a fisherman's breakfast in the Carolina Low Country.

Mussel Stew

6 Lbs Mussels
2 Garlic Cloves – minced
⅓ Cup Chopped Italian Parsley
24 Small Slices Crusty Italian Bread – grilled
An Additional ¼ Cup Finely Chopped

Italian Parsley
1 Cup Extra Virgin Olive Oil
1 Cup Dry White Wine
Salt and Pepper to Taste
1 Additional Garlic Clove

Leave the mussels in their shells and scrub them very well. Heat the olive oil in a medium-sized pot over high heat. When the oil is well heated, add the mussels with the chopped garlic, salt, pepper, and parsley. Toss everything around in the oil for a few minutes (do not let the garlic burn) and then add the wine and cook covered until all the mussels have opened and the liquid is reduced by half. Check and discard any mussels that did not open.

Prepare 4–6 bowls by lining each bowl with slices of the bread rubbed well with the garlic clove. Ladle some of the liquid into each bowl, then add the mussels, and sprinkle with the extra parsley for garnish. Chopped basil is also a good substitute for the parsley garnish.

Mussels in White Wine

Cozza al Vino Bianco

50–60 Mussels – scrubbed
8 Fresh Basil Leaves – torn
4 Tbs Olive Oil
1 Cup Good White Wine
(Wine you will drink while cooking!)

3 Garlic Cloves – chopped
2 tsps Dried Oregano
¾ tsp Red Pepper Flakes – or to taste
Juice of 1 Lemon
Salt and Pepper to Taste

Heat olive oil in a large pan over medium-high heat. Add the mussels and pour the wine over all, cover, and bring to a boil. Add the garlic, oregano, red pepper, salt, and pepper and stir. Cover and cook until the mussels start to open. Add the basil and lemon juice, stir, and cover. Continue cooking until all the mussels are open. Before serving, discard any mussels that are still closed.

Ladle into soup bowls and serve with crusty Italian bread and the remainder of the white wine, if any!

Mussels Marinara

Mitili Marinara, a Recipe from Sicily

2 Dozen Fresh Mussels
¼ Cup Olive Oil
2 Garlic Cloves
2 Tbs Tomato Paste

½ Cup White Wine
Salt and Pepper
2 Cups Cooked Arborio Rice
1 Tbs Freshly Minced Basil

Select mussels that have tightly closed shells. Discard any that don't. Scrub them well with a vegetable brush and scrape off the hairy beard. Rinse well under cold water.

Brown the garlic in hot oil for a few minutes. Add tomato paste, wine (be careful because it will splatter), and seasonings. Stir to blend well. Add the mussels, cover the pan, and cook over a low flame for 10–15 minutes until all the shells have opened. Discard any mussels with tightly closed shells.

Serve the mussels over cooked rice and sprinkle with minced basil.

Oyster Casserole

5 Tbs Salted Butter – divided
¼ Cup Celery – chopped
1 tsp Minced Fresh Garlic
4 Oz Fresh Mushrooms – sliced
½ Cup Heavy Cream
¾ tsp Kosher Salt
¼ tsp Nutmeg

¼ Cup Green Bell Pepper – chopped
2 Scallions – thinly sliced
2 (16 Oz) Containers Fresh Oysters
2 Tbs Flour
1 Oz Parmesan Cheese – grated
Black Pepper – freshly ground
1 Cup Coarsely Ground Breadcrumbs

Preheat broiler. Melt 2 Tbs of the butter in a skillet over medium-high heat. Add onion, bell pepper, celery, scallions, and garlic. (I'm not a green pepper fan, so I use orange or yellow.) Cook, stirring until the vegetables have softened. Add oysters (drained) and mushrooms. Bring to a simmer and cook stirring often for about 5 minutes and then set aside.

Melt 1 Tbs of the butter in a small saucepan over medium heat. Stir in flour and cook, whisking constantly, until smooth and starting to brown a little. Add cream and cook, whisking constantly, until the sauce has thickened and is starting to bubble. Add the nutmeg and mix in well. Add grated cheese and continue cooking and whisking until the cheese has melted. Remove from the heat.

Using a fine wire-mesh strainer, strain the oyster mixture and discard just the liquid. Add the oyster mixture to the cheese sauce and stir well to make sure all is incorporated. Add the salt and pepper and stir again. Spread mixture in a lightly greased 11" x 7" baking dish. Melt the remaining butter, toss in the breadcrumbs and get them well coated, and sprinkle over the oyster mixture.

Broil in middle of oven until the breadcrumbs are a golden brown and the mixture is very bubbly. This should only be about 5 minutes. This is a great dish to serve with popovers.

Paella

1 Quart Chicken Broth – or as needed	2 Cups Paella or Arborio Rice
1 tsp Saffron	½ Cup Dry White Wine
½ Cup Extra Virgin Olive Oil	1 Dozen Littleneck Clams
1 Lb Spanish Chorizo – cut into ½" slices	1 Lb Chicken Thighs – boneless, skinless – cut into small chunks
1 Lb Large Shrimp – peeled and deveined	1 Cup Fresh Parsley – chopped
2 Lemons	1 Loaf Crusty Italian Bread
Kosher Salt to Taste	Freshly Ground Black Pepper
1 Red Bell Pepper – chopped	1 Yellow Bell Pepper – chopped
1 Tbs Tomato Paste – or as needed	3–4 Garlic Cloves – chopped
1½ tsps Paprika	1 Medium Onion – chopped

In a small saucepan, stir together the saffron and broth and bring to a simmer. In a very large skillet or paella pan, heat the olive oil over medium heat. Add the chorizo and chicken and brown all over. Season with salt and pepper. Add onion and peppers and cook until the onion only begins to soften. Add the tomato paste, garlic, and paprika. Cook and stir until fragrant (about 1 minute). Add the rice, stirring well to get everything coated with the oil, and cook for about 2 or 3 minutes. Add the wine and cook until evaporated. Slowly add the broth and bring everything to a simmer. Now, tightly cover the pan and cook until most of the liquid is absorbed but not totally dry (about 10–12 minutes). Add the shrimp and the clams and cook just until the shrimp are pink and the clams have opened. Discard any clams that did not open.

Remove from the heat and sprinkle with the juice from half of a lemon. Fluff the rice. Serve with an authentic Spanish Aioli or Alioli on the side and a few lemon wedges. And, of course, some crusty bread for sopping.

Aioli/Alioli

4 Garlic Cloves – peeled and chopped	½ tsp Salt
2 Eggs – yolks only	1 Cup Extra Virgin Olive Oil
1½ tsps Lemon Juice – freshly squeezed	

Peel and mince the garlic and place in blender with salt and yolks. With the motor running slowly, add the extra virgin olive oil and pulse until thickened, and then slowly add lemon juice. Scrape into a serving bowl and serve on the side.

Note: Alioli, also called Aioli or Ali Oli, is one of the most common Spanish sauces. In Spain you will find it used on a variety of dishes such as fish, meat, and vegetables, along with Paella. In many forms, it is a big accompaniment to Spain's favorite street food, Patata Brava.

Sardines Stuffed Sicilian Style

Sarde a Beccafico

2½ Lbs Fresh Sardines – about 24	8 Tbs Olive Oil – divided
⅓ Cup Raisins or Currants	1 Cup Breadcrumbs
2 Garlic Cloves – minced	⅓ Cup Toasted Pine Nuts
3 Tbs Capers – rinsed	3 Tbs Fresh Parsley – chopped
¼ Cup Pecorino Cheese – freshly grated	Salt and Pepper to Taste
3 Tbs Fresh Lemon Juice	¼ Cup Fresh Orange Juice

Clean the sardines by cutting off the head and fins and removing any scales. Split the fish open along the belly and remove the intestines. Run your finger inside the fish along the length of the backbone and the sardine should open flat like a book. Lift up and remove the backbone, cutting off the tail. Repeat the process with the rest of the sardines. Rinse well, pat dry, and set aside.

Filling:

Add the currants to ⅓ cup of hot water and allow to sit for 10 minutes. Drain them and set aside. Heat 3 Tbs of oil in a small saucepan over medium-high heat. Add the breadcrumbs and cook, stirring constantly until moistened. Add the garlic and continue cooking for another minute or two and then remove from the heat. Add the currants or raisins, pine nuts, capers, parsley, and cheese. Mix all together until well combined.

Assemble:

In a large baking dish that will be large enough to fit all the sardines once they are filled, oil it lightly. Open a flat sardine, skin side down, on your work surface and place a heaping tablespoon of filling in the wide end of the fish. Roll the fish around the stuffing toward the tail.

Place the rolled fish, tail up, in the prepared baking dish. When all are assembled, pack them tightly so that they stay rolled while baking. You can do this all this in advance if you wish, and then refrigerate the fish for several hours until ready to bake.

Cooking:

Preheat the oven to 375°. In a small bowl, whisk together 4 Tbs of oil, lemon, and orange juice. Pour the mixture over the sardines. Bake until the fish are firm (15 minutes or so). Serve hot, warm, or at room temperature, whichever way you prefer.

Note: If you are a fan of sage, place a small sage leaf in between a few rolled sardines just before putting them in the oven. Gives the dish a nice, delicate flavor. Also, a cut lemon rubbed over your hands, ferociously, as well as the surface you worked on, will help eliminate the fish smell. This is a very traditional Sicilian appetizer. You can make it your own by adding things you enjoy to the filling. Instead of baking, they can be floured and carefully fried. As for "Beccafico," it is the name of a tiny bird that becomes fat from gorging on figs. Why? So now you know, and your guess is as good as mine.

Shrimp and Crab Étouffée

¼ Lb Butter
½ Cup Celery – finely chopped
1 Tbs Garlic – minced
2 Lbs Shrimp – shelled and deveined
2 Cups Fish Stock – hot
1 Lb Lump Crabmeat – picked over for shells
⅓ Cup Fresh Parsley – finely chopped

1 Medium Onion – finely chopped
½ Cup Yellow Bell Pepper – chopped
1 Pinch of Salt
Freshly Ground Black Pepper
2 Tbs Cornstarch
⅓ Cup Scallions – finely chopped

1 tsp Cayenne – or to taste

Melt the butter in a large heavy pot. Add the onions, yellow pepper, celery, garlic, salt, black pepper, and cayenne. Cook, stirring frequently until all the vegetables are tender. This should take no more than 10–15 minutes.

Add your shrimp and raise the heat a little and cook just until the shrimp has turned pink. Add 1½ cups of fish stock (it should be hot), and then stir the cornstarch into the remaining stock, mix until all combined, and add to the pot. Bring to a slow simmer and cook until slightly thickened (about 20 minutes).

Add the crab and cook just until warmed through. Ladle into soup dishes, garnish with the scallions and parsley, and put a scoop of hot, cooked rice in the center of each bowl with some extra on the side.

Note: While this is cooking, make a pot of white rice. (See recipe for Sticky Rice.)

Shrimp and Orzo

3 Tbs Olive Oil – divided	1 Onion – chopped
1 Pint Grape or Petite Tomatoes – halved	3 Garlic Cloves – sliced
1 tsp Fresh Oregano – chopped	Sea Salt to Taste
Freshly Ground Black Pepper	3½ Cups Chicken Stock
¾ Lb Orzo	1 Lb Gulf Shrimp – wild caught
¾ Cup Panko	⅓ Cup Freshly Grated Cheese
3 Tbs Butter – or more as needed, melted	2 tsps Fresh Lemon Zest
Several Lemons – cut into wedges	Several Basil Leaves – torn

Clean and devein shrimp. Preheat oven to 400°. Heat some of the oil in a large skillet with a lid that you can also put into the oven. Heat the oil over a medium-high flame and when ready add the onion and garlic and cook until the onions are soft. Stir frequently and do not burn the garlic. Add the tomatoes, oregano, a good pinch of salt, freshly ground black pepper, and cook until the tomatoes are soft. As they are cooking, press down on them a little to release some of their juice. Stir in the chicken stock and orzo, bring to a boil, stirring to get it all combined.

Cover with a tight-fitting lid and bake in the oven until the orzo is al dente and most of the liquid has evaporated. This will take about 15–18 minutes. Carefully check around 12 minutes and give a good stirring.

When ready, remove from the oven, and change the oven from bake to broil. Toss the shrimp with the remaining olive oil, a pinch of salt, and a quick grinding of black pepper. Combine the panko, grated cheese, melted butter, and lemon zest (add more butter if the mixture looks too dry) and sprinkle over the shrimp. Arrange the shrimp over the orzo in the pan and return the pan to the oven and broil, uncovered, just until the shrimp are a nice pink. Garnish with basil and serve with lemon wedges.

Shrimp in Lemon Aioli

1 Lemon – sliced thinly
½ Cup Mayonnaise
1 Tbs Fresh Chives – minced
1 tsp Lemon Juice

1 Lb Large Shrimp – cleaned
2 tsps Extra Virgin Olive Oil
1 tsp Paprika
½ tsp Sea Salt

Finely mince a few slices of the lemon and stir into the mayonnaise with the chives and lemon juice in a bowl. Cover with plastic and set in refrigerator for about 30 minutes.

Preheat your grill and season your grill plate.

Peel and devein the shrimp and put in a bowl, drizzle with olive oil and a sprinkle of paprika and salt. Stir to coat the shrimp so that it is covered all over.

Cook the shrimp on the prepared grill until they are bright pink and the inside is no longer transparent. This will take about 2–3 minutes on each side. Transfer the shrimp to a platter and serve with the lemon aioli with a few lemon slices on the side.

Shrimp Scampi

Scampi Gamberetto

½ Cup Olive Oil
5 Garlic Cloves – peeled, minced
Freshly Ground Black Pepper
1 Cup White Wine
1 Half Lemon
2 Tbs Dried Breadcrumbs – optional

Chopped Parsley – to taste
4 Tbs Butter
½ Lb Large Shrimp – peeled, deveined
Sea Salt – to taste
1 tsp Dried Oregano

Heat a large skillet over medium-high heat and add the butter and oil. Swirl the butter with a wooden spoon until it melts into the oil. Add the garlic and cook, stirring for a few minutes until it becomes aromatic. Do not let it burn. Add the shrimp, a few at a time, with a grinding of black pepper and some salt. Cook on each side until they are pink, and then remove to a plate.

Pour the wine into the hot skillet. Let it cook until it reduces by half. Add the oregano and stir to combine. Return the shrimp to the pot and cook until heated through, about 3–4 minutes, stirring. Squeeze the lemon juice over all. Add the parsley, and optionally, sprinkle some breadcrumbs (pangrattato). Toss to combine.

Note: We like to serve this over pasta, and we always have a slice or two of crusty Italian bread to sop up the juice. And, yes, we pass the grater and cheese wedge! When I've requested this dish in Italy, it was made with langoustines, small lobster-like crustaceans. Juicy and very tasty.

Snails, Lumachi, or Babaluci

Yes, We Ate Snails

Snails – several pounds
1 Large Onion – chopped
4 Cloves Garlic – minced
3 tsps Tomato Paste
1 or 2 Bouillon Cubes in 6–8 Cups Water

1½–2 Glasses Sauterne
1 tsp Bell's Seasoning
Salt and Pepper – generous amount
Olive Oil – for cooking

Rinse snails several times in cold water. In a large pot, brown the onion and garlic. Let soften, but do not let the garlic burn. Add bouillon, broth, and tomato paste and simmer for a few minutes. Add Bell's Seasoning, stir, and then taste for salt and pepper. Simmer for a few minutes and then add snails. Make sure there is enough liquid to cover snails. Simmer on medium heat for about 15–20 minutes. Just before serving add the wine and simmer for 5 minutes. Serve with crusty Italian bread for sopping up the sauce. Pass sturdy toothpicks for picking the snails out of their shells.

Yes, we ate snails and loved them. I am recreating my Father's recipe from memory. When we were newly married and in our first house in Smithtown, NY, we wanted to surprise everyone at a holiday dinner with snails. We put them in a pot in a large sink in the basement with a brick on the lid (Charlie and I have a difference of opinion on this point), and the next morning, when we were getting ready to cook them, we found them climbing up the walls and on the ceiling. I'm talking about dozens and dozens that we had to collect. Hope we found them all!

Spicy Squid

1½ Lbs Whole Squid – cleaned
2 Tbs Each Cilantro and Parsley – chopped
1 Tbs Red Wine Vinegar
Salt and Pepper to Taste
3 Scallions – chopped

½ Red Onion – chopped
¼ Cup Extra Virgin Olive Oil
Juice of 1 Lemon
1 tsp Red Pepper Flakes

Cooking squid is easy. The secret is to grill or sauté it quickly so it does not get dry and rubbery.

Place the squid on a hot grill or sauté in a hot pan, 1 to 2 minutes per side. Remove immediately and cool. Cut cooled squid into ¼-inch rings. Leave the tentacles whole.

Place all ingredients for the marinade in a glass bowl and whisk until well combined. Add the squid and toss thoroughly. Refrigerate for at least 6 hours or overnight.

Sweets

Fig Cake

2½ Cups Fresh Figs – stems removed, figs mashed
½ Cup Light Brown Sugar
4 Eggs, lightly beaten
½ tsp Nutmeg
Pinch of Salt
1 tsp Orange or Lemon Zest – your choice

1½ Cups Sugar
¾ Cup Shortening
2 Full Cups Flour – plus extra if needed
1½ tsps Cinnamon – or more to taste
1 tsp Baking Soda
1 Cup Chopped Pecans or Walnuts

Set oven to 350°. Mix together sugar, figs, and shortening. Stir zest into eggs and stir briskly for a few seconds. Add eggs to fig mixture and beat well. Mix flour, cinnamon, salt, nutmeg, baking soda, and nuts together. Add this to the fig mixture and spread in a well-greased and floured Bundt pan. Bake for about 45 minutes until a tester comes out clean.

Fig Story:

Our love for all things "fig" started with a fig tree in Castrofilippo, Sicily. Many, many years ago, my Father-in-Law somehow was able to bring a small part of that Sicilian tree back home with him to New York City after a visit there. It was planted in the back yard at 321 East Forty-Eighth Street. Over the years, several cuttings were shared with his Children. Our cutting has survived several of our relocations and is now thriving here in Georgia. Not only has it survived, but through multiple cuttings over the years, it has given birth to dozens and dozens of trees which we have shared with Children and Grandchildren and, also, sell at our market, donating the proceeds to USO. We even sent a cutting back to Sicily, where it is thriving, and we do have a picture. But, that's for another story. However, our yield is such that even though we give so many figs away, I am always inventing fig recipes: cakes, pies, breads, crostatas, jam muffins, and so on. Who knows, I might even work on one for ice cream!

A Sicilian Geli

A Chilled Delight

4 Cups Ripe Watermelon Pulp
5 Tbs Cornstarch
¼ Cup Dark Chocolate – finely ground

⅓ Cup Sugar
½ Cup Pistachio Nuts – finely ground
A Pinch of Cinnamon

Pulse the watermelon in the blender and remove excess liquid by passing the puree through a sieve.

Mix all the ingredients—save for the jasmine, chocolate, and cinnamon—placing them in a saucepan. Bring to a boil over medium heat.

As the elements simmer, the cornstarch will begin to thicken the sauce. Remove from the stove and allow it to cool once well blended and quite thick.

Pour the creamy watermelon mixture in martini glasses or muffin molds. Dust the top with powdered pistachio, a dash of cinnamon, and garnish with chocolate shavings and the jasmine flower. Serve chilled and prepare for the applause.

Note: This chilled delight is typical of Palermo's culinary tradition of cornstarch-based desserts.

Sicilian Cream Tart

A Quick and Easy Cassata

1 9" Sponge Cake	¼ Cup Candied Cherries – chopped
1½ Lb Ricotta – drained	½ tsp Cinnamon
6 Tbs Rum	½ Cup Toasted Almonds – chopped
½ Cup Powdered Sugar	2 Oz Chocolate – grated

Occasionally, I have been able to buy a store-bought sponge cake that can be purchased in layers. Otherwise, slice a whole sponge cake into 3 layers. Sprinkle the layers with rum.

In a bowl, stir ricotta with a fork to break it up. Add sugar and beat for 3–5 minutes until creamy. Stir in remaining ingredients until well-blended. Spread evenly over bottom and middle layers. Spread top and sides with frosting.

Frosting:

¼ Cup Butter	2 Egg Whites
2½ Cups Powdered Sugar	1 tsp Almond Extract

Cream butter with 1 cup sifted powdered sugar. Beat egg whites until stiff, and gradually beat into the egg whites the remining 1½ cups of powdered sugar. Fold egg whites into the butter mixture and add the almond extract. Cover sides and top of cassata evenly with the frosting. Store in refrigerator until ready to serve.

Rugelach

4 Tbs Unsalted Butter – softened
½ Cup Sour Cream
¼ Cup Powdered Sugar
5 Tbs Sugar
½ Cup Apricot Jam
½ Cup Currants

4 Oz Cream Cheese – softened
1 Egg
Pinch of Salt
1 Tbs Cinnamon
½ Cup Walnuts – chopped
1 Egg – lightly beaten

Dough:

In a stand mixer fitted with the paddle attachment, beat butter and cream cheese on medium speed. Add sour cream and egg, and continue to beat until very smooth. Add flour, sugar, and salt, and continue beating on low speed until a dough forms. Remove dough from paddle and divide into 4 balls. Wrap each in plastic wrap and refrigerate for 1 hour.

Filling:

Heat oven to 350°. Combine sugar and cinnamon in a small bowl and set aside. Working with 1 ball at a time, using a rolling pin, roll out to a 10-inch circle. Spread 1 Tbs of jam over the entire surface, leaving a ¼-inch border. Sprinkle with 2 Tbs currants and 1 Tbs cinnamon-sugar. Press down lightly on filling to adhere to jam.

Using a knife, cut the dough into 10 wedges. Working with one wedge at a time, roll up wedge from wide end to narrow. Transfer to parchment-lined baking pan. Repeat with remaining dough.

Brush crescents with remaining cinnamon-sugar. Bake, rotating the pans around the 12-minute mark. Continue baking until well browned, about 20–25 minutes. Cool on a rack and let cool completely before serving.

Pissota

An Old-World Olive Oil Cake

4 Eggs
3 Cups Flour

1 Cup Sugar
1½ Cups Extra Virgin Olive Oil

¼ Cup Rum (Grand Marnier) – or your favorite
Zest from 1 Lemon

¼ Cup Milk – plus more as needed
1 tsp Baking Powder

Preheat oven to 375°. Grease and flour a 9-inch tube pan. Place eggs in a bowl. Beat in the sugar until light and fluffy. Slowly add flour until all combined. Whisk in olive oil, rum (or favorite liqueur), milk, lemon zest, and baking powder. If batter seems stiff, whisk in a little more milk, a little at a time, until the batter is more flowing. Pour into the tube pan and bake until golden brown and tester comes out clean, about 40 minutes. Cool in pan for 10 minutes, and then cool completely on wire rack.

A Summer Clafouti

Batter:

3 Eggs
6 Tbs Butter – melted
⅔ Cup Flour
½ tsp Salt

1 Cup Milk or Half-and-Half
1 tsp Vanilla Extract
½ Cup Sugar

Peaches:

4 Tbs Butter
½ Cup Sugar
2 tsps Vanilla – or your favorite flavoring

5 Peaches – peeled, pitted, sliced
2 tsp Sugar
Cinnamon – to sprinkle

Preheat oven to 400°. For the batter, put all the batter ingredients in a blender, blend until smooth, scraping down the sides, and set aside.

Generously butter a 10-inch glass pie plate and set it in the oven to heat. Melt butter in a pan, add the peaches, ½ cup of sugar, and vanilla (or your favorite flavor, maybe almond extract), and cook for about 5 minutes until they are glazed and heated through. Remove the plate, carefully, from the oven, give the blender a quick whirl, and quickly pour half of the batter into the hot pie plate. Arrange the peaches and some of their juices over the batter, spreading them out. Now, pour remaining batter over the peaches, sprinkle remaining 2 tsps of sugar over the batter, and sprinkle with cinnamon and any remaining juices. Bake for about 30–35 minutes or until the Clafouti is golden and set in the middle. Remove from the oven and sprinkle, quickly, with a little sugar or sugar-cinnamon mixture. Serve with a topping of whipped cream or a side of ice cream and you have a winner!

Note: A clafouti is sort of a tart. In summer, when fruit is plentiful, you can use any of your favorite fruits. In autumn, I make this, often using apples. But, in summer, our family likes it made with peaches or figs.

Latte e Polenta Carmellata

Milk and Caramelized Polenta

1½ Cups Whole Milk
1½ Tbs Butter
¾ Cup Heavy Cream
4–5 Whole Coffee Beans
6 Oz Nut Brittle – broken into pieces, optional

⅔ Cups Coarse Polenta
¼ tsp Sea Salt – or to taste
1–2 tsps Vanilla Extract
¼ Cup Sugar + 2 Tbs Sugar
2 Cups Water

In a medium saucepan over high heat, whisk together 2 cups water, ½ cup plus 2 Tbs milk, polenta, butter, and salt. Slowly bring to a boil and then reduce to simmer, stirring often with a wooden spoon (Italians will only use a wooden spoon when working with polenta) until thickened and soft, about 35–40 minutes. Transfer the polenta to an 8½" x 4½" x 3" loaf pan. Spread evenly and press down lightly with a rubber spatula, place on a wire rack, and let cool.

While cooling, in a medium saucepan combine the remaining milk, cream, vanilla, and coffee beans and bring to a boil. Once boiled, cover and set aside.

When the polenta has cooled sufficiently, set oven to broil. Line a small baking dish with parchment paper. Empty the polenta onto a cutting board and cut into 1-inch cubes. Toss the cubes with the sugar and transfer to the baking dish. Sprinkle all the excess sugar on top of the polenta cubes. Broil until the sugar has caramelized, about 12 minutes. Divide the cubes among serving bowls. Gently reheat the milk, but do not bring to a boil. Remove and discard the coffee beans from the liquid and then ladle the liquid into the bowls with the polenta. Sprinkle nut brittle on top, if using.

Note: In the north of Italy, it is common to bake polenta and then fry it in squares until crispy or caramelize and drench in a milk mixture and make a dessert.

Italian Lemon Cookies

1¼ Cups Flour

1 Lemon – juice and zest

¾ CUP + 2 Tbs Unsalted Butter – softened

¼ Cup + 2 Tbs Cornstarch

Pinch of Salt – or more to taste

½ Cup Powdered Sugar

Lemon Glaze

In a medium bowl, whisk together flour, cornstarch, lemon zest, and salt.

In a large bowl, beat on medium speed butter and sugar until fluffy and light. Add half of the flour and the lemon juice, and beat in to combine. Next, add the remaining flour using a wooden spoon or kitchen spatula, combining all to form a dough that should be a little sticky. Transfer the dough to a large piece of parchment paper and roll the dough into a log that measures approximately 1½-inches wide. Wrap the dough in the parchment paper and refrigerate for 1 hour.

Remove the dough from the refrigerator and unroll it, leaving it on the parchment paper. Working quickly, cut in ½-inch slices, placing the slices on a parchment paper–lined cookie sheet. Refrigerate for 20 minutes.

While dough is cooling, preheat oven to 320°. Bake the cookies for 5 minutes and then raise the temperature to 350°. Continue to bake for 8–10 minutes longer. When they are a light-golden color, remove from the oven and let the cookies sit on the cookie sheet for 5 minutes. Then, move carefully to a wire rack to cool completely. When the cookies are totally cooled, you can simply dust with powdered sugar or spread with a lemon glaze.

Lemon Glaze:

3 Tbs Fresh Lemon Juice

Zest of 1 Lemon

1½ Cups Powdered Sugar

In a small bowl, whisk together the lemon juice, zest, and powdered sugar until smooth. Spread on completely cooled cookies.

Flam, Barcelona Style

Crème Caramel

3 Tbs Sugar + 1 Additional Cup	2 Tbs Water
2½ Cups Whole Milk	1 Vanilla Bean or Vanilla Extract
2 Eggs	6 Egg Yolks

In a small saucepan, combine 3 Tbs sugar with the water and bring to a boil over medium heat. Boil, without stirring, until the mixture becomes a golden-brown syrup, about 4–5 minutes.

Pour an equal amount of the caramel syrup into each of 6 (4 Oz) custard cups. Tip and rotate the cups to swirl the caramel until the bottom and sides are coated about halfway up.

Pour the milk into a saucepan, add vanilla, and place over low heat until small bubbles form along the edges of the pan, about 6–7 minutes. DO NOT ALLOW THE MILK TO BOIL!

Preheat oven to 300°. In a bowl, using a wire whisk, beat together the eggs, yolks, and 1 cup of the sugar until a pale, creamy mousse forms. Add a little of the hot milk, whisking constantly to prevent the yolks from curdling. Add the remaining milk a little at a time while continuing to whisk. Strain the custard through a fine-mesh sieve into the prepared molds, dividing it evenly.

(I find it easier to sieve directly into a measuring cup with a pouring spout and then pour evenly into the cups.)

Place the filled cups in a large baking dish that is lined with a dish towel or paper towels for stability. Carefully add boiling water to reach halfway up the sides of the cups.

Bake until the custards are set but the center is still a little jiggly. Remove the baking dish from the oven and lift the cups out of the water. Let cool to room temperature. When cooled, cover and refrigerate until well chilled—4 hours or overnight.

To serve, run a small, sharp knife around the inside of each mold and then turn the cups upside down onto individual plates, letting the caramel run down the sides.

Note: They call it "flam" and we call it "flan," but either way, it's delicious and easy! In Barcelona, this dessert is normally prepared in individual metal pots known as "flaneras."

Chocolate-Chip Cookie Loaf

1 Cup Butter – unsalted, room temperature

2 Eggs

Pinch of Salt

3 Cups Flour

¾ tsp Cinnamon

1 ⅓ Sugar – preferably superfine
   (but regular works, too)

1 tsp Vanilla Extract

1 tsp Baking Powder

1 Cup Mini Chocolate Chips

⅛ tsp Nutmeg – optional

3 Tbs Superfine Sugar – can use regular

Preheat oven to 350° and line two baking sheets with parchment paper.

In the bowl of a stand mixer, using the paddle attachment, combine butter and 1 ⅓ cups sugar. Beat on medium speed until light and fluffy. Add in eggs one at a time, beating in before adding the next one. Add vanilla, salt, and baking powder. Mix just until all well combined, scraping down the sides of the bowl occasionally to make sure all is incorporated.Reduce speed to low (so you don't get a flour shower) and slowly add flour, just until it is combined. Stir in the chocolate chips.

Divide the dough into 4 equal parts. On a lightly floured board, roll each piece into a 15-inch-long log. Place 2 logs at a time onto the parchment paper–lined pan. Press down on the logs to flatten them until they are 2½ inches wide. Repeat with the other two logs and set aside.

Combine the cinnamon, nutmeg (if using), and 3 Tbs of sugar, and sprinkle on top of the flattened logs. Bake one pan at a time for 15 minutes, or just until the edges are lightly golden. Remove from oven, and while still in the pan, immediately cut each log on a diagonal into cookie strips. A pizza cutter works well in doing this. Transfer cookies to a wire rack to cool. Repeat with second pan.

Note: Superfine sugar is easily made by spinning granulated sugar in the processor for several seconds. For a variety, I have sometimes used peanut-butter chips.

Finnish Cardamom Bread

Pulla

¾ **Cup Milk – warmed to 110°**
⅓ **Cup Sugar**
4½ **Cups Flour**
2 **tsps Cardamom**
4 **Tbs Butter – melted and cooled**
Coarse Sugar and Sliced Almonds – for
   topping

¼ **Cup Water – warmed to 110°**
2¼ **tsps Active Dry Yeast – 1 pkg**
2 **Eggs – room temperature**
¾ **tsp salt**
1 **egg – beaten with 1 Tbs water for wash**

In a large bowl in a stand mixer, combine milk, water, and sugar. Sprinkle the yeast over top and let stand for 5 minutes, until foamy. Add 2 cups of flour, eggs, cardamom, and salt. Mix until smooth. Add butter and mix until well combined.

Knead the dough in the bowl, adding enough of the remaining flour to keep it from sticking, until the dough comes clean from the sides of the bowl and does not stick to your hands either.

Shape the dough into a ball in the bowl and cover it with a damp tea towel. Let the dough rise in a warm, draft-free place for 60–90 minutes, or until doubled in size.

Once risen, punch the dough back and divide into 3 even strands for a braid. Roll each strand into a 20-inch-long log. Braid the strands and place the braided loaf on a parchment-lined baking sheet. Brush the top of the loaf with egg wash and sprinkle it with sugar and almonds, if desired.

Let the loaf rise for 30–40 minutes, or until doubled in bulk. (Have your oven preheated to 375° for at least 30 minutes before putting bread in to bake.) Bake the bread for 25–30 minutes, until golden and hollow sounding when tapped.

Remove the loaf from the oven and let it cool slightly on a wire rack before cutting.

Note: To make rolls, divide the dough into 12 even portions. Roll each portion into a round ball and place on a parchment-lined baking sheet. Brush with egg wash and sprinkle with sugar and almonds. Let rise about 20–30 minutes, until doubled. Bake for 10–15 minutes, until golden.

French Apple Cake

8 Tbs Salted Butter
1¾ Lbs Granny Smith or Fuji Apples
12 Tbs Sugar – divided
2 Tbs Calvados – or your favorite brandy
2 Eggs
Butter – to grease pan
¼ tsp Nutmeg

1 Lb Golden Delicious Apples
Pinch of Kosher Salt
½ Cup Flour – add more to dust pan
1 tsp Baking Powder
2 tsps Vanilla Extract
1 tsp Cinnamon

Peel apples (actually any of your favorite, crisp baking apples will work), then core and cut into slim, ¼-inch slices. A mandolin comes in handy to do this. Preheat oven to 375° and place your rack in the middle of the oven. Using a springform pan, grease it with the butter and dust with flour, shaking out the excess.

In a large skillet over medium-high heat, melt the butter, swirling the pan until you see brown solids at the bottom of the pan and the butter is fragrant (2–3 minutes). Pour all of this, including the brown solids, into a small heatproof bowl (just pour; do not scrape the pan). Stir the spices into the butter and set aside.

Add all of the apples to the hot skillet. Sprinkle with 3 Tbs of the sugar and a pinch of salt, and stir to combine the sugar and salt in. Cook, stirring occasionally, until all the moisture released from the apples has evaporated and the slices are just starting to brown a little (13–15 minutes). Add the Calvados (or brandy of your choice) and cook until evaporated, about 1 minute. Transfer to a large platter. Spread out and refrigerate, uncovered, to cool, about 20 minutes.

In a small bowl, whisk together flour and baking powder. In a large bowl, whisk together eggs, vanilla, and the remining sugar. Slowly stir in the browned butter, including the brown solids. Add the flour mixture and stir with a kitchen spatula until smooth. The batter will be very thick. Add the cooled apples and fold in, coating them evenly with the batter. Transfer to the prepared pan, spread out in an even layer, and sprinkle with some extra sugar. Bake until deeply browned (35-40 minutes). Let cool completely in the pan on a wire rack about 2–3 hours. Run a knife around the inside of the pan and remove the sides carefully. Slice and serve. A little whipped cream on top is perfect for this dessert.

Note: You can use unsalted butter, just adjust the amount of salt according to your taste.

Coeur à la Crème

12 Oz Cream Cheese – room temperature
1 Lemon – zested
1 tsp Kosher Salt
1 Bottle Chutney – or any preserves

1 Cup Heavy Cream
1 Tbs Fresh Lemon Juice
½ tsp Ground Black Pepper

Place the cream cheese in the bowl of an electric mixer fitted with the whisk attachment and whip until it is firm like whipped cream. With the mixer on low speed, slowly add the cream, lemon zest, lemon juice, salt, and pepper. Beat on high speed until the mixture is very thick.

Line a sieve with a few layers of cheesecloth, allowing the excess to drape over the sides. Pour the cream mixture into the cheesecloth and smooth the top with a spatula. Fold the excess cheesecloth over the top of the cream. Place the mixture on a plate or suspend the sieve over a small bowl. Cover with plastic wrap and refrigerate overnight.

When ready to serve, unmold the crème upside down onto a plate and pour the chutney over the top, allowing it to drip down the sides. Serve chilled with crackers.

Note: Instead of chutney, any of your favorite preserves would do.

Almond Butter Cookies

1 Cup Butter – softened
2 tsps Almond Extract
Pinch of Sea Salt
½ Cup Sugar
Extra Pinch Salt – optional

½ Cup Sugar
½ tsp Vanilla Extract
2 Cups Flour
Extra Sugar for Dusting

Preheat oven to 350° and line 2 baking sheets with parchment paper. In a large bowl, beat together the butter and sugar until light and fluffy. Add the extracts and a pinch of salt. Mix in well. Add the flour and mix just until all is well combined. Do not overmix.

In a rimmed dish, combine sugar with an optional pinch of salt. Roll the balls into a size of about 1 inch and then roll in the sugar, making sure they are well coated. Place on the lined baking sheets. Press down on them lightly with the back of a soup spoon to flatten just a bit.

Bake until the edges are golden, 12–15 minutes. Cool on a wire rack.

Caramel Rice Custard

½ **Cup Short-Grain Rice**
3 **Eggs**
1 **tsp Salt**
5 **Cups Milk**

¾ **Cup Sugar**
2 **tsps Vanilla Extract**
⅓ **Cup Sugar**

In the top of a double boiler, combine rice and 4 cups of milk. Cook over boiling water, stirring occasionally, for about 45 minutes, until the rice is tender. **(Keep a check on the water in the double boiler so that it does not run out.)** Remove from hot water and let cool slightly for about 10 minutes. Preheat oven to 350°.

Lightly grease a 2-quart souffle dish or casserole and place in a shallow baking pan. In a large bowl using a wire whisk, beat eggs with remaining 1 cup of milk. Add ¾ cup sugar, salt, and vanilla. Mix well. Gradually stir in the hot rice mixture and mix well until all is combined.

Pour the mixture into the prepared pan. Pour enough hot water into the pan to reach depth of 1 inch around the souffle dish. Bake uncovered 50–60 minutes, or until toothpick inserted in the center comes out clean. Carefully, using tongs or potholders, remove the souffle dish from the hot water and place on a wire rack.

Cool at room temperature for 1 hour. Then cover with plastic wrap and refrigerate until completely chilled—best overnight. Next day, 1 hour before serving, make the caramel.

Sprinkle ⅓ cup of sugar evenly over the bottom of a small heavy skillet. Cook slowly over very low heat, stirring occasionally with a wooden spoon just until the sugar melts and turns golden brown. Remove from heat and cool very slightly.

Using a teaspoon, drizzle syrup over the top of the custard. Refrigerate the custard until time to serve.

Cantucci

A Tuscan Dolci

2¼ Cups Flour
2 tsps Baking Powder
2 Eggs
¼ tsp Orange Extract
1 tsp Orange Zest - optional

¾ Cup Sugar
¼ tsp Salt
⅔ Cup Raw Almonds - chopped
2 tsps Vanilla Extract

Preheat oven to 450°. Coat a baking sheet lightly with cooking spray. Mix all ingredients in a bowl with an electric mixer to form a dough. When ready, form logs 12" x 2½" and 1 inch thick. Bake about 20 minutes. Remove and cool on rack.

Cut into ¾-ich slices while still warm. Put them back on the baking sheet and bake for 5 minutes longer. Cool completely on rack. Makes about 24.

Enter any house in Montefollonico and you will undoubtedly be offered one of these with a small glass of Vin Santo. Montefollonico is known simply as "the Town of Vin Santo" to wine connoisseurs who take part in the annual festival appropriately named "Lo gradireste un goccio di Vinsanto" held every December. Wine makers lovingly protect the traditional recipe with patience and dedication. Vin Santo is a syrupy sweet dessert wine very traditional in Tuscany, especially in the Siena area. It is claimed that it was given its name by a Franciscan priest who used the wine, which was the church's sacrament wine, to heal victims of the plague. Whatever, when I open a bottle given to me by my Cousin Andrea in Montefollonico, I proclaim it heavenly.

Almond Pie

Crostata Mandorle

2 Cups Raw Almonds
2 Eggs
½ tsp Almond Extract
1 Recipe Chilled Pie Dough – find
    elsewhere in this book
⅓ Cup Slivered Almonds

½ Cup Sugar
½ tsp Vanilla Extract
¾ Cup Mini Chocolate Chips – optional
1 Egg – for egg wash
1 Tbs Water

Preheat oven to 350°. Grease and flour an 8-inch pie plate.

In a food processor, pulse the almonds and sugar together until they are very fine. Empty the mixture into a large bowl. Add the eggs and vanilla; stir all until well combined. Add the chocolate chips, if using, and stir again.

Remove the dough from the refrigerator and divide in half. On a floured surface, roll out the dough into 2 thick circles, ⅛ inch thick. Place one disc in the prepared pie pan and trim the edges and crimp. Prick the bottom of the crust. Spoon in the filling and top with the second crust. Cut off any excess and pinch the edges together and crimp.

In a small bowl, whisk together the egg yolk and water to make an egg wash. Brush the top crust and sprinkle with slivered almonds, scattering all over the top of the pie. Bake for 35–40 minutes until a nice golden brown. Let the pie cool completely before serving.

Almond Cranberry Quick Bread

An Aunt May Recipe

2 Cups Flour	**1¼ tsp Baking Powder**
½ tsp Salt	**2 Large Eggs**
1 Cup Sour Cream	**¾ Cup Sugar**
½ Cup Canola Oil	**½ tsp Almond Extract**
1 Cup Fresh Cranberries – rinsed, dried, chopped	**1 Cup Sliced Almonds**

Add all ingredients, except the cranberries, into a large mixing bowl and mix well.

Fold in the cranberries. Pour batter into a sprayed 8½" x 4½" loaf pan or 3 mini loaf pans 5 ¾" x 3¼". Sprinkle top with 2–3 Tbs sliced almonds.

Bake 350° for approximately 55 minutes until golden brown. For the mini loaves, bake approximately 40 minutes.

Note: Exactly the way it was written down and given to me.

Almond Pound Cake

Makes 1 Bundt Cake or 2 Loaf Cakes

8 Oz Cream Cheese

3 Cups Sugar

½ tsp Salt

1 tsp Almond Extract

1½ Cups Unsalted Butter – room temp

3 Cups Cake Flour – sifted after measuring

1 tsp Vanilla Extract

7 Large Eggs

Preheat oven to 300° and grease and flour 2 loaf pans or 1 12-inch Bundt pan. In a large mixing bowl of a stand mixer fitted with the paddle attachment, combine the butter and cream cheese until smooth. When well combined, add the sugar and beat until light and fluffy. Add the vanilla extract, the almond extract, and salt. Beat just until all combined. Alternate adding the eggs and flour, beating just until you cannot see the yolk and the flour is mixed in. End with the flour and do not overbeat at this point. Scrape down the sides of the bowl and pour into the prepared pan or pans, smooth the top, and bang the pan a few times on the counter to release any air bubbles.

Bake for 1 hour and 30–45 minutes for the Bundt cake. Check loaf cakes after 1 hour and 15 minutes.

Almond Toffee Tart

Shell:

2 Cups flour

¾ Cup Butter – cold, diced

3 Tbs Sugar

2 Eggs – room temperature

Filling:

1½ Cups Heavy Whipping Cream

½ tsp Lemon Zest

2 Cups Sliced Almonds – toasted, cooled

¼ tsp Almond Extract

1½ Cups Sugar

Pinch of Salt

½ tsp Vanilla Extract

Preheat oven to 325°. Layer the sliced almonds in a single layer on a baking sheet and bake for about 12 minutes. Let cool.

You can very easily make the shell in a food processor, pulsing together the flour, sugar, and butter. When all combined, add the eggs and pulse until it all comes together like wet sand. Be very careful to not overmix. Dump this all into your greased and floured tart pan and press the dough evenly over the bottom and up the sides of an 11–12-inch tart pan that has a removable bottom. Place the tart pan on a baking sheet and bake for about 12–15 minutes and until it is a light golden brown. Remove from the oven, set aside, and raise oven temp to 375°.

To Make the Filling:

In a large saucepan, combine the cream, lemon zest, and salt. Bring this to a boil over medium-high heat, stirring constantly for about 6–8 minutes. Reduce the heat to medium and cook while still stirring for another 5 minutes. Remove from the heat and stir in the nuts, vanilla, and almond extracts and spread the mixture into the pastry shell. Place the shell on a baking sheet and bake until a light brown for 30–35 minutes for 12-inch tart and 35–40 minutes for 11-inch tart. Cool in the pan on a wire rack until warm. Carefully remove the sides and serve. Or cover and serve later.

This is great served with a squirt of whipped cream and makes a very nice dessert or a delicious, sweet, satisfying snack.

Amaretto Soufflé

5 Eggs	**½ Oz Plain Gelatin**
2½ Oz Powdered Sugar	**1½ Oz Amaretto Liqueur**
1 Pint Heavy Cream	**Fresh Raspberries – optional**

Dissolve the gelatin in the Amaretto. Whip eggs and sugar until stiff. Fold in the liqueur, making sure it is well combined, and then fold in the cream, which has been beaten stiff. Pour into a glass bowl and refrigerate for at least 2 hours. Optionally, just before serving, sprinkle the top with some fresh raspberries.

Apple Praline Bread

1 Cup Sour Cream
2 Eggs
2 tsps Baking Powder
½ tsp Salt
1 Cup Nuts – walnut, pecan, or combo –
    divided

2 Cups Flour
2 Cups Flour 1 Cup Brown Sugar
2 tsps Vanilla Extract
½ tsp Baking Soda
1½ Cups Granny Smith Apples – peeled,
    finely chopped

Preheat the oven to 350°. Lightly grease a 9" x 5" x 3" loaf pan. Set aside. Using an electric mixer, beat together the sour cream, sugar, eggs, and vanilla on low speed for a couple of minutes until well blended. Stop the mixer and then add in the flour, leavening agents, and salt. Continue to beat on low until well combined.

Fold in the apples and half the nuts into the batter. Transfer the batter into the greased loaf pan.

Sprinkle the rest of the nuts on top and then press them lightly into the batter. Bake for about 60 minutes or until a toothpick inserted into the center comes out clean.

Cool in the loaf pan for about 20–30 minutes and then transfer to a wire rack to cool completely.

Praline Sauce:

¼ Cup Brown Sugar

¼ Cup Butter

In a small saucepan, place the butter and brown sugar. Using medium heat, bring to a boil. Lower the heat and then simmer lightly for about one minute, stirring constantly until the sauce thickens. Remove from heat and then drizzle over the bread. Cool completely.

Augello Holiday Cranberry Mold

1 Lb Bag Fresh Cranberries – rinsed and
    picked over
1 Cup Granulated Sugar
2 Large Green Apples – cored and roughly
    chopped in food processor

1 Cup Walnuts – chopped
1–2 Envelopes Unflavored Gelatin –
    dissolved in ½ cup liquid such as water
    or apple or orange juice

Chop cranberries in a food processor and pour into a bowl. Gradually add 1 cup of sugar, a little at a time, and stirring well after each addition. Let sit for about 45 minutes to an hour. Put apples in the food processor but only rough chop. Do not make small pieces. After the cranberries have melded with the sugar, add the apples and chopped nuts. Then slowly dissolve the gelatin in the water or juice over low heat. When clear and slightly cooled, toss with the cranberry mixture and pour into a mold. Cover and let set in the refrigerator for at least 6 hours or overnight. Unmold on a plate with a lip.

This is a recipe from West Milford days, and I don't think we have ever had a holiday or special occasion since then when this salad wasn't served. It is a family favorite and it looks so pretty when unmolded. Sometimes we even save it for dessert.

Aunt May's Pastierra di Grano

Easter Wheat Pie

1 Container (3 Lb) Whole-Milk Ricotta	**Orange Peel**
9 Eggs	**1 Oz Orange Flower Water**
2½ Cups Sugar	**1 Tbs Vanilla**
Cinnamon (powder or oil)	**½ Lb Cooked Wheat – drained**
Citron	

Beat sugar and eggs well until the sugar is dissolved. Add ricotta, citron, cinnamon, orange peel, orange flower water, vanilla, and grain. Pour into pie shell—optional lattice across the top.

Crust – Pasta Frolla:

2 Cups Sifted Flour	**¼ Cup Sugar – optional**
2 tsps Baking Powder	**¼ Lb Butter**
2 Extra-Large Eggs	

Add dry ingredients into processor; add butter until the pasta resembles cornmeal. Add eggs. Beat eggs and pour slowly, adding 1 drop water into bowl until a ball forms. Let rest 10 minutes.

Arrange in pie dish. Pour in filling. Bake at 325° for 1 hour for Pyrex; 350° for 1 hour for metal or other type pans.

Note: This is the way it was written and given to me many years ago.

Baked Crespelle

¾ Cup Flour
¼ Cup Sugar
½ tsp Salt
¼ tsp Baking Powder

2 Large Eggs – slightly room temperature
1 tsp Vanilla Extract
1½ Cups Whole Milk
2 Tbs Unsalted Butter

Place a 12-inch iron skillet or other heavy skillet in oven and set heat to 450°. In medium bowl (for ease in pouring I use a large measuring cup), add first 7 ingredients. Whisk together until smooth. You can also add all this to a blender to blend until smooth, making sure you scrape down the sides. Add the 2 Tbs butter in the hot skillet and let melt to golden (about 1 minute). Carefully pour the batter into the hot skillet and let bake until puffed and set and a golden brown.

Remove skillet from oven and place on stove grates for about 3 or 4 minutes to set. It will deflate. At this point you can serve it from the skillet and cut into 4 pie-shaped pieces and let each person spread with jam, jelly, honey, or syrup, as desired. Or, if you can, slide it onto a large plate and you can fill it with a thinned-out Nutella, roll like a jelly roll, sprinkle with powdered sugar, and cut into 4 large slices. Either way, very filling served with bacon or sausage.

Note: Crespelle are thinner, lighter crepes.

Banana Pudding Layer Dessert

2 Cups Graham Cracker Crumbs
8 Oz Cream Cheese – room temperature
¼ Cup Sugar
16 Oz Cool Whip Topping – divided
2 (3.4 Oz) Boxes of Banana Cream Instant
   Pudding
Nuts – optional
1 (20 Oz) Can Crushed Pineapple – drained

½ Cup Butter – melted
½ tsp Vanilla
2 Tbs + 3½ Cups Cold Milk – divided
1 (23 Oz) Container Frozen Sliced
   Strawberries – thawed, drained well
Chocolate Syrup
Maraschino Cherries – optional, but
   encouraged

Grease a 9″ × 13″ baking dish; set aside. In a medium bowl, combine the graham cracker crumbs and melted butter. Stir the mixture until it's evenly moist. Then, dump the crumbs into your baking dish and press them into an even layer. Then, place the baking dish into your refrigerator until you've prepared your next layer.

In another medium bowl, combine the cream cheese, sugar, 2 Tbs of milk, and vanilla with a hand mixer on a medium speed. Mix together until fluffy and light. Then, using a rubber spatula, completely mix in 8 Oz of the Cool Whip. Once the mixture is completely combined, remove your baking dish from your refrigerator and evenly spread the cream cheese mixture on top of the graham cracker crust.

Pour your drained strawberries and pineapple on top of the cream cheese mixture and spread it evenly. It doesn't matter which fruit you put in first.

Mix the 2 boxes of banana cream instant pudding with 3½ cups of cold milk. Whisk for a few minutes until the pudding starts to thicken. Then, use a rubber spatula to spread the pudding over the fruit layer. Let the dessert sit for about 5 minutes so that the pudding can firm up a bit more.

Spread the remaining 8 Oz of Cool Whip over the top of the dessert as evenly as possible. Drizzle (or pour, your choice) the chocolate syrup on top of the Cool Whip layer. Allow the dessert to chill for at least 4 hours before serving or overnight.

Black and Whites

More Like a Little Cake

Black and Whites were a staple in most neighborhood bakeries during all my growing-up years. My Mother never bought them, but they always intrigued me. Finally, as a teenager when I had a part-time job, I purchased my first Black and White and thoroughly enjoyed it. They disappeared for a little while, but they have recently started making a comeback. This younger generation thinks they are a new invention! But basically, I think this is really just a New York City cookie.

Cookie:

1 ⅓ Cups Sugar
½ Cup Unsalted butter – room temperature
2 tsps Light Corn Syrup
2¼ Cups Cake Flour
2 tsps Baking Powder
⅔ Cup Whole Milk
½ tsp Lemon Extract

1 Cup Vegetable Shortening – room temperature
4 Large Eggs – room temperature
2 Cups Regular Flour
½ tsp Salt
2 tsps Vanilla Extract

Preheat oven to 400°. Cover baking pans in parchment paper. In a large bowl of a stand mixer, cream together the sugar, shortening, and butter until light and fluffy. Slowly add the corn syrup and then the eggs one at a time, making sure each egg is well incorporated before adding the next.

In another bowl, combine the flours, baking powder, and salt.

Add the dry ingredients to the creamed mixture and beat on medium speed, mixing with milk and beginning and ending with the dry ingredients. Add the vanilla and lemon extracts and mix in until well combined.

Make 4-inch cookies. This is easily done if using a Silpat pan covering. Otherwise, draw 4-inch circles on the parchment paper, leaving a little room between each cookie. Place ½ cup of mix in the middle of each circle and spread evenly with a spatula to fill the circle and smooth the top a little. Bake approx. 10 minutes or until the bottoms are golden.

Icing:

1½ Lbs Powdered Sugar – sifted to eliminate lumps
¼ Cup Warm Water

⅓ Cup Light Corn Syrup
½ tsp Vanilla Extract

Chocolate Icing:

1 Recipe Vanilla Icing

4 Oz Semisweet Chocolate – melted

To make the icings, combine the ingredients for the vanilla recipe in the top of a double boiler over very slightly simmering water, making sure the water does not touch the bottom of the top pan. Stir until well combined and the mixture is thick. Cook until your candy thermometer reaches 100°. If getting too thick, add a few drops of water. Remove from heat, but keep the icing over hot water to keep it warm.

To make the chocolate icing, add the melted chocolate to the vanilla icing.

Frosting the Cookies:

Only frost cooled cookies. Turn the cookies over and frost one half of the flat side with the vanilla icing. Yes, the rounded side will be the bottom. You can use a spatula or a broad knife, but if you have a pastry brush, the brush will give the smoothest finish. Don't work it too much or it will not be glossy. Place on a rack to thoroughly dry and then repeat with the chocolate icing. Dry thoroughly. Makes approx. 12–14 large cookies.

Caprese Cake

¾ Cup Butter – softened
¾ Cup + 2 Tbs Sugar
6 Large Eggs
10 Oz White Chocolate
10 Oz Almonds – peeled
Zest of 3 Lemons

Juice of 1 Lemon
1 tsp Baking Powder
1 Tbs Limoncello
Powdered Sugar – for dusting
Lemon Zest or Curls – for garnish

Preheat oven to 350°. In a large bowl, cream butter with an electric mixer for about 10 minutes until foamy. Add the sugar and continue to beat for an additional 10 minutes. Add the eggs one at a time while continuing to mix. Meanwhile, while all this beating and mixing is going on, chop the white chocolate (use a good quality) with the almonds in a food processor until finely ground. Add to the butter mixture and mix well. Add the lemon zest and lemon juice and mix well, making sure it is all combined. Lastly, add the baking powder and Limoncello (if you have homemade Limoncello, all the better) and mix until all combined. Prepare a 12-inch round baking pan with butter and flour or butter and slightly buttered parchment paper. Pour the batter into the prepared pan and bake for 40–50 minutes until golden. Remove from oven and allow to cool completely on a wire rack. Once cooled, carefully flip it out of the pan onto a large serving plate. Dust with powdered sugar and garnish with lemon zest or lemon curls.

Cardamom Cake

3 Sticks Butter – unsalted
3 Cups Sugar
6 Eggs
2 tsps Vanilla or
2 tsps Cardamom

1 Cup Milk – not low-fat
3 Cups Flour
1 tsp Baking Powder
½ tsp Salt

Cream 3 sticks of butter gradually with 3 cups of sugar. When soft, add the 6 eggs 1 at a time along with the vanilla or cardamom. Sift together 3 cups flour, 1 tsp baking powder, ½ tsp salt, and add slowly 1 cup of milk and then add slowly to egg mixture. Spoon into well-greased Bundt or tube pan and put into a COLD oven. Bake at 325° for 1 hour and 15 minutes. Turn oven off and leave inside for 1 more hour. Remove from pan and when totally cool, sprinkle with powdered sugar or make a glaze of powdered sugar and a few drops of milk

Note: This is a recipe from our West Milford era, and it is a favorite of Dad's. It was given to me by Edie Katalinas, who was our next-door neighbor and my Lamaze partner when I was expecting Claudia.

Carrot Cake Glazed

Serves 15 or More

2 Cups Flour – all purpose
½ tsp Salt
3 Large Eggs – well beaten
¾ Cup Vegetable Oil
¾ Cup Buttermilk
2 tsps Vanilla
2 Cups Carrots – grated

1 Cup Walnuts – chopped
2 tsps Baking Soda
2 tsps Cinnamon
2 Cups Sugar – granulated
1 (8 Oz) Can Crushed Pineapple – drained
3½ Oz Flaked Coconut

Cake:

Combine flour, baking soda, salt, and cinnamon and set aside. Combine eggs, oil, buttermilk, sugar, and vanilla, and beat until smooth. Stir in flour mixture, pineapple, carrots, coconut, and chopped walnuts. Pour into large greased and floured Pyrex pan. Bake at 350° for 35–40 minutes or until a tester inserted in the middle comes out clean and the top is golden brown. Remove from oven and immediately spread buttermilk glaze over the entire cake while still in pan. Cool in pan 15 minutes and remove and let cool completely.

Buttermilk Glaze:

1 Cup Sugar – granulated
½ Cup Buttermilk
1 Tbs Light Corn Syrup

½ tsp Baking Soda
½ Cup Butter
1 tsp Vanilla

While cake is baking, add all ingredient in a small saucepan and cook over low heat just until it comes to a boil. Remove from heat and let sit until ready to pour over cake.

Orange Cream Cheese Frosting:

½ Cup Butter – softened
1 tsp Vanilla Extract
1 tsp Grated Orange Rind

8 Oz Cream Cheese – softened
2 Cups Powdered Sugar – sifted
1 tsp Orange Juice

Combine butter and cream cheese, beating until light and fluffy. Add vanilla, powdered sugar, orange rind, and orange juice and beat until smooth. Frost cooled cake.

Zucchini Orange Bundt Cake

1½ Sticks Butter – melted
2½ tsps Baking Powder
¼ tsp Cardamom
2 Medium Zucchini – 2½ cups
Eggs
Orange Glaze

2½ Cups Flour
¼ tsp Cinnamon
½ tsp Orange Zest
1 Tbs Orange Juice
1½ Cups Sugar

Preheat oven to 325°. Brush a 6 cup Bundt pan with butter and dust with flour. Whisk together the flour, baking powder, spices, and 1 tsp of salt. Grate zucchini on the large holes of the grater, then squeeze dry in a kitchen towel. Stir together the eggs and sugar, and stir in the melted butter, zucchini, and orange zest and juice. Pour batter into prepared Bundt pan and bake for 55–60 minutes until a cake tester comes out clean. Cake will rise quite a bit and then fall back down during baking.

Transfer pan to a wire rack and let cake cool for 10 minutes in the pan. Run a knife around the edges of the pan to loosen, and then turn out onto the rack to cool for at least 30 minutes.

Brush several layers of the orange glaze evenly all over the cake.

Orange Glaze:

1¼ Cups Powdered Sugar – sifted
¼ tsp Finely Grated Orange Zest
Good Pinch of Cardamom

3 Tbs Fresh Orange Juice
Milk – optional if needed for thinning

Whisk together the sugar, cardamom, orange zest, and orange juice. Keep whisking until the mixture is the consistency of honey. If too thick, whisk in a tiny bit of milk, ½ tsp at a time.

Cassata Siciliana

A Very Traditional Sicilian Dessert

Cake:

5 Large Eggs – separated
½ tsp Salt
1½ Cups Sugar

Rind of 1 Lemon – grated
1½ Cups Flour
½ tsp Cream of Tartar

Preheat oven to 350°. Butter and flour 2 8-inch cake pans. Beat the egg whites until they are stiff but not too dry, folding in the salt and ½ cup of the sugar halfway through the beating. Beat the egg yolks with the remaining 1 cup of sugar and the lemon rind. Fold the yolks into the whites with a rubber spatula. Sift the flour with the cream of tartar twice and then fold into the eggs. Pour the mixture into the prepared cake pans. Bake for about 40 minutes, until the tops are golden. Let cool.

Filling:

2 Lbs Ricotta
2 Cups Confectioner's Sugar
2 tsps Cinnamon

¼ Cup Semi-Sweet or Bittersweet Chocolate Pieces
¼ Cup Chopped Candied Fruit
½ Cup Chopped Pistachios or Pine Nuts

Force the ricotta through a sieve. Combine with the remaining ingredients and set aside.

To Assemble:

6 Tbs Liqueur (your favorite, such as Grand Marnier, Cointreau) or Marsala – your choice

Confectioner's Sugar

Cut the cooled cake into strips or slices and sprinkle with liqueur or marsala. Line the sides and bottom of a 10-cup round mold completely and tightly with strips of cake, saving enough to cover the top. Fill the mold completely with the creamy ricotta mixture. Top with a layer of cake, pressing down to fill the mold solidly. Cover with plastic wrap and chill for at least 6 hours. Unmold the cake and sprinkle with confectioner's sugar before serving. This works best if you have a large glass bowl. While chilling, place a little weight on top of the plastic wrap to help compress. I've read suggestions to line the mold with Saran or other plastic wrap for ease in unmolding, but I have not tried that.

Celebrating Santa Lucia

And Remembering My Little Nonna

Santa Lucia was born in Italy in the year 283 AD and suffered the death of a martyr in 304 AD. The Feast of Santa Lucia is celebrated on December 13, the day of her death. Lucia, meaning light, Santa Lucia is the patron saint of the blind. In her paintings or her statues, she is often depicted holding her eyes on a golden plate. I was always told that when she was martyred, her eyes were gouged out. However, I have never been able to confirm that. But she is the patron saint of eyes.

In Italy, there are special devotions to Santa Lucia (St. Lucy), and it is because of this devotion and tradition that her Feast Day continues to be celebrated.

In northern Italy, Santa Lucia arrives in the company of a donkey and sometimes brings gifts to good Children in the night between December 12 and 13. (No donkey or gifts ever arrived at my house in New York City! However, there was Cuccia.)

In Tuscany, where my Little Nonna was raised, they ate boiled wheat on this feast day. Some areas called this Cuccia. My Little Nonna's Mother's name was Lucia (Vigliari), and so when I made my confirmation at the age of six, I was asked by my Father to take that name as I was confirmed. I think it pleased my Dad and Little Nonna. I can remember a few years when I was little, my Little Nonna would make me Cuccia, sweetened ,and, I think, only with sugar, on that Feast Day. Our youngest Daughter, Claudia, embraced that name at her confirmation, but I am remiss as I have not made Cuccia for her. Cuccia is actually a Sicilian name, and I remember, as a Child, this dish only being called Cucci!

Cucci Recipe

2 Cups Wheat Berries – after soaking   **2 Lbs Ricotta – drained**
½ cup Sugar – or to taste   **½ tsp Vanilla**
¼ tsp Nutmeg   **½ tsp Cinnamon – optional**
½ Cup Whole Milk – optional

Soak the wheat berries for 2 days, making sure you change the water often. When ready to cook, rinse the berries and put in a covered pot, in slightly salted water, bring to a boil, and then lower heat and simmer for about 3 hours. At this point they should be tender but a little chewy.

Put the ricotta, sugar, vanilla, nutmeg, and cinnamon (if using) in a bowl and beat with a hand mixer until smooth. If you like it thin, add some milk. Taste and adjust for sugar. I remember it being thick, so I don't think my Little Nonna added milk. Add the ricotta mixture to the wheat berries and stir in until all incorporated. This can be eaten warm or cooled. I remember eating it at lunchtime and it was warm. Such a good memory. Think I'll whip up a batch this year and share with Claudia.

Little Nonna and me, late 1940s

Chocolate Oreo Poke Cake

Cake:

1 Box Chocolate Cake Mix
½ Cup Vegetable Oil
8 Oz Sour Cream
30 Oreos – divided

¾ Cup Whole Milk
3 Eggs
1 Tbs Vanilla Extract

Topping:

1 (16 Oz) Jar Hot Fudge Sauce
1¾ Cup Whole Milk

1 Package (3.4 Oz) Instant Chocolate Pudding
1 Extra-Large Container Cool Whip

To Assemble:

Preheat oven to 350°. In a large mixing bowl, combine the chocolate cake mix with ¾ cup milk, vegetable oil, eggs, sour cream, and vanilla. Mix well until all combined and pour into 9" x 13" pan. In a plastic bag, crush 10 Oreos until crumbly but not small crumbs. Sprinkle all over cake. Bake 20–30 minutes until a cake tester comes out clean. Cool for 20–30 minutes. With the handle of a wooden spoon, poke holes all over the cake. Heat hot fudge until it is pourable (add a little vanilla) and pour over the cake.

Prepare instant pudding (using only 1¾ cup milk), combining milk and pudding mix. Pour all over cake and refrigerate just until cool.

Topping:

Crush 10 Oreos and fold into the Cool Whip. Pour mixture all over cake. Chill at least 2 hours and top with the remainder of the Oreos, crushed, and a drizzle of the hot fudge.

Note: This is our favorite beach dessert. You never can have too much chocolate!

Christmas Eve Cake

Torta Vigilia di Natale

1 Cup Water
1 Cup Seedless Raisins or Currants
¼ Cup Walnuts – chopped
¼ Cup Pecans – chopped
1 Cup Sugar

½ Cup Butter – salted
1 Egg – lightly beaten
1 tsp Vanilla or Rum Flavoring
1 tsp Baking Powder
½ Cup Sifted Flour

Simmer, all together, the raisins or currants and the nuts in the water for about 5 minutes and then let cool. (I like to add a tiny pinch of salt to the water and a pinch of sugar.) Cream the butter and sugar until light and fluffy; add the egg and beat in until just combined. Add the flavorings and stir in. Sift baking powder and flour together and add to the creamed mixture. Beat until well blended. Add the cooled fruits and a bit of the liquid and stir well. Pour into a greased 8-inch pan (I have a square glass one that I use, so I serve it to family straight from the pan) and bake for 25 minutes. Cool, remove from the pan, and cut into squares.

Ciambellone

A Sicilian Holiday Dessert

4 Cups Flour
3 Eggs
1 tsp Vanilla
1 Cup Sugar – plus extra for sprinkling on top
1 Cup Milk – plus extra for brushing tops

1 tsp Cinnamon
½ Cup Oil – vegetable or canola
1 tsp Baking Powder
Lemon Zest – from one large lemon

Preheat oven to 350°. Make a mound with the flour on a board, creating a well in the center. Using your fingers, begin alternating and incorporating the liquid (add eggs to milk and mix slightly, next add oil) and the dry ingredients into the well, mixing until all are combined. Add lemon zest, making sure to distribute evenly. Add additional flour as needed, kneading to make a smooth dough. Divide into two equal parts, roll each part into 2 or 3 ropes and shape each into circular, fat rings. Brush each with some milk and sprinkle tops with sugar. Place the coils on a buttered baking sheet and bake for about 40 minutes until golden brown.

Crumb Cake or Crumb Bun

That Is the Question

There is no doubt that, whether you call it Crumb Cake or Crumb Buns, this favored breakfast sweet is particular to New York City. Or that very few people outside of the city, unless transplanted, have ever indulged in it. But it has been a favored item in New York City since the mid-nineteenth century. Cushmans and Hanscoms and many little neighborhood bakeries would be remiss if this sweet was not available, most especially for weekends.

As a rare treat, on a Sunday morning, I was given a few quarters with which to stop by Hanscoms on my way home from Mass at St. Agnes. Hanscoms was on Second Avenue between Forty-Second and Forty-First Streets. We were a family of six, and I was entrusted with the money to buy six Crumb Buns. Not easy concentrating on Mass while caressing the quarters in my pocket, thinking of those delicious buns, and all the while my empty stomach is gurgling. This was indeed a treat. Fortunately, over the years I have been able to obtain several recipes. Here is one for Crumb Cake.

Crumb Mixture:

1 Cup Unsalted Butter	2½ Cups Flour
1 Cup Dark Brown Sugar	½ Cup Granulated Sugar
½ tsp Salt	2 tsps Vanilla Extract
2 Tbs Cinnamon	

Melt the butter in a medium saucepan and then let cool for a few minutes, but not long enough to harden. Mix together the flour, sugars, salt, vanilla, and cinnamon with a fork until this mixture resembles medium-sized crumbs. Set aside.

Cake Mixture:

2¼ Cups Flour	Powdered Sugar – for dusting
½ tsp Baking Soda	2 tsps Baking Powder
10 Tbs Unsalted Butter – diced	½ tsp Salt
2 Eggs – room temperature	1 Cup Super-Fine Sugar* – or regular sugar
1 tsp Vanilla	1 Cup Sour Cream – drained

Note: You can spin regular sugar in a processor to make super-fine sugar!

Assembly:

Set oven to 350°. Butter and flour a 9″ x 13″ pan. In a large bowl, combine the flour, baking powder, baking soda, and salt and whisk all together making sure they are well combined.

In the bowl of a stand mixer, add the cut-up butter and mix with paddle on low speed until the butter is soft, creamy, and light in color. Add the super-fine sugar a little at a time and continue beating for 5 or 6 minutes, making sure it is well blended in and making sure to scrape down the sides of the bowl in the process.

Add the eggs 1 at a time, making sure the egg is well blended in before adding the next. Add the vanilla and beat for another minute.

On low speed, carefully and slowly (or you will be covered), add the flour mixture alternately with the sour cream, starting and ending with the flour. All the while, make sure you keep scraping down the sides of the bowl. Pour the batter into the prepared baking dish and smooth the top.

Take a handful of crumb mixture and, squeezing your hand a little to produce good-sized crumbs, scatter the mixture all over the cake, making sure to cover the entire cake. Pat them down gently to push them just slightly into the cake mixture to make sure they adhere and don't roll off.

Bake for 25–35 minutes until the top of the cake is golden and the sides pull away slightly from the pan. When cool, sprinkle generously with powdered sugar. Cut into squares, and now your Crumb Cake is Crumb Buns! Breakfast will never be the same. An alternate recipe for Crumb Buns is also in this cookbook. It is one that we save for breakfast.

Cuccidatti

Definitely a Sicilian Christmas Cookie

Dough:

2 Cups Shortening
2 Lbs Flour – and extra if needed
3 Tbs Baking Powder
3 Eggs – well beaten

1 Pinch Salt
2 Cups Sugar
8 Oz Beer

Combine shortening, flour, salt, sugar, and mix well. Take beaten eggs and beer and add to the dry ingredients. Mix well, as you would a pie dough. Wrap in plastic wrap and let rest.

Filling:

1 Box Golden Raisins	3 Tbs Cinnamon
1 Lb Dried Figs	½ tsp Nutmeg
1 Lb Almonds	12 Oz Jar of Orange Marmalade
½ Lb Walnuts	2 tsps Whiskey – your favorite
½ Lb Pecans	½ Cup Sugar – adding water to make this
2 tsps Vanilla	into a thick syrup

Bake nuts in a 325° oven until brown. Cool completely and mix with raisins and figs. Grind all together. Add the remaining ingredients and let sit in the refrigerator overnight or even a day or two.

Preheat oven to 350°. Take the filling out of the refrigerator and let it sit for a while so that it becomes pliable and easy to work with. Roll the dough about ⅛ inch thick and cut into rectangles about 2" x 4". Place a teaspoon of filling in the center and close the pastry. When all are rolled, place on cookie sheets, seam side down. Bake in a 350° oven for 12–15 minutes until browned. When cooled, glaze with your favorite icing mixture and, if desired, top with colored sprinkles.

Little holiday treats made by the dozen

Very Easy Chocolate Cake for a Crowd

Cake:

2 Cups Flour

2 Sticks Butter

5 Tbs Cocoa Powder

½ Cup Buttermilk

1 tsp Vanilla

2 Cups Sugar

1 Cup Water

2 Eggs

1 tsp Baking Soda

Mix flour and sugar in a large bowl. In a medium saucepan, combine butter, water, and cocoa over medium heat. Bring mixture to a boil and pour over the flour/sugar mixture. Mix well.

Add eggs, buttermilk, baking soda, and vanilla. Pour into a well-greased 9″ × 13″ pan and bake at 350° for 30 minutes or until a cake tester comes out clean.

Fudge Icing:

1 Stick Butter

4 Tbs Cocoa Powder

1 tsp Vanilla

4 Tbs Milk

1 (16 Oz) Box Powdered Sugar

1 Cup Pecans – chopped or your favorite

In a medium saucepan, combine butter, milk, and cocoa and bring mixture to a boil. Remove from heat and add powdered sugar, stirring well with a whisk or wooden spoon until the sugar melts and the mixture is smooth. Stir in vanilla and pecans, then pour over hot cake. Serves 12 to 16.

Easy Peach Cobbler

1 (29 Oz) Can Sliced Peaches – drained

1 Cup Milk

½ tsp Cinnamon

1 Cup Sugar

1 Cup Bisquick

½ tsp Nutmeg

½ Cup Butter – melted

Preheat oven to 375°. In an 8″ x 8″ baking dish, stir in Bisquick, milk, nutmeg, and cinnamon. Stir until all are well combined. Stir in the melted butter.

In a medium mixing bowl, stir together the peaches and the sugar. Spoon this mixture over the Bisquick mixture. Bake for about 60 minutes or until the top is a golden brown. Best served warm with ice cream, Cool Whip, or a dollop of freshly whipped cream.

Note: You can use Pioneer or even self-rising flour if you prefer. I just always have good results with Bisquick. Also, I double the recipe and bake it in a 9" x 13" glass pan. And the juice I drain from the peaches I just pour into our bottle of orange juice.

Flan Recipe

½ **Cup Sugar**	2 **Tbs Water**
2 **Eggs**	3 **Egg Yolks**
¼ **tsp Lemon Zest**	2 **tsps Vanilla Extract**
1 **Can Sweetened Condensed Milk**	1½ **Cups 2% Milk**

Preheat the oven to 350°. Place a kitchen towel in the bottom of a large baking dish and place a 9-inch cake pan in the center. Bring the sugar and water to a boil in a small saucepan, swirling the pan gently until the sugar has dissolved (about 3 minutes).

Reduce to a simmer and cook, swirling the pan occasionally (but not actually stirring), until the mixture has caramelized and turned a deep mahogany (7–10 minutes). Slowly pour the caramel into the 9-inch cake pan. Let caramel cool until slightly hardened.

Bring a large saucepan of water to boil. Meanwhile, whisk eggs and egg yolks together in a medium bowl until combined (about 1 minute). Whisk in the zest, vanilla extract, condensed milk, and low-fat milk.

Pour the mixture into the cake pan, then transfer the baking dish with the cake pan inside to the oven. Pour the boiling water into the baking dish until the water reaches halfway up the side of the cake pan.

Bake for about 30–40 minutes, or until the custard has just barely set and is no longer sloshy. You want the center of the custard to be 170–175°. Don't worry if the flan hasn't entirely set, it will finish setting during cooling.

Remove the baking dish from the oven and transfer the cake pan to a wire rack and let cool for about 2 hours.

Wrap the cake pan with plastic wrap and refrigerate until the custard is completely chilled (more than 2 hours and up to 24 hours).

Run a knife around the edge of the cake pan to loosen the custard, then invert a large serving platter over the top of the cake pan. Holding both the plate and pan, flip the custard over onto the platter. Drizzle any extra caramel sauce over the top of the flan and serve.

Note: You may want to make extra caramel sauce for the flan, which is easy to do by just repeating the directions above.

Fluffy and Light Lemon Pie

Crust:

1¾ Cups Flour
¼ Cup Cornstarch
12 Tbs Butter – cooled to slightly less
    than room temperature.

⅔ Cup Powdered Sugar
¾ tsp Salt

Filling:

4 Eggs – lightly beaten
3 Tbs Flour
¾ Cup Fresh Lemon Juice – 4 lemons
⅛ tsp Salt

1 ⅓ Cups Brown Sugar
2 Tbs Grated Lemon Zest
⅓ Cup Whole Milk

Preheat the oven to 350°. Butter a 13" x 9" baking dish and sprinkle with flour. Mix the flour, powdered sugar, cornstarch, and salt in a blender. Once it's mixed together, cut the butter into 1-inch pieces and add it to the mixture. Process the mixture until it's a pale yellow and has a coarse texture. Put the mixture into the baking dish and press it to the bottom and sides.

Refrigerate the crust for about 30 minutes, then bake for 20 minutes.

While you're waiting for the crust, mix the eggs, brown sugar, and flour in a medium-sized bowl. Then, stir in the lemon zest, lemon juice, milk, and salt. Once the crust is done baking, reduce the oven's temperature to 325°. Stir up the filling mixture, then pour it into the crust. Bake the pie until the filling feels firm (about 20 minutes).

Move the baking pan to a wire rack and let it cool for about 30 minutes. Sprinkle some confectioner's sugar on top, cut, and devour.

Note: This fluffy treat is both simple and tasty. You might want to make two of these, because it will disappear quickly!

Francesca's Sugar Sticks

From My Dear Friend Francesca German in Erie, Pennsylvania

6 Egg Whites
1 Cup Flour – sifted
¾ Cup Sugar – plus extra for second baking

2 tsps Vanilla Extract
1 Cup Walnuts – whole
8 Tbs Butter – unsalted, melted, and cooled

Beat egg whites until stiff. Then add small amounts of sugar and vanilla alternately with flour and butter. Beat in slowly until all used up. Add whole nuts. Line a cookie sheet with foil and pour batter in, shaping the foil so that the batter is 1 inch deep. Bake at 350° for about 45 minutes until the top is browned. Remove from pan, foil and all. When cool, wrap in foil and freeze. When ready to use, remove from freezer and, while still frozen, slice very thin. Dip in granulated sugar and bake in single layer in 325° oven until golden brown. Start at 10 minutes and watch carefully, as they burn easily. Sometimes I double the recipe and bake in a large casserole dish. The results are a wider cookie, whereas in the cookie sheet the cookie will only be about 1 inch or maybe 1½ inches.

Note: The best part about this recipe is it is easily doubled and baked in foil in a 10" x 13" pan. Before freezing, cut into smaller sections that you can take out only what you need. You now have a quick dessert in the freezer to finish in a hurry. This is a great way to use leftover egg whites. I always serve Francesca's Sugar Sticks at a party and remember my Erie friend.

Fresh Peach Melba

2¼ Cups Sugar – divided
½ Vanilla Bean – cut (or 2 tsps Vanilla Extract)
5 Lbs Peaches – peeled and cut into slices
2 Tbs + 1½ Cups Flour

¼ tsp Baking Soda
4 Eggs – Large
¼ Cup Milk – not low fat
3 Tbs Triple Sec or Orange Juice

2¼ Tbs Baking Powder
½ tsp Salt

1½ tsps Vanilla
¾ tsp Almond Extract
6 Tbs Butter – melted

Preheat oven to 325°. Blend ¾ cup sugar and vanilla in processor until well blended. Sift the sugar into large bowl, add peaches and 3 Tbs flour, tossing to coat. Transfer to 13" x 9" dish and bake until bubbly, about 25 minutes. Whisk remaining 1½ cups sugar and 1½ cups flour, baking powder, salt, and baking soda in a large bowl. Whisk eggs and next 4 ingredients in small bowl and add to dry ingredients, whisking until smooth. Fold in the melted butter. Pour batter over hot peaches and continue baking until topping is brown and center is cooked, about 45 minutes longer.

Note: For a real treat serve this with homemade vanilla ice cream. Another delicious anniversary dessert.

Grand Marnier Chocolate Mousse

8 Oz Bittersweet Chocolate – finely chopped
¼ Cup Light Brown Sugar – packed
1 Cup Heavy Cream

2 Eggs and 2 Egg Yolks
½ tsp Fresh Orange Zest
3 Tbs Grand Marnier

Microwave chocolate in a glass bowl, slowly, stirring often and scraping the sides until melted.

Stir and let cool.

In a blender, add eggs, yolks, sugar, and orange zest and blend until foamy and light in color (about 1 minute). Add cream and Grand Marnier and cooled chocolate and blend until combined and slightly thickened. Divide evenly among 4–6 custard cups or fancy glasses.

Cover with plastic wrap and refrigerate at least 4 hours or overnight. Before serving, uncover and let sit for about 15 minutes. Add a dollop of whipped cream on top and maybe some chocolate shavings.

Note: This is a great Valentine's Day dessert. You can substitute Framboise (a raspberry liqueur) for the Grand Marnier and top it off with a few peaks of whipped cream and fresh raspberries.

Or add 2 tsps vanilla instead of the liqueur and top with fresh strawberries drizzled with Fragola Fabbri, which is strawberries in a heavy syrup imported from Italy. So delicious!

Grano Dolce

A Great Dish for the Feast of Santa Lucia

½ Cup Wheat Berries (Farro) – soaked
¼ Cup Walnuts – chopped
2½ Tbs Honey
¼ Cup Currants
1 Cup Whipped Cream

Pinch of Salt
¼ Cup Almonds – chopped
¼ Cup Sweet White Wine
2 Oz Semisweet Chocolate – chopped

Soak the wheat berries over night or for at least 12 hours in a pot of slightly sweetened water to cover. Then, drain the berries and pour into a large pot filled with enough water to cover by an inch or two, add a little salt, and bring to a boil. Reduce heat to medium and cook for about 30 minutes or until berries are tender but not overcooked and mushy. For the last 10 minutes of the cooking, toss in the currants. Drain and set aside.

In a large skillet, combine walnuts and almonds and gently toast on medium for about 5 minutes. Transfer nuts to a large bowl and stir in the honey, wine, and wheat berries and currants. Let the mixture cool to room temperature and then stir in the chocolate pieces.

Serve with whipped cream.

Holiday Cranberry Dessert

1 Package Fresh Cranberries
1 Medium Can Pineapple Tidbits – drained
1 (10 Oz) Package Large Marshmallows

1 Pint Whipping Cream
¾ Cup Sugar
¾ Cup Walnuts – chopped

Whip cream, adding some of the sugar for sweetness. Grind the cranberries with the nuts and marshmallows. Do this in segments or the marshmallow will clog the processor. Mix the pineapple with the remaining sugar and mix in with the cranberries, marshmallows, and the nuts. Fold all into half of the whipped cream. Gently scoop into a glass bowl so as not to mash everything. When ready to serve, top with the remaining whipped cream.

Note: When cranberries are in season, I freeze a bag or two to use in the warmer months. Then I make the same recipe and freeze in an oblong baking dish. When ready to serve, just cut into squares and top with a little whipped cream. Very refreshing.

Hot Cross Buns

Pane Dolce Pasquale

1 Package Active Dry Yeast	**¼ Cup Warm (110–115°) Water**
½ Cup Warm (110–115°) Low-Fat Milk	**3 Eggs – room temperature**
4½–5 Cups King Arthur All-Purpose Flour	**½ Cup Sugar**
8 Tbs Butter – unsalted, room temperature	**1½ tsps Salt**

In a small bowl, sprinkle the yeast over the water and mix with a spoon until the yeast dissolves. Let the mixture ferment for about 5 minutes. Small clusters of chalky-looking bubbles should appear on the surface. Stir in the milk. With a fork, beat in the eggs, 1 at a time. Set the mixture aside.

In a food processor, mix together 4½ cups of the flour, the sugar, and salt. Break up the butter over the dry ingredients and work it in until a crumbly mixture is obtained. Add the yeast mixture and mix until a ball of dough is formed. Add additional flour if necessary to obtain a dough that is soft but not too sticky.

Turn the dough out onto a floured board and knead for about 3 or 4 minutes until a smooth ball of dough forms. Let the dough rest on the work surface for 10 minutes, covered with a towel or inverted bowl.

Knead the dough again for 5 minutes until smooth and no longer sticky. Lightly spray a large bowl with cooking oil or lightly coat with butter. Gather up the dough and place it in the bowl, turning to coat. Cover the bowl tightly with plastic wrap and let the dough rise until doubled in size (2–2½ hours).

When the dough has risen to approximately double the size, use 2 fingers to make 2 indentations into the center of the dough. If the indentation does not close up, the dough has sufficiently risen and is ready to use.

Break off pieces the size of small oranges and form into balls. Place them on lightly greased baking sheets about 2 inches apart. Cover and let rise about 30 minutes.

Bake in a preheated oven set at 375° for about 20–25 minutes or until nicely browned. Cool on a wire rack.

Make a powdered sugar icing, using 1 cup powdered sugar and 3–4 Tbs half-and-half. Mix until smooth. Then make a decorative cross on the top of the buns with the icing.

Note: Hot Cross Buns were found everywhere during Lent and right up to Easter when I was growing up and even newly married. Now I think it is a forgotten pastry, as I haven't been able to find them around Easter time.

Hummingbird Cake

3 Cups Flour
2 Cups Sugar
1 tsp Baking Soda
1 tsp Salt
1 tsp Cinnamon
¼ tsp Nutmeg
2 Cups Mashed Bananas

1 Cup Walnuts or Pecans – chopped
1 Can (8 Oz) Crushed Pineapple – undrained
2 tsps Vanilla Extract
½ Cup Raspberry Jam
3 Eggs – room temperature
1 Cup Vegetable Oil
Cream Cheese Frosting

Preheat oven to 350°. Grease 3 9-inch cake pans, line the pans with parchment paper or wax paper, and grease and lightly flour the paper too.

Combine flour, sugar, baking soda, salt, cinnamon, and nutmeg in a large bowl. Add eggs and oil and stir until all the ingredients are well combined. Stir with a wooden spoon—**do not beat!**

Stir in bananas, nuts, pineapple with liquid, and vanilla. Mix all in very well. Pour batter into prepared pans and bake for 25–30 minutes until the tops are lightly browned and slightly puffed and a cake tester comes out clean.

Cool in the pans for about 10 minutes and then remove from the pans and cool completely on wire racks.

Spread jam on bottom layer, making sure that you don't get it too close to the edge or it will bleed into the frosting. Frost with cream cheese filling and refrigerate for at least 3–4 hours before serving.

Cream Cheese Frosting:

8 Oz Cream Cheese – room temperature
½ Cup Butter – softened

1 (16 Oz) Package Powdered Sugar
1–1½ tsps Vanilla Extract

Beat cream cheese and butter with an electric mix until smooth. Gradually add powdered sugar and continue beating on low speed until light and fluffy. This should make about 3 cups.

Note: This cake is great for breakfast or brunch, too. When I add nuts to a recipe, I like to bake them for about 8–10 minutes on a baking pan in an oven preheated to 325°. Remove from the oven and cool completely before adding to a recipe or they will just steam and get mushy. Baking gives the nuts a richer flavor.

Italian Cream Cake

1 Stick Butter – softened
½ Cup Crisco – solid
2 Cups Sugar
5 Eggs – separated
1½ tsps Vanilla Extract

1 Cup Walnuts – baked and crushed
1 tsp Baking Soda
1 Cup Buttermilk
1 Small Can Coconut

Grease and flour 2 9-inch round cake pans. Cream butter and Crisco, add sugar, and beat until smooth. Add yolks, 1 at a time, and beat until well incorporated. Combine flour and soda and add to the creamed mixture alternately with buttermilk. Stir in vanilla; add coconut and nuts. Beat egg whites until stiff peaks form and fold in. Pour batter into prepared pans. Bake at 350° for 35–40 minutes until a cake tester comes out clean.

Frosting:

1 (8 Oz) Package Cream Cheese – softened
½ Stick Butter – unsalted
1 (16 Oz) Box Powdered Sugar

1 tsp Vanilla
1 Cup Raspberry Jam – or as necessary

Beat cream cheese and butter until smooth. Add sugar and vanilla and beat until all well combined. Spread jam on bottom cake layer. Don't get it too close to the edge or it will bleed into the frosting. Add top layer and frost cake. Garnish with nuts and coconut, if desired. My family likes lots of frosting, so I make it to 1½ times.

Italian Rice Puffs

Riso Sfinge

¼ Cup Rice – uncooked
2 Cups Milk
1 tsp Butter
2 Cups Peanut or Canola Oil

3 Eggs – separated
1 Oz Rum or Vin Santo
⅓ Cup Flour
Powdered Sugar – for dusting

Cook rice in milk over a low flame just until the rice is tender—do not overcook. Season with salt and pour into a dish without draining. Add butter and mix well. Add slightly beaten egg yolks, rum or Vin Santo, and flour, and blend thoroughly. Beat egg whites until stiff but not dry and fold them into the rice mixture.

Heat oil to 375°. Make rice puffs by carefully dropping 1 heaping tsp of the mixture into the hot oil. Do not fry more than 3 or 4 at a time, or the oil will cool down and the rice will just absorb the oil and not brown. Fry puffs until golden, turning to brown evenly.

Remove from the oil with a slotted spoon, sprinkle with powdered sugar, and serve immediately.

As a young bride, I had a very embarrassing experience with another sfinge recipe. I made them early in the day, as I wanted to surprise my in-laws at a holiday dinner. I refrigerated them in a sealed Tupperware bowl, and when I opened the cover after dinner, all that was in the bowl was a big glob of mush soaked in oil. Good thing I always make several desserts.

Italian Ricotta Cookies

2 Cups Sugar
1 Container (15 Oz) Whole-Milk Ricotta
2 Eggs – room temperature
2 Tbs Baking Powder
1½ Cups Powdered Sugar

1 Cup Butter – softened
2 tsps Vanilla Extract
4 Cups Flour
1 tsp Salt
3 Tbs Milk

Preheat oven to 350°. In large bowl, with mixer at low speed, beat sugar and margarine or butter until blended.

Increase speed to high; beat until light and fluffy, about 5 minutes. At medium speed, beat in ricotta, vanilla, and eggs until well combined.

Reduce speed to low. Add flour, baking powder, and salt; beat until dough forms. Drop dough by level tablespoons, about 2 inches apart, onto ungreased large cookie sheet. Bake about 15 minutes or until cookies are very lightly golden (cookies will be soft). With pancake turner, remove cookies to wire rack to cool. Repeat with remaining dough.

When cookies are cool, prepare icing. In small bowl, stir powdered sugar and milk until smooth. With small metal spatula or knife, spread icing on cookies; sprinkle with sugar crystals. Set cookies aside to allow icing to dry completely, about 1 hour.

Note: You can give these cookies a lemon flavor by using lemon extract instead of vanilla, or just put a drop of lemon extract in the frosting.

La Torta della Mamma

5 Eggs – room temperature, separated   **1 Cup Sugar**
2 Tbs Fresh Lemon or Orange Juice   **Zest from Either Lemon or Orange**
1 Tbs Vanilla or Almond Extract   **1 Cup Flour**
Pinch of Salt

Preheat oven to 350°. Beat egg yolks in a large bowl with an electric mixer until thick and lemon-colored. Gradually beat in half of the sugar until it is combined. Beat in the flour until well blended. Stir in the lemon or orange juice, extract of your choice, and salt. Stir in the zest and set aside.

In another bowl, with a whisk, beat the whites until foamy. Slowly beat in the remaining sugar, 2 Tbs as a time, until soft and glossy peaks form. Set aside.

Fold the beaten egg whites gently into the yolk mixture with a wide spatula. Be careful to not deflate the whites. Scoop the batter into a 9" x 3" tube pan. Tap the pan on the counter to remove any air bubbles and also to make sure the batter is evenly distributed.

Bake for 30–35 minutes or until a cake tester comes out clean and the cake is evenly browned. It should spring back when slightly touched with your finger.

Invert the cake pan over the neck of a sturdy bottle and cool completely. Loosen cake all around the inside of the pan and around the tube with a knife. Gently shake the cake out and set on a serving dish. Enjoy it plain, or make it fancy with a thin glaze or just a dusting of powdered sugar.

Note: There are as many recipes for Torta della Mamma in Italy as there are Mammas. Some are plain, some are fancy, some are fruit or cream filled. All are delicious because they are made with love. This is one of several that I have, but this one was given to me by a relative in Tuscany and I serve it with just powdered sugar.

Lemon Crumb Pie

Crostata al Limone

2 Cups Graham Cracker Crumbs
½ Cup Ground Almonds
1½ Cups Mascarpone Cheese
⅓ Cup Greek Yogurt – not low-fat
Zest of 1 Lemon

½ Cup Butter – melted
½ Cup Heavy Cream
½ Cup Sugar
½ Tbs Freshly Squeezed Lemon Juice

Crumb Crust:

Combine the cookie crumbs, butter, and ground almonds in a medium bowl. Grease and flour an 8-inch cake, an 8-inch springform pan, or an 8-inch deep-dish pie plate. Place ⅔ of the crumb mixture on the bottom of the pan, even out, and press down to form the crust. Place in refrigerator for about 30 minutes.

Filling:

While the crust is chilling, make the filling. In a medium bowl, whip the heavy cream until stiff peaks form.

Add the mascarpone cheese, sugar, and yogurt and beat at medium speed until all is well combined. Add the lemon juice and zest and beat until all is well mixed in. Scrape down the sides of the bowl and fold in the whipped cream.

Remove the crust from the refrigerator and add the filling. Smooth the top when finished, but do not pack down. Sprinkle the remaining crumb mixture, scattering them evenly over the top of the filling. Refrigerator for at least 6 hours before serving.

Note: This is a delicious summer dessert and so perfect in the hot weather because you never have to turn on your oven and the dessert is light and refreshing.

Lemon Meringue Pie

7 Eggs – separated
1¼ Cups Sugar
½ Cup Lemon Juice – freshly squeezed
1 Tbs Flour

Zest from 2 Lemons
½ tsp Cream of Tartar
3 Tbs Cornstarch
1 (9 or 10-inch) Pie Crust – prebaked

Preheat oven to 350°. In a double boiler (not aluminum), with simmering water, add the egg yolks and whisk slowly while adding 1 cup of sugar, 3 Tbs cornstarch, 1 Tbs flour, and lemon juice. When all is incorporated, continue to whisk until the mixture is quite thick. Stir in the lemon zest and remove from the heat to allow to cool. Beat the egg whites until they hold soft peaks, incorporate ⅓ of the egg whites into the cooled lemon mixture using a spatula, and mix in thoroughly. Pour into the baked pie crust. Add the remaining sugar with the cream of tartar to the remaining egg whites, a little at a time, beating after each addition until almost stiff but not dry. Pile it on the lemon filling, covering it completely to seal the edges. Swirl the top to make it fluffy and not flat. Place the pie on the middle shelf of the oven and bake until you see the meringue starting to brown. Be careful, as it can easily burn. Depending on your oven this can take between 5 and 10 minutes. Remove from oven and let cool completely before serving or refrigerating.

Note: Since my family likes mile-high meringue, if I have additional egg whites in the refrigerator, I will add a few more and increase the sugar a little and use 1 tsp cream of tartar. This makes a very nice presentation.

Lemon Mousse

1 Envelope Unflavored Gelatin
½ Cup Water
3 Eggs – separated

1 Cup Sugar
⅓ Cup Freshly Squeezed Lemon Juice

2 Tbs Fresh Lemon Zest
1 Cup Whipping Cream
Lemon Wedges – optional, cut in half and
    sliced very thin
2 Tbs Sugar

Sprinkle gelatin over ½ cup water in a small saucepan, let stand for about 2 minutes. A sort of film will form. Then simmer uncovered over low heat, stirring often until the gelatin dissolves and the liquid is clear. Remove from the heat and cool just until slightly warm. Do not let it get cold and set. Beat egg yolks in a small mixing bowl, adding sugar, until thick and lemon-colored. Add the lemon juice and zest gradually. Beat on high speed for about 7–8 minutes, and then stir in the gelatin mixture making sure it is well combined. Refrigerate this mixture, covered, for about 30 minutes or until it mounds when dropped from a teaspoon. Beat the egg whites in a medium-sized bowl until stiff, gradually adding the 2 Tbs of sugar. Whisk the refrigerated gelatin mixture in a large bowl to remove any lumps. Whip 1 cup of cream until stiff. Fold the whipped cream and the beaten egg whites into the gelatin mixture. Pour all into a 1½-quart serving or souffle bowl and refrigerate until firm, at least 4 hours, but not longer than 12 hours. Garnish with more whipped cream and the lemon wedges, if desired.

Note: This is a great desert to make with Meyer lemons. Also, if you have time, frost the lemon wedges with egg white and sugar for a very attractive appearance. If you don't want to use lemon wedges, you can just sprinkle lemon zest over the whipped cream for more color and extra lemon flavor.

Maddalena

Sponge Cake

5 Eggs – room temperature
½ Cup Unsalted Butter – melted and warm
1 Cup Sugar

¾ Cup + 2 Tbs Flour
Extra Butter – for greasing 10-inch pan

Heat oven to 400°. Lightly butter a round 10-inch cake pan. Sprinkle with flour and tap out the excess. Set aside.

Beat eggs in a large mixing bowl at high speed until foamy. Gradually beat in sugar, 2 Tbs at a time, and continue to beat until mixture is pale and tripled in volume, about 6–7 minutes.

Remove 1½ cups beaten egg mixture and pour into medium bowl. Drizzle melted butter over mixture and gently fold in with a rubber spatula. Gently fold butter-egg mixture back into egg mixture in mixing bowl. Sift flour in three batches over mixture while gently folding in with large rubber spatula.

Fold just until all is incorporated. Do not overfold. Gently pour batter into prepared pan in a spiral moto, working from the outer edge of the pan toward the center. Bake on center rack of oven until top springs back when lightly pressed and a tester comes out clean (about 30 minutes).

Cool cake on wire rack for 5 minutes. Turn out of pan; continue to cool on rack until it reaches room temperature. If not using immediately, wrap securely in plastic wrap until ready to use.

Note: This is a very rich sponge cake and calls for an unusual technique where part of the melted butter is folded into part of the beaten egg mixture.

Coconut Cake

A Sweet Recipe from Our Friend Marty

5 Eggs – room temperature	2 Cups Sugar
1 Cup Oil	2 Cups Self-Rising Flour
½ Cup Whole Milk	1 tsp Vanilla Extract
1 tsp Coconut Extract	1 Package or Medium Can Flaked Coconut

Note: Bring eggs to room temperature and add 1 at a time while stirring all ingredients in with a wooden spoon. Best to not use an electric mixer.

Beat sugar, oil, and eggs with a wooden spoon or wire whisk. Blend in flour, milk, and flavorings and stir with a wooden spoon until all are well incorporated. Stir in flaked coconut. Bake for 1 hour at 350° in a greased and floured Bundt pan. When a cake tester comes out clean, remove from the oven and place pan on wire rack. With a wooden skewer, punch holes all over the cake and pour glaze all over, slowly and carefully. (Try not to let the syrup get too close to the edge of the pan or the tube, as it makes it a little difficult to unmold by becoming sticky.)

Leave cake in pan until completely cooled. When ready to unmold, slide knife around the inside of the pan and around the tube to help loosen.

Glaze for Coconut Cake:

½ Cup Water	1 Cup Sugar
¼ Cup Butter	1 tsp Coconut Flavoring

Mix all together in a saucepan and bring to a boil and boil for 1 minute. Carefully pour all over cake and let it sink in.

Mascarpone and Amaretti Trifle

½ Cup Toasted Almonds – finely chopped
¼ Cup Amaretti Liqueur
15 Oz Ricotta Cheese – drained
1 tsp Lemon Zest
1 tsp Vanilla
1 Cup Raspberry Preserves – strained of seeds

2 Cups Amaretti Di Saronno Cookies –
crushed
8 Oz Mascarpone Cheese
½ Cup Sugar
1 tsp Orange Zest
4 Oz Chocolate Chips

Mix the chopped almonds and crushed cookies together with the liqueur and toss well to make sure all well combined.

In a large bowl, combine the mascarpone, ricotta, sugar, zests, and vanilla with electric beaters until well mixed. Fold in the chocolate chips. I prefer to use the mini chocolate chips, but either works.

In a 1-quart serving bowl, layer ½ of the cookie mixture on the bottom, then ½ of the cheese mixture; repeat with cookie mixture and then cheese mixture.

Cover and refrigerate for at least 5 hours, then top with raspberry preserves. Cover and refrigerate overnight.

Note: You can also top with a Raspberry Sauce found elsewhere in this book. However, the sauce is a little thinner.

Mostaccioli

These are one of Campania's several Christmas spice cookies. They are sometimes half covered with chocolate fondant, half with white, and sometimes only with chocolate. They are also made "imbottiti," that is, stuffed with dried fruits or a chocolate cream, which seems always to be chocolate-coated and shaped more like bonbons than cookies. Having eaten many over the years, I think that these days they are most often more chocolate truffle, with the thinnest layer of spice cookie, than a cookie with a filling. This recipe is from New York–based, Neapolitan-American pastry chef, Nick Malgieri, who worked out a great recipe in his book *Great Italian Desserts*. Recipe makes 36 cookies.

Cookie Dough:

2 Cups Bleached Flour
⅓ Cup Water
½ tsp Baking Soda
¼ tsp Ground Pepper
Grated Zest of 2 Oranges

1 Cup Sugar
½ tsp Baking Powder
¼ tsp Cinnamon
¼ tsp Ground Cloves

Chocolate Icing:

6 Oz Semisweet Chocolate
¼ Cup Light Corn Syrup

¼ Cup Water
¼ Cup Sugar

Preheat oven to 325°. In a mixing bowl, combine the flour and the sugar. Pour the water into a small bowl and stir in the remaining dough ingredients. Stir the water mixture into the dry ingredients and continue mixing until the dough begins to hold together. If it seems dry, add more water, no more than a tablespoon at a time, sprinkling the water on the dough. Do not add so much water that you will have to add more flour.

Turn the dough out onto a lightly floured surface and knead a minute or so just until the dough becomes homogenous and smooth. Do not knead too much or the dough will be difficult to roll and the cookies will be tough.

Shape the dough into a flat disk about 6 inches in diameter and then wrap it in plastic. Let the dough rest at room temperature for at least 30 minutes before shaping and baking it. (Other Campanian bakers suggest letting the dough "ripen" for 1–3 days in the refrigerator.)

Place the dough on a lightly floured surface, dust the top very lightly with flour, and then roll it out to a 12" x 9" rectangle and no more than ¼ inch thick.

With a floured knife or pizza or pastry cutting wheel, cut the dough into 6 strips, each 2" x 9". Cut each strip diagonally at 2-inch intervals to make 6 diamonds. You should get 36 in all. (It is suggested that you do not mass the scraps back together—the resulting cookies will be overly tough—but bake them as they are.)

Transfer the Mostaccioli to greased cookie sheets or to cookie sheets lined with greased parchment paper. Brush them lightly with cold water. Bake in the middle level of the oven for about 20 minutes, until they are very lightly colored. Remove the cookies to a cooling rack and let cool completely.

Icing:

Chop the chocolate finely and set aside.

In a small saucepan, combine the water, the corn syrup, and the sugar. Bring to a boil, stirring often. Remove the pan from the heat and add the chopped chocolate, swirling the mixture around the pan to make sure the chocolate is immersed in the syrup. Allow to stand 3 minutes.

Whisk the icing smooth. With a pastry brush, paint icing on the underside of each Mostaccioli. Allow the Mostaccioli to dry, icing up, on a rack for 5 minutes.

Turn the cookies over and brush the tops with the icing. (If, as you work, the icing becomes firm, add 1 Tbs water and reheat it gently over low heat, stirring constantly.) Allow the icing to dry at room temperature for at least 1 hour, then ice them again and let dry again. Pack them into a tin between layers of wax paper. They keep well.

Note: I was happy to find this recipe, as this is one of those cookies that I remember from years gone by that you really don't see anymore. It would be a shame to lose them.

Nutella Sweet Bread

Pane Dolce alla Nutella

2 Cups Flour	**2 tsps Baking Powder**
¼ tsp Baking Soda	**½ tsp Salt**
1 Cup Sugar	**3 Large Eggs**
¾ Cup Plain Yogurt – not low-fat	**½ Cup + 2 Tbs Vegetable Oil**
1 tsp Vanilla Extract	**½ Cup Nutella Spread**

Preheat oven to 350° and butter and flour a loaf pan. In a large bowl, whisk together the flour, baking powder, baking soda, and salt.

In another bowl, beat the eggs together with the sugar for about 5 minutes on medium speed until light and fluffy. Scrape down the sides of the bowl and add the yogurt, oil, vanilla, and flour mixture, beating to combine well. Pour half the batter into the prepared loaf pan and drizzle in the Nutella. Run the tip of a knife through the batter a few times, then add the remainder of the batter over the top to cover. Bake for 50–55 minutes, until a tester inserted in the center comes out clean. Let the loaf cool completely before cutting. Sprinkle with powdered sugar or a little cinnamon sugar.

Note: Nutella can be a little thick, so you can thin it out in your microwave, set on low and stirring every minute or so, or set the jar in a small pan of hot water set over a low flame and stir until you get the right consistency to pour. Do not let the bottom of the Nutella burn while trying to dilute, so stir often.

Oatmeal Chocolate-Chip Cookies

1 Cup Butter – room temperature	1½ Cups Dark Brown Sugar
2 Eggs	1 Tbs Vanilla
1 tsp Baking Soda	1 tsp Sea Salt
1¾ Cups Flour	3 Cups Quick Oats
2 Cups Chocolate Chips	

Preheat oven to 350°. Line a baking sheet with parchment paper and set aside.

In an electric mixer, mix the butter and sugar together for about 2 minutes, until the butter is light and fluffy. Add the eggs, 1 at a time, baking soda, and salt. Mix until just combined. With the mixer on low, add in the flour and mix just until all is incorporated. Add the oats and, again, mix just until all combined. **Best not to overmix.**

Stir in the chocolate chips.

Using a medium-sized tablespoon, scoop a portion of the cookie dough and drop on prepared cookie sheet. Place the cookies 2 inches apart to allow for spreading. Bake for 8–10 minutes until golden around the edges, but still a little soft in the center. **Do not overbake**. Let cool on baking sheet for 2–3 minutes and transfer to a rack to cool. Don't store until totally cooled.

Old-Fashioned Rice Pudding

5 Cups Whole Milk, or 3 Cups Whole Milk and 2 Cups Half-and-Half	½ tsp Cinnamon
	2 tsps Vanilla Extract
⅔ Cup Rice	¼ tsp Nutmeg – optional
⅓–½ Cup Sugar	⅓ Cup Raisins
3 Tbs Butter – unsalted	2 Large Egg Yolks

Combine 4 cups of milk or milk combination, rice, butter, cinnamon, nutmeg, and salt in a large, heavy saucepan. Simmer over low heat until rice is tender and the mixture is creamy, stirring often for about 1 hour. Remove from heat and stir in the raisins and vanilla. Pour remaining milk into a small, heavy saucepan and bring to a simmer. Whisk egg yolks in a medium bowl and gradually whisk the hot milk into the beaten eggs. Do this very slowly at first so as not to cook the eggs. Return the mixture to the same saucepan. Stir over medium heat until a thermometer registers 160°. This should take about 3 or 4 minutes. Be very careful to not let this boil. Stir egg mixture slowly into the rice mixture. Transfer entire mixture to a glass or ceramic bowl. Cover and chill before serving. If too thick, add a little more milk.

Original Cheesecake

4 (8 Oz) Packages Cream Cheese
6 Eggs – large
1½ Cups Sugar
2 Tbs Cornstarch
½ Cup Butter – unsalted, melted

1 Tbs Lemon Juice – freshly squeezed, preferably
2 Cups Sour Cream – not low-fat
Pinch of Salt

Preheat oven to 450°. In blender, add ingredients in order given and blend until smooth. This might have to be done in 2 batches. If using mixer, put ingredients into large bowl and beat for about 15 minutes. Pour into a large 10 or 12-inch springform pan that has been lightly greased. Put this pan in a larger pan, adding hot water until it reaches halfway up the side of the springform pan. Bake for 1–1½ hours until top is slightly brown. Allow to cool to room temperature and then chill thoroughly for several hours and preferably overnight.

Note: This was one of the first cheesecakes I attempted to bake for a holiday sometime in the 1960s. It remained my favorite go-to cheesecake recipe until I became more adventurous.

Pan di Spagna

Sponge Cake

5 Large Eggs – room temperature
2½ Cups Flour

1 Cup Sugar
2 tsps Baking Powder

Preheat your oven to 350° and grease and flour a 9-inch springform pan. In a large bowl of an electric mixer, beat the eggs and sugar for 2–3 minutes on medium speed. Add the flour and baking powder and beat for an additional 3 minutes until the batter is smooth. Pour the batter into the prepared pan and bake for 40–50 minutes, until a toothpick inserted into the center comes out clean. Cool on a wire rack and then cool completely before serving.

Note: Pan di Spagna is the basis for many Italian desserts, like tiramisu, and can also be eaten alone with coffee or at breakfast.

Panna Cotta

Cooked Milk

1 Cup Whole Milk	2½ tsps + ⅛ tsp Plain Gelatin
3 Cups Heavy Cream	1 Vanilla Bean or Vanilla Extract
6 Tbs Sugar	Pinch of Salt

Sprinkle the gelatin over the milk in a medium saucepan and let sit until the gelatins softens, about 10 minutes.

Meanwhile, fill a large bowl halfway with ice water. Place cream in a 4-cup measuring cup. Cut vanilla bean in half lengthwise. Using tip of paring knife, scrape out seeds. Add vanilla bean and seeds to cream and set aside. Set 8 4-Oz ramekins on a baking sheet.

Heat milk and gelatin mixture over high heat, stirring constantly, until the gelatin is dissolved and the mixture registers 135° (about 1½–2 minutes). Take off heat, add sugar and salt, and stir until dissolved.

Stirring constantly, slowly pour cream mixture into milk mixture, then transfer to medium bowl and set over the bowl of ice water. Stir frequently until slightly thickened. This will take about 10 minutes. Strain mixture into 8-cup liquid measuring cup, and then distribute evenly among the ramekins.

Wrap baking sheet in plastic wrap, but do not let the plastic touch the surface of the cream. Refrigerate overnight or for at least 12 hours.

To unmold, fill a small bowl with boiling water. Dip the ramekin into the water for 3 seconds. Loosen the edges of the Panna Cotta. Dip again and invert onto serving plate with a ridge.

Pastia

A Traditional Italian Easter Dish

½ Lb Thin Egg Noodles
6 Eggs
1¼ tsp Crushed Cinnamon
½ tsp Vanilla

2¾ Cups Milk
½ Stick Butter
2½ Cups Sugar
Pinch of Nutmeg

Preheat oven to 350°. Boil the egg noodles and then rinse quickly in cold water to cool. Put ½ stick of butter in the noodles and mix in ¾ cup milk. Mix an additional 2 cups of milk with the eggs, cinnamon, nutmeg, sugar, and vanilla.

Spread the noodles out in a well-greased baking pan. Pour the liquid evenly over the noodles and bake 1–1½ hours. Remove from oven. Cool and then refrigerate to set.

Pastia con Ricotta

A Little Heavier Dish with Ricotta

1 Lb Thin Egg Noodles – Cooked
½ Cup Butter
1½ Cups Sugar
1 Quart Milk
1 Pint Heavy Cream

1 Oz Anise Extract – optional
3 Tbs Vanilla Extract
12 Eggs
8 Oz Whole-Milk Ricotta – drained

Preheat the oven to 350°. In a large mixing bowl, combine the noodles, butter, sugar, milk, cream, anise (if using), vanilla, eggs, and ricotta. Mix well and spoon into a 9" x 13" glass baking dish. Bake for 1¼ hours until the top is golden and a knife inserted in the center comes out clean. Cool and then set in refrigerator to set. Cinnamon or cardamom can be substituted for the anise.

Pasticciera Crema

A Very Basic Pastry Cream

1½ Qts Whole Milk – not low-fat or skim
1½ tsps Vanilla Extract
Peel of 2 Large Lemons – cut into long strips
8 Large Egg Yolks – at room temperature*

2¼ Cups Sugar
⅔ Cup Cornstarch
*Save the egg white for Francesca's
  Sugar Crisps

Over low heat, slowly bring the milk, vanilla, and lemon peel to a boil in a large, heavy-bottomed pot, stirring often. Beat the egg yolks and the sugar together in a large bowl until light and fluffy. Add the cornstarch and blend well until all incorporated. Remove milk mixture from the heat and remove the lemon peels. Very slowly stir ¾ cup of the hot mixture into the eggs, constantly stirring so as not to cook the eggs. Then slowly stir this egg mixture into the remaining hot milk, again stirring constantly. Stirring is key in this recipe. When all is thoroughly incorporated, return the pan to a high heat and let it come to a boil and boil for about 2 minutes, always stirring constantly until it becomes thick and creamy.

Note: This is a basic recipe for any dessert that calls for a pastry cream filling. It can be made chocolate simply be eliminating the lemon peel and stirring ¾ cup of unsweetened cocoa powder into the hot milk, making sure it is well blended before adding it to the egg mixture. Also, different liquors can be added to achieve different flavors. A great cream-puff filler.

Pasticciotti

Pasticciotti are Sweet Italian Cream-Filled Pastries

Pastry:

2 Cups Flour
½ Cup Sugar
1 Egg
1 tsp Vanilla
Pinch of Salt

1 tsp Baking Powder
¼ Cup Butter
¼ Cup Crisco
¼ Cup Whole Milk

Filling:

3 Tbs Cornstarch	½ Cup Sugar
½ Cup Heavy Cream	1 Cup Whole Milk
2 Egg Yolks	1 Tbs Butter
1 tsp Vanilla Extract	1 Egg – beaten for brushing

Making the Custard:

Sift the cornstarch and sugar and spoon into a saucepan. Add the milk, heavy cream, and whisk lightly until you have a smooth mixture free of lumps. Whisk in the egg and then heat on medium, whisking constantly, until the custard thickens.

Mix the butter and almond extract. Remove from the heat and cover the custard with plastic wrap set directly on the custard to prevent the custard from forming a skin as it cools.

To Make the Pastry:

In a food processor, add the flour, sugar, salt, and baking powder. Pulse until all is mixed. Add the butter and Crisco and pulse again until the mixture looks like crumbly cornmeal. Add egg, milk, and vanilla and mix until the dough starts to form into a ball and pulls away from the sides of the bowl.

Turn the dough out onto a lightly floured board and lightly work the dough until it is smooth. Divide the dough into 2 flattened rounds, cover with plastic wrap, and refrigerate for 1 hour.

Starting with the first ball, place it onto a floured board and roll it out to ¼ inch thick. Using a 3-inch pastry cutter or a thin glass, cut out 12 rounds. Place each round into a fluted mold or a muffin mold and press all around well to remove all air. Add 2 Tbs of the custard to each of the molds and then cover each with a 3-inch round of dough. Let chill in refrigerator for a least 1 hour or overnight. Brush tops with egg wash and bake at 425° for 15–18 minutes.

Pastry Dough #2:

(Makes a lighter pastry)

1¾ Cups Flour	Pinch of Salt
½ Cup Sugar	1 Egg + 1 Egg Yolk
1 tsp Vanilla Extract	1 tsp Baking Powder
½ Cup Butter	2 Tbs Butter – cubed

Work in food processor same as #1. Divide in 2 and chill for 1 hour.

Pastiera di Riso

Although Pastiera di Riso is generally associated with Easter, our family enjoys it at other holidays or family get-togethers, too!

3¼ Cups Flour	⅓ Cup Sugar – or to taste
1½ tsp Baking Powder	¾ tsp Salt
2 Sticks Butter – cold, diced	3 Eggs – beaten

Pastry:

Pulse flour, sugar, baking powder, and salt in food processor until well combined. Add butter and pulse until the mixture resembles coarse meal with some pea-sized lumps. Add eggs and pulse until all just incorporated and dough begins to form large clumps or ball.

Turn out dough onto a work surface and divide into 6 portions. With the heel of your hand, massage each portion a few times in a forward motion to help distribute fat. Gather dough together using a pastry scraper and form into a thick log. Cut off ⅔ of the log and form into a large rectangle for the bottom of the pie. Form the remaining piece into a smaller rectangle for the top. Chill each, wrapped in plastic wrap, until firm, at least 30 minutes. This recipe is for a 9" x 13" baking pan.

Filling:

¾ Cup Arborio Rice	4 Cups Water
5 Egg Yolks – divided	⅔ Cup Sugar
1½ Tbs Cornstarch	¼ Cup Flour
2 Cups Whole Milk	1½ tsp Vanilla or Almond Extract – your choice
1 Lb Ricotta – drained	1½ tsps Orange Zest – grated
1½ tsps Lemon Zest – grated	¼ tsp Cinnamon
¼ tsp Nutmeg	1 Large Egg – lightly beaten
Pinch of Salt to Taste	

Bring rice and well-salted water to a boil in a 2-quart saucepan, then reduce heat and simmer, covered, until rice is tender (about 20 minutes). Drain in strainer and rinse quickly under cold water. Drain well, shaking several times to release excess water.

Whisk together 3 yolks and sugar in a heatproof bowl, then whisk in cornstarch and flour until smooth (this mixture should be very thick), then boil, whisking for 1 minute. Remove from heat and whisk in butter and vanilla or almond extract. Transfer to a bowl and chill, covering the surface with plastic wrap, for about 2 hours.

Stir together ricotta, custard, and remaining yolks, then stir in zests, nutmeg, cinnamon, salt, and cooked rice.

Assemble:

Preheat oven to 350°. Generously butter a 9″ x 13″ baking dish and line the bottom with an overlapping double layer of foil, leaving at least 2 inches of overhang on both ends, then generously butter foil.

Roll out larger piece of dough between 2 sheets of wax paper or plastic wrap to a 11″ x 15″ rectangle (about ⅛ inch thick). If dough becomes too soft, chill or freeze until firm. Remove top sheet of paper and invert dough into baking pan, patting it gently to fit into pan. Chill while working with second piece of dough. Roll out remaining dough again between sheets of wax paper the same way. Cut 12 (¾-inch-wide) long strips. (The pastry dough is soft and tears easily when it gets too soft but patches easily too. Best to keep it chilled.)

Spread filling in pan, smooth top, and arrange 6 strips diagonally across filling, trimming ends. Arrange remaining 6 strips, diagonally across first strips to form a lattice effect on top with diamond-shaped spaces. Alternately, you can just cut strips to go across short end and then across the long end. Trim lattice to fit pan, then fold outside crust over filling, crimping to make a border. Brush pastry evenly with a beaten egg.

Bake pie on middle rack of oven until pastry is golden brown and filling is puffed and set, about 1½ hours, loosely covering top of pie with foil after 45 minutes to prevent the crust from becoming too brown. Transfer to a rack to cool. When completely cool, carefully lift pie out of pan using foil and transfer to serving dish. Chill if not serving immediately, but bring to room temperature or a bit warm to serve.

Note: Pastry dough can be made and chilled 1 day in advance and kept chilled. Rice can also be prepared 1 day in advance and kept chilled.

Pastierra di Arancia

4 Cups Flour	1 Cup Sugar
2 tsps Baking Powder	4 Eggs
1 Stick Unsalted Butter – melted	½ Cup Whole Milk
1 Additional Stick Unsalted Butter – room temperature	2 Cups Sugar
	3 Lbs Whole Milk Ricotta
1 Cup Heavy Cream	14 Eggs
5 tsps Vanilla Extract	2 Cups Cooked Arborio Rice – or your favorite
Zest of 1 Large Orange	

First make the crust: Place the flour, sugar, baking powder, eggs, melted butter, and milk in a large bowl of an electric mixer and beat on medium speed for 5 minutes until smooth.

Lightly butter a 10″ x 15″ baking dish. Press the dough into the bottom and up the sides of the dish as evenly as possible. Set aside. Note: If your kitchen is very warm, refrigerate the pan until the filling is ready.

Next, make the filling: Preheat the oven to 350°. Beat the butter and sugar in a large bowl with an electric mixer on medium speed until combined for 3–4 minutes. Add the ricotta, heavy cream, eggs, and vanilla and continue beating until all are fully incorporated, scraping down the sides with a rubber spatula several times. Fold in the rice and orange zest with the spatula.

Pour the filling over the prepared crust and bake until the edges are golden brown and set but the center is still a little jiggly—1 hour 45 minutes to 2 hours 15 minutes. Let cool thoroughly before slicing.

Pesca Semifreddo

Iced Peach Souffle

3 Large Fresh Peaches – peeled and sliced	⅓ Cup Sugar
1 tsp Fresh Lemon Juice	1½ Cups Whipping Cream
½ Cup Greek Yogurt	½ tsp Vanilla Extract

Reserve some extra peaches for decorating.

In a small saucepan over medium-low heat, combine the peaches, sugar, and lemon juice. Stir to incorporate the sugar and bring the mixture to a slow boil. With the back of a fork, mash the peaches while they are cooking, stirring until the mixture is hot and the sugar is dissolved. Transfer this peach sauce to a bowl and let cool. When cool enough, refrigerate for about an hour until very cold (about 30–45 minutes).

When the peaches are almost ready, in a large bowl, whip the cream until stiff. Add the vanilla to the yogurt and fold into the whipped cream. Next, gently fold in the peach sauce. Pour the mixture into an 8-inch loaf pan or individual freezable serving dishes. For the loaf pan size, freeze about 8 hours.

Note: You can make this using a 15-Oz can of sliced peaches, drained. Use ¾ of the peaches for the sauce and reserve the rest for decorating the top of the souffle. For years our anniversary dessert has been Peach Melba or some form of it. This is as close as I can get to Peach Melba this year. I made a trial batch using canned peaches and it was delicious. It won't disappoint.

Pistacchio e Limone Cantucci

1¾ Flour – plus extra for dusting
1½ tsp Baking Powder
½ Cup Lemon Zest – or to taste
3 Eggs – lightly beaten

¾ Cup Sugar
Pinch of Sea Salt
¾ Cup Shelled Pistachios – unsalted

Preheat oven to 350°. In a large bowl, whisk together flour, sugar, baking powder, and salt. Stir in the lemon zest and nuts until well combined. Add eggs, one at a time, and stir dough until it all comes together. Divide dough into 3 pieces.

On a board that has been lightly floured, shape each piece into a log that is about 9 inches long and 1½ inches wide. Place each log on a baking pan lined with parchment paper. Do not place them too close together, as they will expand while baking.

Bake logs, rotating the pans halfway through baking, and continue baking until they are golden and fairly firm to the touch (about 22–25 minutes). Transfer baking pans to a wire rack to let cool for about 5–7 minutes. Using a serrated knife, cut the logs crosswise, slightly on an angle, into ½-inch slices. Arrange the slices standing upright, leaving room in between each slice, on the baking sheet and bake for 20 more minutes. Remove from oven and baking pan and cool completely on wire rack.

Pistachio Delight

Dolce di Pistachio

1 Envelope Unflavored Gelatin	2 Eggs – well beaten
¼ Cup Cold Water	1 Tbs Liqueur – your favorite
1¼ Cups Milk	½ Pint Heavy Cream
⅓ Cup Sugar	¼ Cup Chopped Pistachios

Soften gelatin in cold water. Scald milk in the top of a double boiler, add gelatin, sugar, and nuts and stir until the gelatin and sugar are dissolved. Pour hot milk mixture slowly over well-beaten eggs, stirring as you do so that the eggs do not cook. Return to the double boiler.

Cook over high, but not to boiling, heat until slightly thickened. Do not allow the custard to boil.

When slightly thickened, remove from heat, cool just a bit, and then chill until thickened but not completely set.

Whip cream until stiff and fold into the custard mixture. Fold in desired liqueur (I use Amaretto) and pour into a 1-quart mold or individual serving cups and chill at least 4 hours before serving.

Torta al Pistacchio

Un Dolce Siciliano

Cake:

1⅔ Cups Shelled Pistachios	6 Eggs – divided, room temperature
Pinch of Kosher Salt or Sea Salt	¾ Cup Sugar
Zest of 1 Large Lemon	Powdered Sugar – for dusting

Cream Filling:

1 Cup Whole-Milk Ricotta – drained	⅔ Cup Heavy Cream
½ Cup Mascarpone – see note*	¼–⅓ Cup Powdered Sugar
½ tsp Vanilla Extract or Vanilla Paste	

Putting It Together:

First, make the cake. Preheat the oven to 325° with your rack in the center of the oven. Butter the bottom and sides of a 9-inch springform pan with at least 2¾-inch-high sides. Process the pistachios in a food processor in 2 batches until they are the texture of fine cornmeal. Leave a few slightly larger pieces for interest. Set aside. Take care to process most of them finely and not coarsely, as coarsely ground nuts will affect the delicate texture of the cake.

Using a stand mixer fitted with the whisk attachment, beat the egg whites and salt at low speed until frothy, then raise the speed to medium and beat until they hold soft peaks. Increase the speed to medium-high and gradually add 6 Tbs of the granulated sugar and continue to beat until medium-firm peaks form.

In a separate bowl, beat the yolks with the remaining 6 Tbs granulated sugar at medium speed until they are thick and pale (about 4 minutes). Mix in the lemon zest. Use a large spatula to gently fold the egg yolk mixture into the whites. Gently fold in the ground pistachios in 3 additions, folding each time just until the nuts are incorporated. Do not overmix.

Spread the batter evenly in the prepared pan. Bake until the cake is golden and firm to the touch and pulls away from the sides of the pan (about 40 minutes). A toothpick inserted near the center should come out clean. Cool the cake in the pan on a wire rack for 20 minutes, then carefully remove the sides of the pan and let cool completely. Before loosening the sides, I like to run a small metal spatula around the inside of the pan to make sure nothing is sticking.

Transfer the cooled cake on its base to a serving platter, or carefully run a large, metal cake lifter under the cake and slide it directly onto the platter.

Making the Ricotta Cream:

Using a mixer with the whisk attachment, briefly beat the ricotta on medium speed until creamy. Add the heavy cream, mascarpone, ¼ cup powdered sugar, and vanilla extract (or paste and beat briefly on low to combine the ingredients). Increase the speed to medium-high and beat until the mixture begins to thicken. Taste and add the rest of the powdered sugar, if needed. Beat until just stiff.

Note: If you don't want to use mascarpone, just add an additional ½ cup well-drained ricotta.

Putting It All Together:

Using a large serrated knife, slice the cake horizontally into two layers and set the top layer aside. Spread the ricotta cream over the bottom layer. Place the top layer carefully over the filling. Press down very lightly to hold firmly, but not too hard because the filling will ooze out. Or, as an alternative, because this cake is not very tall, just cut into wedges to serve and put a generous dollop of the cream mixture on top. Dust with powdered sugar and serve.

Praline Cream Puff Ring

1 Cup Water	**4 Egg Yolks**
½ Cup (1 Stick) Butter – unsalted	**1 Egg – beaten for glazing**
¾ tsp Salt	**⅓ Cup Almonds – sliced**
1 Cup Flour – sifted	

Preheat oven to 400°. Combine water, butter, and salt in heavy saucepan and bring to a boil. Remove from heat. Add the flour all at once and beat with a wooden spoon until all incorporated. Set pan over medium heat and beat until the mixture pulls away from the sides of the pan. Let cook for 5 minutes. Beat in the egg yolks one at a time until the mixture is smooth. Set aside. Draw 8 4-inch circles on parchment paper. Turn paper over and fit onto baking sheet. Spoon dough into pastry ring inside the circle. Pipe a third ring atop the middle of the 2 circles. Brush lightly with glaze and sprinkle with almonds. Repeat the same process with the remaining circles. Bake for 45 minutes and then turn off the heat. Open the oven door halfway and let the pastry stand until dry and cool for about 1 hour. Remove from oven and if perfectly cool, cut the lids off the rings and reserve.

Praline:

½ Cup Powdered Sugar	**¼ Cup Sliced Almonds**

Grease baking sheet. Cook sugar and almonds in heavy small saucepan over medium heat until caramelized, stirring constantly for about 10 minutes. Immediately pour onto the greased baking sheet and let cool completely. Break into pieces and transfer to a food processor and grind to a powder. This can be prepared a day or two ahead of time and stored in an airtight container.

Pastry Cream:

1 Cup Milk	**2 Tbs All-Purpose Flour**
3 Egg Yolks	**1 Cup Whipping Cream**

¼ Cup Sugar	1 Pint Strawberries – rinsed, drained dry,
1 tsp Vanilla	and thinly sliced

Bring milk to a boil in a heavy saucepan. Whisk yolks, sugar, and vanilla in a bowl until thick and light. Blend in flour. Gradually whisk in milk. Return to saucepan. Set over medium heat and bring to a boil, stirring constantly. Reduce heat and simmer until thick, 2–4 minutes, always stirring constantly. Transfer to bowl. Rub a piece of butter over the surface to prevent a skin from forming. Cool completely. Fold the praline into this mixture. This also can be prepared a day ahead of time and kept refrigerated. Beat cream until slightly stiff and holding shape and fold into the praline pastry cream mixture.

Assembly:

Praline Cream – already prepared	Powdered Sugar
Strawberries – already drained and sliced	

Spoon praline cream mixture into pastry bag fitted with a plain tip. Pipe into the bottom half of each in cream puff ring. Arrange strawberries in the cream. Top with pastry lid, sprinkle with powdered sugar, and serve. A little bit of work, but this makes an impressively delicious dessert.

Pumpkin Cake Roll

A Thanksgiving Day Dessert Must

3 Eggs – Large	1 tsp Baking Powder
1 Cup Sugar	2 tsps Cinnamon
⅔ Cup Canned Pumpkin	½ tsp Salt
1 tsp Lemon Juice – freshly squeezed	¾ tsp Nutmeg
¾ Cup Flour	Powdered Sugar

Beat eggs at high speed for about 5 minutes while gradually adding the sugar. Stir in the pumpkin and fresh lemon juice. Combine the flour, baking powder, cinnamon, salt, and nutmeg and fold into the pumpkin mixture. Spread in greased and floured sheet pan, approx. 15" x 10" x 1". Bake at 375° for 15 minutes. Turn out immediately onto a kitchen towel that has been sprinkled with powdered sugar. Roll towel and cake together, from the short end, and allow to cool. Carefully and slowly so it does not crack, unroll and fill.

Filling:

1 Cup Powdered Sugar

8 Oz Cream Cheese or 12 Oz Mascarpone*

1 Cup Chopped Walnuts

4 Tbs Butter – softened

1 tsp Vanilla

Combine all ingredients except the nuts and beat until smooth. Spread the cheese mixture on the cake roll and sprinkle evenly with the chopped nuts. Reroll and put on platter, seam side down, and sprinkle with more powdered sugar.

Note: For a richer filling, use 12 Oz Mascarpone cheese and mix with 1¼ cups sifted powdered sugar, 2 Tbs heavy cream, 1 pinch of salt, ½ cup chopped nuts, and 1½ tsps vanilla. Combine as above and spread on cake. This dessert is so popular that I have to make two at Thanksgiving.

Quaresimali

For the Dough:

1¼ Cups Whole Unblanched (with Skins) Almonds – toasted and roughly ground (easily done in processor)

1 Cup Sugar

1½ Cups Flour

For the "Pisto":

1 tsp Fine Ground White Pepper

¼ tsp Ground Cinnamon

2 Eggs

⅓ Cup Finely Chopped Orange Peel and Candied Citron

½ tsp Finely Grated Nutmeg

¼ tsp Ground Cloves

1¼ Cup Whole Unblanched (with Skins) Almonds – toasted

1 Egg Beaten – for wash

Preheat the oven to 325° and line a baking sheet with parchment paper. On a board or in a large bowl, mix together the ground almonds, the sugar, flour, and the "pisto," which is the white pepper, nutmeg, cinnamon, and cloves combined. Make a well and break the eggs in. Using a fork, or your fingers, gradually incorporate the eggs into the dry ingredients, as if you were making pasta dough.

Once you have obtained a sticky dough, work in the whole almonds and the candied peels. If you are using a bowl, turn the dough out onto a lightly floured board.

Shape the dough into 3 logs, each 9" x 1½" and about ¾ inch high. Place the logs on a cookie sheet lined with parchment and brush them with beaten egg. Bake for 35 minutes. Remove from the oven and let cool on the pan for 15 minutes. Reduce the oven temperature to 300°.

With a metal spatula, remove the logs from the paper and place them on a cutting board. Cut them into ½-inch-wide, crosswise slices. Return the biscotti to the baking sheet, arranging them standing up and not touching each other.

Bake for another 25 minutes and then cool the cookies on a rack. Store in a tin. Makes about 50–54 Biscotti, 1½ inches wide by ½ inch thick.

Note: This is another one of those recipes that is almost forgotten and why I am including it. Quaresima is Italian for lent, and Quaresimali qualify as Lenten because they are made without fat—or at least no butter, oil, or lard. More than making up for that lack, however, is the fat in the huge amount of almonds. Ground almonds are the base of the dough, which is seasoned both sharply and sweetly with a "pisto" of white pepper, nutmeg, cinnamon, and clove. Whole almonds stud every bite. Similar quaresimali are made in various regions of Italy, often with hazelnuts.

Rice Custard, Tuscan Style

Torta di Riso alla Tuscano

1¼ Cup Sugar – plus extra to dust pan	½ Cup Arborio Rice – not rinsed
1 Scant tsp Salt – divided	6 Eggs
¼ Cup Rum, Brandy, or Vin Santo	Zest of 1 Large Orange
1 tsp Vanilla Extract	2 Cups Milk – room temperature or warm

Butter or grease a 9 or 10-inch cake pan and sprinkle the pan with sugar. Use one with a solid bottom and definitely not a springform pan or the liquid will leak out. Set oven temperature to 350°.

Cook the rice in boiling water, adding ½ tsp of salt. You want the rice to be al dente, as it will cook further in the oven while baking, so remove the rice after 9 or 10 minutes.

In a large mixing bowl, whisk together, eggs, sugar, rum (or your favorite), orange zest, vanilla, and ½ tsp of salt. Mix well, making sure all is combined. Add the warm milk and the rice. Stir well to get all incorporated.

Pour the mixture into the prepared pan. The rice will settle along the bottom, so do not worry when you see that happen. During the baking, the top will become like a custard, which is what makes this unique. Bake for 50–60 minutes or until the top is lightly browned. It should feel firm to the touch. A tester inserted in the center should come out clean. Remove from the oven and let cool in the pan. This is good served cold or at room temperature, but not hot, or it will be loose.

Note: On different occasions, I've made this with Amaretto, Grand Marnier, and even just orange juice.

Ricotta Cake

Una Ricotta Dolce

1¼ Cups Flour	2 Eggs – room temperature
¼ tsp Salt	1 Cup Ricotta – drained
¾ Cup Sugar	¼ Cup Vegetable Oil
Zest of 2 Oranges	2 Tbs Milk
1¼ tsp Baking Powder	

Preheat your oven to 350°. Grease and flour an 8-inch Bundt pan. In a small bowl, whisk together the flour, baking powder, and salt.

In a large bowl, beat the eggs with the sugar until light and fluffy on medium speed for about 5 minutes. Slowly incorporate the ricotta a little at a time, beating continuously. Add in the orange zest and oil a little at a time and beat for 1 minute. Add the flour mixture and continue beating. Add the milk and beat the batter until it is very smooth. Spoon the batter into the prepared Bundt pan and bake for 50–60 minutes until a cake tester comes out clean. Let the cake cool completely on a wire rack before serving.

Ricotta Orange Cake

Torta all' Arancia di Ricotta

1½ Cups Flour
¼ tsp Salt
¾ Cup Sugar
Zest of 2 Large Oranges
2 Tbs Milk

1½ tsp Baking Powder
2 Large Eggs
1 Cup Ricotta – drained
¼ Cup Vegetable Oil

Preheat oven to 350° and grease and flour an 8-inch Bundt pan and set aside. In a small bowl, whisk together the flour, baking powder, and salt.

In another bowl, beat the eggs with the sugar for about 8 minutes until light and creamy. Then add the ricotta a little at a time, beating constantly. Next, add the orange zest and oil slowly for about 1 minute until well combined. Add the flour mixture while still beating and slowly add the milk.

Beat the batter until it is smooth and then pour it into the prepared Bundt pan. Bake for 50–60 minutes until a cake tester inserted into the middle comes out clean. Cool in pan for 10–12 minutes. Cool completely on a rack.

Note: My Aunt's recipe called for an 8-inch pan. I haven't seen one that size, and my pan measures 10 inches. This works out just fine.

Savoiardi Handmade

Savoiardi Fatti con Mane

2 Eggs – separated
1 Cup + 2 Tbs Flour
1 Tbs Cornstarch

¼ Cup Sugar – plus a little extra
½ tsp Baking Powder

Preheat your oven to 350° and line a 10" x 14" pan with parchment paper. Combine the egg yolks and sugar in a bowl, and with an electric mixer, beat on medium speed for about 12–15 minutes.

In a clean bowl, with clean beaters, beat the egg whites until they hold stiff peaks and then gently fold them into the egg yolks.

In a small bowl, sift together all the flour, baking powder, and cornstarch. Fold the mixture a little at a time into the egg mixture until all completely combined.

Spoon the batter into a pastry bag fitted with a large, round tip and form 1½-inch-long logs on the baking sheet, spacing them so that they do not stick together as they spread while baking. Sprinkle with a little additional sugar and bake for 10–12 minutes (checking after 8) until they are golden. Let the cookies cool completely before serving or storing or using to make a dessert.

Note: These cookies can be used for many desserts and especially for tiramisu! If just serving as a dessert cookie, sprinkle with powdered sugar after completely cooled.

Savoiardi II

A Little Lighter Version of Italian Lady Fingers

5 Egg Whites	**4 Egg Yolks**
⅔ Cup Sugar	**1 tsp Vanilla Extract**
½ tsp Baking Powder	**1 Cup Flour**

Preheat oven to 350°. Separate eggs into two bowls. Beat the egg whites on high speed until foamy. Slowly add 2 Tbs of the sugar to the egg whites and continue to beat until still peaks form. Set aside.

Add the remaining sugar to the egg yolks and beat until pale yellow; set aside.

Sift together the flour and the baking powder onto a piece of wax paper.

Gently fold ½ of the egg whites into the egg yolks. Fold the flour mixture into the yolks and then fold in the remaining egg whites.

Scoop batter into a pastry bag with a wide tip or you can use a plastic bag with a corner snipped off.

Pipe the dough onto a greased cookie sheet in the shape of a long finger about 4 inches in length and 1¼ inches wide.

Bake for about 5–6 minutes or just until only the edges are golden brown.

Sfingi

A Sicilian Dolce

1 Lb Ricotta – whole milk, drained	2 tsps Baking Powder
3 Eggs – large	Pinch of Salt
3 Cups Presto Flour	Hot Vegetable Oil – for frying
3 Tbs Sugar	Powdered Sugar – for dusting

This is a type of Sicilian fritter very similar to Zeppole. Mix ricotta, eggs, flour, sugar, baking powder, and salt all together in a large bowl. In large pot or deep fryer, heat oil to 375°. Drop by spoonfuls carefully into the hot oil. Not too many at a time. If crowded, they will not brown and crisp. And, if the oil is not kept hot, they will just absorb the oil and be soggy. Remove from the oil, carefully, with a slotted spoon or metal strainer and sprinkle with powdered sugar. I'm not sure if Presto flour is still available. If not, any all-purpose flour should do.

Note: This is a Sicilian treat that I learned from my Mother-in-Law. For our first Christmas in our house in Smithtown, I wanted to surprise everyone at dessert time. I made several batches and carefully put them in an airtight container. When I opened the container, all that was in there was a soggy mess in a sea of oil. They must be eaten right away. Big disappointment for the new cook.

Sfogliata

Pastry Crust

1½ Cups Sifted Flour	¼ Cup Butter – unsalted
¾ tsp Salt	½ Cup Shortening
2 Tbs Sherry	

Chill all ingredients for 30 minutes before starting to make the Sfogliata. Also, it's a good idea to chill the pie plate and rolling pin.

Put flour, butter, salt, and shortening in a bowl and cut the shortening into the flour with a pastry blender or, as my Grandmother did it, using two knives. Do this until what you have resembles the size of very coarse crumbs. Add only enough sherry to make everything stick together. Wrap pastry in waxed paper and chill in refrigerator for 30 minutes.

Divide dough into 2 parts. Roll bottom crust little larger that the top crust, if you are making a 2-crust pie. Otherwise, roll even. Roll out on a lightly floured board from the center to the edges. Place the crust in chilled pie pan and press flat with fingers. Prick bottom and sides well with a fork. Flute the edges. Place shell in refrigerator until ready to bake.

Meanwhile, preheat oven to 450°. Place shell in oven and bake for 10 minutes until brown. Cool completely. Fill with any desired filling.

Note: This is an old-fashioned recipe, and this is how it was given to me. The recipe makes a dough for 2 9-inch pie shells or 1 9-inch double-crust pie. The sherry is said to make the crust flaky and light. I've read that some people now use vodka.

Snickerdoodles

1¼ Cups Flour	1 tsp Cream of Tartar
½ tsp Baking Soda	¼ tsp Salt
¾ Cup Sugar	1 Egg – room temperature
1 tsp Vanilla	1 Tbs Ground Cinnamon – or to taste
½ Cup Butter – softened	Extra Sugar and Cinnamon – for rolling

Cream butter and sugar until light and fluffy. Beat in egg. Sift all dry ingredients together and add to creamed mixture and mix in very well. Refrigerate for at least 1 hour or even overnight.

Preheat oven to 375° (convection) or 400° (regular oven). Line a baking sheet with parchment paper. Whisk cinnamon and the sugar (your choice of amounts) in a separate bowl. Using a 1-inch ice cream scoop, portion out cookies and roll into little balls, the size of large walnuts, using your hands. Roll the balls in the cinnamon-sugar mixture and place on prepared baking sheet. Space them apart as they will spread while baking.

Bake just until edges are slightly browned and firm, but the centers are puffed (about 8–10 minutes). Let cool on baking sheets for 10 minutes before transferring to a wire rack to cool completely.

St. Lucy Cookies

A December 13 Cookie

4½ –5 Cups Flour
1 Cup Sugar – divided
½ tsp Salt
2 Eggs – large and room temperature

1 Cup Milk – whole
1 tsp Vanilla
Vegetable Oil – for deep frying
Powdered Sugar – to sprinkle

In a bowl, mix together 4 cups of flour, 2 Tbs of sugar, and the salt. In a medium bowl, whisk the eggs and milk together and add the vanilla. Stir this mixture into the flour, adding enough additional flour to make a soft ball of dough. On a floured surface, knead the dough until smooth and no longer sticky. Divide the dough in half and roll out each piece to a 12" x 15" rectangle. Sprinkle each rectangle evenly with half the remaining sugar and roll up tightly like a jelly roll. Cut the rolls into ½-inch-thick slices. In a deep frying pan or electric deep fryer, heat the oil to 375°. Fry the cookies a few at a time until golden brown. Remove with a slotted spoon to a paper-covered dish to drain and cool. Sprinkle with powdered sugar and serve. This day honors St. Luci as the Patron Saint of Eyesight because her eyes were gouged out just before she was martyred. Her face was believed to have been veiled in white lace after her death, and that's the reason for the powdered sugar.

Note: December 13 Feast Day of St. Lucy. My confirmation name is Lucia, after my Great-Grandmother. She was my Little Nonna's Mother. On December 13, a cookie very similar to this was made for me (well, probably for the entire family) by my little Nonna Agnese, or sometimes she made me a wheat dish called Cuccia.

Strawberry-Rhubarb Tart

1 9" Pie Shell
2 Cups Fresh Strawberries
1 tsp Lemon Juice
Pinch of Salt

2½ Cups Fresh Rhubarb – chopped
1¼ Cups Granulated Sugar
3 Tbs Butter – cubed

Chill the prepared pie crust for one hour. Preheat the oven to 375°. Rinse, destem, and cut the strawberries in half. For the filling, combine the rhubarb, strawberries, sugar, salt, and lemon juice in a bowl and toss to combine all. Pour into the chilled crust. Dot the top of the filling with the butter cubes. Bake in a preheated oven for 50–60 minutes, or until the filling begins to bubble and the rhubarb is tender.

Tiramisu

Pick Me Up

11 Oz Italian Lady Fingers or Savoiardi	**4 Eggs – yolks only**
11 Oz Mascarpone Cheese	**2 Egg Whites – beaten stiff**
3 Oz Powdered Sugar	**1 Cup Espresso**
¾ Cup Heavy Cream – whipped	**2 Tbs Brandy or Rum – or your favorite liqueur**
3 Tbs Cocoa	**¾ Cup Sugar**

Beat the egg yolks with the powdered sugar until creamy and thick. Slowly add the rum, cognac, or your favorite liqueur while beating.

Whisk the mascarpone until smooth and fold into the egg yolk mixture. Beat the egg whites until they hold stiff peaks, but not too dry, and gently fold into the egg mixture. Whip the cream and gently fold into the egg mixture.

Divide the lady fingers or savoiardi into 2 groups (each group suitable for 1 layer placed close enough so that there are not any gaps). Cut as necessary to fill in holes. Place first layer of "dry" savoiardi on bottom of pan, leaving no spaces or holes, and spread evenly with ½ of the mascarpone mixture. Top this with 1 layer of soaked savoiardi, again leaving no holes or spaces, and spread with remainder of the mascarpone mixture.

Sprinkle with cocoa powder and a little shaved dark semisweet chocolate (optional). Refrigerate for at least 6 hours before serving.

Note: I know some recipes call for topping the last layer with whipped cream. That is not the way I've had it in Italy, but do so if that's the way your family likes it.

Torta di Montefollonico

3 Eggs	**1 Envelope Lievito Pane degli Angeli**
¾ Cup Sugar	**Pinch of Salt**

⅓ Cup Oil – mix ½ vegetable oil
with ½ olive oil
1 Lemon – zested and juiced
1½ Cups Flour

1–2 tsps Vanilla or Almond Extract
4 Oz Greek Yogurt – drained
Powdered Sugar – for dusting

Preheat oven to 360°. Beat eggs with sugar until yellow and creamy. Add oil slowly to egg mixture while beating. Blend in lemon zest and juice. Add yogurt and blend in well. Add flour, salt, and Lievito. Bake in buttered and floured 10-inch round pan (I use a 10-inch glass deep-dish pie plate) for 20–25 minutes. Top should be a light golden color. Cool and dust with powdered sugar.

Note: Lievito Pane degli Angeli is a vanilla-flavored rising agent for pastries and can be found in Italian specialty stores. I learned how to make this dessert when visiting my Cousins in Montefollonico. Sometimes pignoli are sprinkled on top just before baking. It can be eaten for breakfast or served for dessert with Vin Santo. It can even be sliced in half, when completely cooled, and filled with a pastry cream.

Torta di Riso

Italian Rice Cake

4 Cups Whole Milk
Pinch of Salt
1 tsp Vanilla Extract
⅓ Cup Raisins
2 Tbs Cognac, Marsala, or Vin Santo
Breadcrumbs – mixed with 1 Tbs sugar for
dusting pan

1 Cup Arborio Rice – uncooked
1 Lemon – peel only
½ Cup Sugar
2 Eggs + 2 Egg Yolks
Butter – to grease pan
Powdered Sugar – for dusting cake

In a saucepan, over low heat, add the milk, rice, lemon peel, vanilla, and a pinch of salt. Bring the milk to a slow simmer and cook the rice until al dente (about 20–30 minutes). Pour all into a medium bowl stirring occasionally until it cools down. Remove the lemon peel.

Soak the raisins in the liqueur of your choice.

Add the sugar to the rice mixture along with the lightly beaten eggs, raisins, liqueur, and stir very well.

Butter very well a 9" x 13"glass baking dish and dust with the breadcrumbs. Pour the batter into the prepared dish and sprinkle with more breadcrumbs.

Place in the oven and cook for 45–40 minutes. It should be golden on top. Insert a tester into the middle of the cake, and if it comes out clean, the cake is done.

Turn off the oven and let the cake rest inside to dry out a bit more for about 5 minutes. Remove and let cool completely. When cool, sprinkle with powdered sugar.

Tres Leches Cake

½ Cup Flour	2 tsps Baking Powder
¾ Tsp Kosher Salt	3 Large or Extra-Large Eggs
1 Cup + 5 Tbs Sugar	2 tsps Vanilla Extract
½ Cup Whole Milk	1¼ Cups Heavy Cream
1 (12 Oz) Can Evaporated Milk	1 (14 Oz) Can Sweetened Condensed Milk
½ tsp Almond Extract	¾ tsp Vanilla Extract
Powdered Sugar – for dusting	2 tsps Vanilla Extract

Preheat oven to 350°. Sift flour, baking powder, and salt into a bowl and set aside. Place eggs, 1 cup of sugar, and vanilla in the bowl of an electric mixer fitted with the paddle attachment. Beat on medium-high speed for 8–10 minutes until very light yellow and fluffy. Reduce the speed to low and slowly add ½ of the flour mixture, then milk, and then the rest of the flour mixture. Scrape the inside and bottom of the bowl to make sure the batter is well mixed. Give it another stirring with the electric mixer and pour into a buttered 9" x 13" baking dish. Bake for 25 minutes, until the cake springs back when the top is touched lightly, and a cake tester comes out clean. Let cool in the pan for 30 minutes.

In a 4-cup measuring cup, whisk together heavy cream, evaporated milk, condensed milk, almond extract, and vanilla extract. Using a skewer, poke holes all over the cooled cake and slowly pour the cream mixture over the cake, allowing it to be absorbed completely before continuing to pour more liquid. Cover the cake with plastic wrap and refrigerate for 6–8 hours.

To serve, sprinkle with powdered sugar. You can cut into squares and top with whipped cream and serve with fresh fruit on the side, or you can make a cream cheese frosting or chocolate glaze.

Tuscan Ricotta Cake

A Traditional Easter-Time Dessert

1 Qt Whole Milk – do not use low-fat
¾ cup Arborio Rice
1 tsp Cinnamon
¼ tsp Nutmeg
1 tsp Vanilla
1¼ Cups Sugar

3 Large Eggs
3 Large Egg Yolks
Unsalted Butter and Flour – to prepare pan
Confectioner's Sugar – for dusting
3 Lbs Whole-Milk Ricotta – well drained

Bring milk to a boil in a large saucepan over medium heat. Stir in rice, cinnamon, nutmeg, and vanilla. Reduce heat to medium-low and cook, stirring occasionally with a wooden spoon until rice is very tender and has absorbed all the liquid (about 30 minutes). Remove from the heat. Stir in ¾ cup sugar and then cover and let cool, stirring occasionally. Preheat oven to 350°. Butter and flour an 8-inch springform pan. In a large bowl, combine the rice mixture, ricotta, whole eggs and egg yolks, and the remaining ¼ cup of sugar. Mix well, but do not mash the rice, and pour into the prepared pan. Bake until the top is golden brown and almost set in the middle (about 65–75 minutes). At this point, if it is starting to get too brown, just cover with foil and continue baking until it is set in the middle. Transfer pan to a rack to cool and then cover with foil and refrigerate to cool completely. To serve, run a knife around the edge of the rim before loosening. Gently remove the rim and sprinkle with powdered sugar.

Note: Sometimes I sprinkle cookie crumbs over the buttered pan shaking out the excess. Also, this can be served with a Raspberry Sauce on the side, which is 1 pint raspberries, 2 Tbs sugar, 1 Tbs freshly squeezed lemon juice. Combine all ingredients in a medium saucepan. Cook over low heat until berries are soft, stirring constantly. Serve warm or room temperature.

Uncle Vinnie's Famous Cheesecake

A Recipe from My Favorite Brother-in-Law

8 Graham Crackers – crushed
3 Pints Sour Cream – drained
7 Large Eggs – separated
4½ Tbs Cornstarch

4 (8 Oz packages) Cream Cheese
2½ Cups Sugar
4½ Tbs Flour
¼ Stick Butter

3 Tbs Freshly Squeezed Lemon Juice   1½ tsps Vanilla Extract

Grease pan with the ¼ stick of butter and sprinkle pan with cracker crumbs to coat the pan.

Blend egg yolks, vanilla, and lemon juice. In another bowl, whisk egg whites until stiff and don't slide down the side of the bowl. Cut cream cheese into cubes in a very large bowl (one that is large enough to handle total liquid). Add sour cream to the large bowl and blend until very smooth. While blending, add sugar, then egg yolk mixture, flour, cornstarch, and melted butter. Blend each in separately before adding the next ingredient. Fold in the beaten egg whites.

Fill prepared pan with the mixture—should be to just about the top of the pan. Cook for 55 minutes at 350° and check for even golden coloring. Give another 5 or 10 minutes, if necessary.

Turn off oven and leave in oven for 2 more hours.

Note: This recipe makes a very large cheesecake and requires a 12-inch springform pan. We have enjoyed Uncle Vinnie's cheesecake on many special occasions, and there is none better and none that can compare.

One was made for every special occasion

Viennese Quick Dessert

1 Cup Sugar
2 Egg Yolks
1 Cup Chopped Nuts – your favorite
1 Cup Butter – almost room temperature

2 Cups Flour
¾ Cup Raspberry Preserves – or your
favorite

Preheat oven to 350°.

Beat together butter and sugar until light and fluffy. Add yolks and blend 1 at a time until well combined. Add flour gradually, and when all combined, add the nuts.

In a 9″ x 13″ pan where the bottom is very slightly greased, spoon ½ of the batter. Top with preserves and cover all with remaining batter. Bake for 30 minutes and the top should be golden brown.

Note: For a special dessert, top with freshly whipped cream.

Zabaglione

½ Cup Sugar
1 Tbs Orange Zest – optional
8 Yolks – room temperature

½ Cup Vin Santo – or sweet dessert wine of
your choice
Pinch of Salt

In a bowl, whisk together the yolks, Vin Santo or sweet wine of your choice, and sugar. Whisk until pale and creamy. (If adding orange zest, add it now.) Add salt and whisk again and scrape sides of the bowl.

Set the bowl over a pan of simmering water and whisk until the mixture thickens and doubles in volume. This will take about 10–15 minutes of constant whisking. Make sure that while the water is simmering, it does not touch the bottom of the bowl. Serve warm, poured into fancy glasses.

Note: This was a specialty of my Grandmother Giovanna at her restaurant in the tiny town of North Branch. She made her Zabaglione in a copper bowl and always used cognac or Vin Santo.

I don't remember her putting in orange zest, but I do remember my Uncle Armando, who was a super cook, preparing it that way.

Zaleti

A Rustic Farmhouse Polenta Cookie from the Veneto Region

2 Eggs
7 Oz Butter – room temperature
1 Small Lemon Zest – grated
1¼ Cups Sifted Flour
1 Cup Yellow Cornmeal

Pinch of Salt
½ Cup Sugar
½ tsp Vanilla Extract
3 Tbs Baking Powder
¾ Cup Raisins or Currants

Preheat oven to 350° and line a baking sheet with parchment paper. In a bowl, beat the eggs lightly with the salt. In a larger bowl, mix butter, sugar, lemon zest, and vanilla. Add the eggs, 1 at a time, until the dough is smooth. Add the sifted flour, baking powder, cornmeal, and then knead the mixture until well blended. Add the raisins, making sure they are well incorporated.

Roll the dough into a cylinder and then flatten, so it becomes a long rectangle. Slice into ½-inch pieces (you should be able to get 24 or 25 slices) and arrange on prepared baking sheet. Bake about 15–20 minutes, until the edges are slightly brown. Allow to cool for about 20 minutes before removing to rack to cool completely.

Note: Zaleti is the Venetian word for Gialetti, meaning "little yellow ones," and is usually served with a chilled glass of Prosecco.

Zeppole

A Sicilian Dolce

1½ Cups Warm Water
1 Envelope Yeast
4 Tbs Sugar
4 Cups Flour – all purpose

2 Eggs – large, slightly beaten
Confectioner's Sugar – for dusting
Vegetable Oil – for frying

Stir sugar and yeast in warm water to dissolve and set aside way from drafts to get frothy. Sift the flour into a large bowl. When yeast is ready, add to flour along with the eggs and mix well to form a dough. Cover bowl and set in a warm area that is free of drafts. Check in about an hour to see if dough has risen. If dough looks good, heat oil and drop by teaspoons into the oil until golden brown. Drain on paper towel and sprinkle with sugar.

Note: This is a dessert made traditionally for the Feast of St. Joseph on March 19. For this Feast Day, the dough is piped into a ring, deep fried, and cooled. Then the ring is split in half and a custard ream is put in the center and topped with a stemmed cherry.

Zeppoles and Fava Beans
for the Feast of St. Joseph

March 19 is a very special day for Italians because it honors the Feast of St. Joseph. In some parts of Italy, it is also celebrated as a sort of Father's Day. Now, we know that St. Joseph was not Italian. In fact, he was Judean. But St. Joseph is very important to Italians, especially Sicilians. In the Middle Ages, there was a drought in Sicily. Italians are very religious people and they prayed to St Joseph to bring them rain. In return, they vowed that they would celebrate with a large feast to honor him. Their prayers were answered, and they kept their word. They feasted on local foods such as fava beans, which thrived after the rains, as well as many sweets. Because the cattle at the time of the first feast were lean, the meal was meatless and that is the way it is still celebrated in many Italian homes today.

Orange Fritters

Frittelle di Riso all' Arancia

2 Cups Milk	½ Cup Rice
2 Tbs Butter – unsalted	¼ tsp Salt
¼ Cup Sugar	⅓ Cup Flour
Zest of 1 Orange – grated	3 Eggs – separated
½ Cup Diced Candied Orange	2 Tbs Orange Liqueur
2 Cups Peanut or Vegetable Oil	

Bring the milk to a gentle boil in a 1-quart pot; add rice. Cook 10 minutes, then add butter, salt, 2 Tbs of sugar, flour, and orange zest.

Remove from the heat and let cool. Fold in the yolks, candied orange, and orange liqueur. In another bowl, beat the eggs whites until peaks form. Gently fold into rice mixture.

Heat the oil until it registers 375° on a thermometer. Drop in the rice batter by spoonfuls (a few at a time, otherwise the oil will get cold and the fritters will be soggy) and fry until puffed and golden on all sides, turning once.

Remove with a slotted spoon and place on paper towels to dry. Roll the fritters in the remaining sugar in small shallow bowl. Serve hot.

Orange Chiffon Cake

6 Tbs Frozen Orange Juice Concentrate – pulp free
½ Cup Canola Oil
1½ tsps Vanilla Extract
1 Tbs Baking Powder
1½ Cups Sugar
½ tsp Cream of Tartar

7 Eggs – separated + 1 Egg White
1 Tbs Butter – melted
Zest of 2 Medium Oranges – 1½ Tbs
2 Cups Flour
1 tsp Salt
1 ⅓ Cups Powdered Sugar

Preheat oven to 325°. Line the bottom of a 10-inch tube pan with parchment paper. In a small bowl, mix orange-juice concentrate with ½ cup water and set aside. In another bowl, whisk together egg yolks, oil, half of the orange zest, vanilla, and ¾ cup reserved orange juice mixture. Set aside.

In a large mixing bowl, sift together flour, sugar, baking powder, and salt. Whisk in the reserved egg-yolk mixture until the batter is very smooth. Set aside.

In a large bowl, using an electric mixer, beat the egg whites on high speed, adding cream of tartar. Beat until stiff peaks form. Add about ⅓ of the egg whites to the batter and whisk gently to combine. Using a rubber spatula, carefully fold in the remaining whites.

Pour batter into prepared pan. Bake in center of oven (**do not open door while baking!**) until golden brown and the top springs back when lightly touched, 50–60 minutes.. Invert pan over the neck of a bottle to completely cool the cake. When cool, run a knife around the edge of the pan and down as far as you can. Also do this around the tube. Invert cake over plate and give it a few shakes to slowly drop onto a rack.

Meanwhile, in a medium bowl, combine powdered sugar, butter, and remaining orange-juice mixture and orange zest. Place plastic wrap directly onto the surface of the glaze and set aside until ready to use. Place completely cooled cake on a serving dish and drizzle glaze over the top, letting it slide down the sides. Let sit for about 10 minutes before serving.

Note: This is a great breakfast or brunch cake.

Neopolitan Cookies

1 (8 Oz) Can Almond Paste	1 Cup Butter or Margarine
1 Cup Sugar	4 Egg Yolks
2 Cups Sifted Flour	4 Egg Whites
20 Drops Red Food Coloring	12 Drops Green Food Coloring
½ Cup Seedless Raspberry Jam	½ Cup Apricot Preserves
1 (12 Oz) Package Semisweet Chocolate Chips	

Preheat oven to 350°. Grease 3 9″ x 13″ pans and line with parchment paper. Grease paper.

Using a fork, break up the paste until fine. Add butter or margarine, sugar, and egg yolks, and with mixer at medium speed, beat until light and fluffy. With a spoon, beat in flour.

In another bowl, beat egg whites until soft peaks form when beater is raised. Add to almond-butter mixture. Remove 1½ cups of batter. Add red coloring, mix thoroughly until evenly blended, and spread evenly in a prepared pan.

Repeat with green coloring and add it to 1½ cups batter and spread evenly in second prepared pan. Put remaining batter in third prepared pan and spread evenly. Bake 10–12 minutes until edges are golden brown. Set on wire racks to cool.

Carefully remove green layer from pan and place on the back side of a parchment-lined baking pan. Spread evenly with raspberry jam. Carefully top this with yellow layer and spread evenly with apricot preserves. Finally top with pink layer. Cover with plastic wrap. Set a baking pan on top and weigh it down with a heavy can or two. Refrigerate for 6 hours or overnight.

Melt chocolate chips slowly in a double boiler until smooth enough to spread. Spread all over the top. Let dry completely. Cut into 12 1-inch strips and then cut each strip into 4 pieces. Make sure to clean knife edge between each cutting.

Note: These are those lovely little multicolored cookies that you always see at weddings and on party platters.

Petite Almond Biscotti

1 Cup Butter – room temperature	1 Cup Sugar
2 Eggs – room temperature	3–4 tsps Orange Zest – or more to taste
2 tsps Vanilla Extract	2 tsps Almond Extract
¼ Cup Grand Marnier	1½ tsp Salt
4 Cups Flour	1 Cup Almonds – whole

In a large bowl, cream the butter and sugar until light and fluffy. Add the eggs, 1 at a time, beating well after each addition to make sure they are well combined. Add the orange zest, both extracts, and Grand Marnier. Beat well. While continuing to beat, add in the salt and flour, slowly. When almost completely mixed, add the almonds and mix just until combined. Divide the dough into 4 pieces. Roll each into a log and then slightly flatten with a rounded top so it looks like a small slice of bread. Wrap in parchment paper and chill for at least 2 hours.

Preheat oven to 375°. Remove logs from the refrigerator and slice to any thickness that you feel comfortable with—usually about ⅓-inch is good. Place on parchment paper–lined baking sheets and bake for about 10 minutes. Turn over and bake for another 10–12 minutes just until both sides are golden brown. This should give about 50–54 Biscotti.

Note: You can use chopped or slivered almonds, if you prefer, but they will have a little different appearance. The whole almonds look prettier but can be a little difficult to slice.

This and That

A Great Ganache

In a large bowl, over hot water that is not touching the bottom of the bowl, add 8 Oz semisweet chocolate chips, 1 tsp instant coffee (optional but gives a more intense flavor), and ½ cup heavy cream. Stir constantly until fully melted, all combined, and smooth. Cool to set, but use at room temperature.

Alli Oli

12 Garlic Cloves – peeled
1 Cup Good Quality or Extra Virgin Olive Oil

1 tsp Kosher or Sea Salt
1 tsp Fresh Lemon Juice

Combine garlic with ½ tsp salt (to start) in food processor and process to a paste. With the motor on, drizzle oil through the tube slowly until the sauce thickens. Pulse in lemon juice. Pour into a jar, stir, and taste for salt and maybe a little pepper.

Note: This is excellent on fish and oven-roasted potatoes. This is a street-food recipe for Patata Brava in Spain. You have to be a garlic lover!

Almond Cream

Crema di Mandorla

1 Envelope Unflavored Gelatin
3 Tbs Water
¼ Cup Almonds – toasted and chopped

2 Tbs Powdered Sugar
1 tsp Almond Extract
6 Maraschino Cherries

Soften gelatin in cold water, and when soft, heat very gently until the gelatin is dissolved.

Combine dissolved gelatin, nuts, sugar, and almond extract and chill until mixture thickens. Whip cream until stiff and fold into gelatin mixture. Chill for at least 3 hours, then serve in pretty glasses garnished with a maraschino cherry. Makes 6 servings.

Aperol Spritzer

1 Part (3 Oz) Aperol
Orange Slices – for garnish

1 Part (3 Oz) Prosecco
Ice

Add ice to a large, stemmed glass until it is almost half filled. Pour in the Aperol and then pour in the Prosecco. Stir and add a slice of orange.

Note: If you like it sweeter, add a little more Aperol. Some recipes call for an ounce of sparkling water. Add that only if you want some fizz (we don't). This is our family-favorite, get-together drink.

Bagna Cauda

Antipasto

An Assortment of Raw Vegetables Such as Peppers, Celery, Cauliflower, Fennel, Broccoli, Steamed Artichoke Leaves
6–8 Anchovy Fillets – rinsed

½ Cup Butter
1 Cup Extra Virgin Olive Oil
4 Cloves Garlic – peeled and minced

Bagna Cauda translates to hot bath! Cut the fresh vegetables into slices and arrange on a plate. Artichokes work well, but they have to be steamed first. Heat the butter and oil over low heat until the butter melts. Add the garlic and gently sauté for a few minutes being very careful to not let the butter burn. Add the anchovies and stir until they dissolve. Pour the mixture into a small deep bowl. Dip the vegetables into the Bagna Cauda, scooping up bits of the anchovy.

Note: This works best if you have a way to keep the mixture from getting too cold. I never remember having a meal at my Aunt and Uncle's house when this wasn't served with the antipasti. We could be many people and I can't remember how my Uncle Armando kept it warm. Maybe it was the constant stirring and passing around that did it. Or maybe it didn't last long enough to cool!

Butter and Sage Sauce

1½ Sticks of Butter – or more to taste   10 Freshly Picked Whole Sage Leaves
¼ tsp Ground Black Pepper   Pinch of Salt

Melt the butter in a small pan until melted and just foaming. Place the sage leaves in the pan and heat until the leaves are slightly crisp about 1 minute or 2. Grind in the black pepper, add a pinch of salt, and stir well. This is a great sauce to sprinkle over grilled fish or a grilled meat. Also great over pasta. Just add to 1 cup of pasta water and then stir into the cooked pasta, adding a good amount of grated cheese.

Butterscotch Sauce

1 Cup Light Brown Sugar – packed   1 Stick Butter – unsalted
½ Cup Light Corn Syrup   2 Tbs Heavy Cream
½ tsp Vanilla Extract   ⅛ tsp Salt

In a heavy-bottomed, nonreactive saucepan, bring the brown sugar and 4 Tbs of the butter to a slow boil on very moderate heat. Whisk in the corn syrup, cream, vanilla, and salt and boil until the mixture registers 235° on a candy thermometer. Immediately remove from the heat and whisk in the remaining 4 Tbs of butter. Whisk until smooth. Best served warm or at room temperature.

Note: This sauce will keep for a few months in the refrigerator in a tightly covered jar.

Campari Spritzer

1 Tbs Orange Juice – chilled   ½ Oz Chilled Campari
1 Tbs Powdered Sugar   Raspberry for Garnish
5 Oz Chilled Prosecco

Combine orange juice and sugar and mix until sugar liquefies. Take a champagne flute, place a raspberry or two on the bottom, top with orange juice, then Prosecco, and lastly, top with Campari. Makes a very refreshing aperitif on a warm evening.

Note: Prosecco is an Italian sparkling white wine.

Cheese Wafers

1 Cup Butter – cubed	**2 Cups Flour**
8 Oz Sharp Cheddar Cheese – grated	**Pinch of Salt to Taste**
½ tsp Red Pepper Flakes	**2 Cups Rice Krispies**

Preheat oven to 350°. Cut butter into flour until mixture resembles coarse meal. Stir in cheese, red pepper, and salt. Fold in cereal.

Shape into 1-inch balls and place on an ungreased baking sheet, 2 inches apart. Flatten each ball.

Bake in batches for 15 minutes. Refrigerate remaining cheese balls while one batch is baking. Makes about 48.

Chimichurri Sauce

½ Cup Olive Oil	**¼ Cup Fresh Basil – chopped**
2 Tbs Lemon Juice – freshly squeezed	**1 Garlic Clove**
⅓ Cup Fresh Parsley – chopped	**2 Shallots – chopped**
Salt and Pepper to Taste	

Starting with the olive oil, place all ingredients in a blender or processor and whirl until it creates a nice thin sauce. If necessary, add more olive oil a little at a time.

Note: Great over meat or fish. You will find a multitude of uses for this sauce, and it saves well refrigerated in a covered jar.

Chocolate Glaze

¼ Cup Light Corn Syrup
2 Tbs Butter
½ tsp Vanilla

3 Tbs Water
8 (1 Oz) Squares Semisweet Chocolate

Combine syrup, water, and butter in a small saucepan and slowly bring to a boil. Remove from the heat, stir in vanilla, and add chocolate. Stir until the chocolate melts and the mixture is very smooth. Let stand until the glaze reaches room temperature before spreading over cake.

Cinnamon Orange Honey Butter

A Delicious Spread for Toast or Pancakes, Etc.

½ Cup Butter – softened
1½–2 tsps Orange Zest

⅓ Cup Honey
½ tsp Cinnamon

In a small bowl, combine all ingredients. Stir to mix well. Refrigerate if not serving immediately, but best enjoyed at slightly room temperature.

Cream Custard Sauce

½ Cup Sugar
4 Egg Yolks
1 tsp Cornstarch – sifted

1 tsp Cognac, Amaretto, or Triple Sec
1 tsp Vanilla
1¾ Cups Milk – scalded

Combine sugar, egg yolks, and cornstarch in medium-sized saucepan. Gradually stir in the scalded milk. Do this slowly so as not to cook the eggs. Heat over low heat, stirring constantly, until the custard thickens and can coat the back of a spoon and registers to 168° on a candy thermometer. Remove from heat. Stir in the liqueur of your choice, then the vanilla, stirring until cool. Refrigerate covered until cold.

Note: This will make any cobbler, pie, pound cake, etc. special and elegant. It is easy to make in a pinch.

Creamy Parsley Dressing

¼ Cup Parsley Leaves
1 Small Onion, Peeled, or 1 Small Red
    Onion, Peeled
1 Cup Olive Oil

2 Tbs Red Wine Vinegar
1 tsp Salt
½ tsp Black Pepper – freshly ground
2 Tbs Sour Cream or Heavy Cream – your choice

Roughly chop onion of choice. Add all ingredients in the bowl of a food processor. Process until all ingredients are incorporated and mixture is creamy, adding more cream and/or oil as necessary. Refrigerate until ready to use.

Note: A red onion will turn this dressing a pretty pink color.

Crema di Limoncello

A Lemon Cream Liqueur

1 Cup Vodka – unflavored
2¼ Cups Whole Milk
½ tsp Vanilla Extract

Peel of 3 Lemons – no white pith
¾–1 Cup Sugar – adjust to your taste
¼ Cup Whipping Cream

Combine vodka and lemon peels in a large glass jar. Cover, give a good shake, and place in a dark cool place for 1 week. However, you must stir the mixture once every day to get a good lemon flavor.

After 1 week, strain and save ½ of the peels.

In a medium pot, combine the milk and the reserved peels and slowly bring to a boil. Remove the pot from the heat, add the sugar, vanilla, and heavy cream, return pot to a low heat, and stir until the sugar dissolves. Remove from heat. Let the mixture cool completely and then remove the lemon peels and discard. Stir into the vodka and place in freezer until ready to serve. It has to be in the freezer for at least 3 hours before serving. As an alternative, you can just keep it in the refrigerator and serve over ice. Makes about 3¼ cups.

Note: I love anything lemon. We have 5 lemon trees outside on our deck that we nurture and bring into our screened porch every winter. The smell of the lemon blossoms is wonderful, and it is so much fun to watch the little lemons develop. This drink is very refreshing.

Crème Fraiche

So Easy to Make Your Own

2 Cups Heavy Cream mixed with 2 Tbs of Buttermilk. If you want some sweetness,

stir in 1 tsp Sugar.

Let sit at room temperature for 12 hours, and there you have it.

Crepes

Pancake Tuesday Special

1½ **Cups Whole Milk**	**3 Eggs**
⅔ **Cup Flour**	**2 Tbs Butter – melted,**
½ **tsp Salt**	**plus extra for coating the pan**

In a medium bowl with a wire whisk, beat 2 Tbs butter with the remaining ingredients until smooth. This can also be done in a blender. Cover and refrigerate for about 2 hours. Remove from the refrigerator and whisk again for a few seconds. When ready, brush the bottom of an 8 or 9-inch crepe pan or nonstick skillet with a little melted butter. Over medium heat, heat the pan, then pour ¼ cup of batter into the pan, quickly tipping the pan to coat the entire bottom. Cook for about 1–1½ minutes until the top is set and the bottom is very slightly browned. Carefully loosen the crepe and turn over to cook the other side for about 30 seconds. Slide out onto wax paper and proceed with cooking the next crepe. Continue until all the batter is used. Usually the first crepe is a throwaway. Should make about 12 crepes.

I make these on the Tuesday before the beginning of Lent and we refer to that day as Pancake Tuesday. This is a dinner item and we fill the crepes with a combination of any of the following: warmed cottage cheese, various preserves, and Nutella, and cover with syrup. My

Grandmother would make a prune jelly that we filled the crepes when I was a Child. Unfortunately, I don't have that recipe.

Fig Preserves

3 Lbs Figs – freshly picked
4½ Cups Sugar
1½ Cups Water

1 Lemon – cut in half
2 tsps Vanilla

Gently rinse figs and remove any little stems that are attached. Place figs in a large bowl filled with cold water and let sit for about 15 minutes. Meanwhile, make a simple syrup by boiling the sugar and water in a pot that is large enough to hold all the figs. When the syrup is thick and clear (about 15 minutes), gently add the figs, vanilla, and lemon. Bring to a boil over high heat and let boil for a few minutes. Lower heat and simmer for 30–40 minutes. Once or twice during the process, give the figs a stir to make sure none are sticking to the bottom of the pot. At this point I usually taste and adjust for sugar.

When the figs are soft and the syrup has thickened, remove the figs from the stove and discard the lemon. Very carefully, using a large slotted spoon, add the figs to a blender jar, and give a few pulses before adding more figs. (I put a towel over the lid and hold it down when pulsing hot stuff.) When all the figs are pulsed, add as much of the liquid as you wish to loosen the preserves and then pulse again. As the preserves cool, it will thicken. After all are blended, ladle into clean, hot sterilized jars. Let cool a little and refrigerate.

Note: The remaining juice is flavorful and sweet, so I save it in the refrigerator and find other uses for it. We have several fig trees in our yard, and sometimes they ripen faster than we can eat or share them. To save them from the squirrels, I pick and make preserves.

Focaccia Dough

½ Cup Water – heated to 105–115°F
1 tsp Sugar
4 Tbs Olive Oil – divided
Pinch of Salt

2 tsps Active Dry Yeast
1½ Cups Warm Water
3½ Cups High-Gluten Flour

In a large bowl, combine ½ cup heated water, yeast, and sugar. Whisk to mix well. Cover with plastic wrap for at least 5 minutes until the yeast is foamy. Stir in additional 1½ cups of water and 3 Tbs olive oil. Stir in the flour and salt. You can use a mixer with a dough hook, or, if you prefer, a large wooden spoon.

Mix dough until it is well blended and slightly sticky. Remove and hand-knead for a few minutes. If dough seems too moist, add a little extra flour. Transfer dough to a large bowl, coat with a little olive oil, cover, and let sit for an hour.

Place dough on a lightly floured 10" x 15" baking sheet and gently press out with your fingers until flat. Cover with a clean cloth and let sit for about 30 minutes.

Proceed with your favorite focaccia recipe.

Garlic Aioli

1 Cup Mayonnaise
2 Garlic Cloves – minced
1 tsp Chopped Fresh Chives
1 tsp Chopped Fresh Parsley
1 tsp Chopped Fresh Basil

1 tsp Chopped Red Onion
1 tsp Lemon Juice – freshly squeezed
Zest of ½ Lemon
1 tsp Prepared Horseradish

Mix all ingredients well with a whisk. Chill for several hours before using.

Note: Great over steak, chops, and fish. Very versatile.

Greek Yogurt Spread

2 Cups Plain Whole Greek Yogurt
3 Tbs Finely Minced Herbs – chives,
    tarragon, parsley
Cheesecloth

½ Cup (or slightly more) Extra Virgin Olive Oil
½ tsp Finely Grated Lemon Zest
Kosher Salt and Freshly Ground Pepper

Line a large sieve with cheesecloth and sit it over a medium bowl. Gather edges of the cloth and cover the yogurt and place in refrigerator to drain for 2–3 days. Gently squeeze out any excess moisture and discard with the extra liquid that accumulated in bowl. At this point the yogurt will be very thick and resemble goat cheese. Roll yogurt into ¾-inch balls and place in an 8-Oz glass jar.

Whisk oil and herbs and lemon zest together. Pour over all the yogurt in jar to cover. Place in refrigerator to marinate for at least 8 hours and up to 2 weeks.

Gumba Boys Grolla

3 Oz Brandy
2 Oz Bourbon
1 Oz Grand Marnier

1 Oz Sambuca
12 Cups Espresso
2 Tbs Sugar

Make the espresso and keep it hot. Add all the liquor together in a small pot and bring it slowly to a boil. Put the hot coffee in the Grolla, add the sugar, and then add the hot liquors. Pass the Grolla around, taking sips, as you wish each other good luck in the form of Cent Anni, Salute, Merry Christmas, etc. The Grolla should be seasoned with hot coffee before its initial use or if it has not been used for a long time. Fill the Grolla with hot coffee and let it set overnight. Drain coffee and rinse with hot water before filling with the Grolla mixture. Never use soap. Rinse after each use with hot water and store with the lid on. Sipping from the Grolla is a symbol of friendship.

Note: A grolla is a multispouted, ornately carved wooden bowl with a small lid. They are always round and usually shallow with an interior capacity for holding liquid proportioned to the number of spouts.

A primitive, wooden, hand-carved friendship drinking vessel

Kahlua

Making Your Own Liqueur

4 Cups Sugar
3 Cups Water
1 Vanilla Bean

2 Oz (¼ Cup) Instant Yuban Coffee
1 Cup Boiling Water
1 Quart Vodka

Boil hard for 20 minutes 4 cups of sugar and 3 cups of water. Let cool. Take 1 cup boiling water and add 2 Oz of instant Yuban coffee. Stir well to dissolve. Split 1 vanilla bean lengthwise and drop it into a ½-gallon clean jug. Pour in sugar mixture and stir well. Pour in coffee mixture and when all is cool, pour in the vodka. Let stand for 2 weeks, stirring (rotate the bottle up and down) the bottle every few days.

Note: I have made this recipe many times, filled small bottles, made special labels, and given as presents at Christmas.

Lemon Cream Sauce

¾ Cup Sour Cream – not low fat
1 Garlic Clove – minced
1 Tbs Fresh Chives – chopped
1 tsp Lemon Zest

1½ Tbs Lemon Juice
¼ tsp Salt
Freshly Ground Black Pepper

Mix all together and serve over cooked vegetables.

Lemon Mayonnaise

2 Egg Yolks
1½ Tbs Freshly Squeezed Lemon Juice
2 tsps Dijon Mustard – or similar

Pinch of Salt
Freshly Ground Black Pepper
1½ Cups Olive Oil

Combine egg yolks, lemon juice, mustard, salt, and pepper in a blender. With the blender on high speed, slowly add ½ cup of oil through the cover opening and continue blending until the mixture thickens and is a light yellow. Turn blender off and scrape down sides. Then, again at high speed, add the remaining oil, a little at a time, and stopping to scrape down the sides. Cover and refrigerate until cold.

Note: This is delicious over vegetables, cooked cubed potatoes, or cold chicken, to name a few ways to enjoy. If the dressing doesn't have to be very smooth, I will add the zest from the lemons and stir in after blending.

Limonata

Fill a tall glass or a shaker partway with ice. Add 2½–3 Oz vodka. If you have citrus-flavored vodka, all the better. Add a generous splash of Limoncello and then add your desired amount of sour mix. Shake well and pour into a high-ball glass. Serve with a thin slice of lemon or a lemon peel.

Sour Mix:

1 Cup Sugar	**1 Cup Water**
2 Cups Fresh Lemon Juice – strained	**½–1 Cup Lime Juice – strained**

Combine the water and sugar in a small pot and cook over medium heat until the sugar dissolves. Lower the heat to a light simmer and add the strained citrus juices.

Let simmer for a few seconds while stirring to incorporate all. Remove from the heat and let cool before pouring into a jar to keep until needed in the refrigerator.

Note: Several years ago, when we were in Tuscany, sitting out on a little outdoor terrace overlooking incredible serene, verdant hills and valleys, we escaped the heat with a delicious drink that refreshed and calmed our tired feet and bodies. We have since been able to closely remake this drink at home. However, the key to the success is that we always have a bottle of homemade Limoncello in our freezer. If you do, too, indulge yourself and think of rolling hills and green pastures and let yourself be carried away.

Limoncello

12 Thick-Skinned Ripe Lemons	4 Cups Grain Alcohol or Vodka
1½ Cups Sugar	3 Cups Water

Wash the lemons and dry the skin. Peel with a vegetable peeler making sure you are not getting any white pith. Do not use lemons that are overripe. The quality of the lemon is the success of the Limoncello.

Fill a bottle with the grain alcohol or unflavored vodka. Add the peels and shake to mix.

Seal the bottle and store for 14 days in a cool, dark place until the liquid has become slightly lemon-colored.

Combine the sugar and water in a saucepan and slowly bring to a boil. Lower to a simmer and cook until the sugar has melted and the liquid is clear. Stir every few minutes.

Let the syrup cool completely and then pour into the lemon mixture. Stir to mix well and let all sit together for 3–4 days. Strain the mixture, separating the peels from the liquid, and discard the peels.

Pour the liquid into a bottle that will seal well and can be kept in the freezer.

Note: You can make a large batch, pour into little bottles, and give as presents. I usually like to find a little recipe that uses Limoncello and tie it with ribbon to the bottle.

Manhattan

1½–2 Oz Rye Whiskey
½–¾ Oz Sweet Vermouth
1 Dash Bitters – or to taste
1 Stemmed Maraschino Cherry

Add all, except cherry, in a cocktail shaker filled with ice. Shake well and pour into glass. Serve with maraschino cherry.

This was the daily 5 o'clock cocktail for Aunt May and Aunt Ann. Usually, they were together, but if they weren't, they were on the phone with each other, catching up while enjoying their drink.

It's five o'clock somewhere

Peach Orange Preserves

2 Lbs Ripe Peaches – unpeeled, pitted, and cut in 1" pieces
3 Cups Sugar
2 tsps Fresh Lemon Juice

1 Whole Unpeeled Orange – cut into ½" pieces, seeds removed
½ tsp Salt
2½ Cups Water

Combine peaches, sugar, water, orange, and salt in a soup pot and slowly bring to a boil over medium-high heat, stirring occasionally. Reduce heat to medium-low and simmer until the fruit has broken down. Stir often during this process to make sure that nothing is sticking to the bottom of the pot and scorching. This will take about 30 minutes and the mixture should be fluid. It will thicken as it cools.

Off heat, stir in the lemon juice, and cool for about 2 hours before pouring into air-tight containers and refrigerating.

Pecans

Candied Pecans:

Preheat oven to 325°.

Spread 2 cups pecan halves on a parchment paper–lined baking sheet. Bake until lightly toasted and fragrant (about 10 minutes) and set aside.

Boil ½ cup packed light brown sugar with 2 Tbs balsamic vinegar and 2 Tbs olive oil in a large skillet set over medium-high heat. Cook until mixture is foamy and slightly thickened. Watch carefully because this will happen in about 2–3 minutes. Carefully add pecans and cook stirring constantly until well coated, about 3–4 minutes. Spread out on prepared baking sheet and sprinkle with ½ tsp sea salt. Break into bite-sized pieces when cooled.

Glazed Pecans:

Line a baking sheet with parchment paper and set aside.

Whisk ¾ cup sugar and ¼ cup sour cream in a large saucepan until smooth. Cook, stirring constantly, until mixture is bubbling and thick (about 5 minutes).

Remove from the heat and stir in 2 cups lightly toasted pecan halves. Sprinkle with ¾ tsp vanilla extract until well coated. Spread out on the prepared baking sheet and let cool completely. Break into bite-sized pieces.

Spiced Pecans:

Heat oven to 300°. Line a baking sheet with parchment paper and set aside.

Mix 2 Tbs packed dark brown sugar with 2 Tbs smoked paprika, 1 tsp cayenne pepper, 1 tsp sea salt, ½ tsp ground coriander, ¼ tsp granulated garlic, ¼ tsp ground cumin, and ⅛ tsp ground allspice in a bowl. Mix 2 cups pecans and ½ a beaten egg white in a bowl until very well combined. Toss nuts into the spice mixture and coat completely. Spread on prepared baking sheet and bake until browned and crisp, about 23–30 minutes. Cool completely before serving.

Pinzimonio

Combination of Finely Minced Ingredients

1 Cup Good Olive Oil
1 Tbs Fresh Parsley – minced
½ tsp Freshly Grated Lemon Zest
Pinch of Salt

1½ Tbs Fresh Basil Leaves – shredded
2 Anchovy Fillets – very finely minced
¼ tsp Garlic – minced
Twist of Finely Ground Black Pepper

Combine all ingredients in a container with a tight-fitting lid. Shake until thoroughly blended. Let rest at room temperature for at least 2–4 hours. Shake again just before using to make sure it is well blended.

Note: This is a very delicate sauce for seafood, cold roast beef, and some vegetables. However, it should be used the same day it is made, for maximum flavor.

Pissaladiere

Something between a Pizza and a Tart

Crust:

1¼ Cups Flour
½ Stick Unsalted Butter – chilled
2 Tbs Water – or more as needed

Pinch of Salt
2 Tbs Olive Oil

Mix flour and salt in processor. Add butter (that has been diced) and oil. Using pulse options, process until the mixture resembles coarse meal. Pulsing, mix in enough water, 1 Tbs at a time, to form moist clumps. Gather dough into a ball, flatten into a disc and wrap in plastic. Chill for at least 2 hours.

Filling:

3 Tbs Olive Oil
2 Garlic Cloves – finely chopped
1 tsp Fresh Thyme – chopped
20 Niçoise Olives

2½ Lbs Onions – thinly sliced
1 Bay Leaf
1 Tbs Capers – drained
16 Anchovy Fillets

Heat oil in a heavy-duty skillet over medium-low heat. Add onions, garlic, bay leaf, and thyme; stir to blend. Cover and cook until onions are very tender, stirring occasionally for about 45 minutes. Uncover and sauté until most of the liquid evaporates and the onions are golden in color, about 10 minutes longer. Stir in the capers. Season with salt and pepper. Cool completely; discard bay leaf.

Preheat oven to 425°. Lightly oil large baking sheet. Roll out dough on floured surface to an 11-inch round. Transfer dough to prepare sheet. Crimp edges of dough to form a thick border. Spread filling evenly over the dough. Scatter the olives and anchovies on top of the filling.

Bake the Pissaladiere until crust is crisp and golden, about 30 minutes. Transfer to platter and serve.

Note: This can also be done on a pizza stone, but the temperature and time will change.

Pizza Dough

Charlie's Favorite

1½ Cups Water
2–3 tsps Instant Dry Yeast
2 tsps Sea Salt
1¾ Cups Bread Flour – see note, or
    1¾ Cups All-Purpose Flour – see note

2 Tbs Olive Oil – helps in stretching
    dough
1–2 tsps Sugar – gives dough rich brown
    color

Charlie's Method:

In your mixing bowl, place water, olive oil, flour, sugar, and yeast to blend. Add salt and continue to mix until the dough pulls away from the bowl. If the dough is wet (sticky), add flour 1 Tbs at a time until the dough pulls away from the bowl. If the dough seems too dry, add water 1 Tbs at a time until the dough pulls away from the side of the bowl.

Remove the dough from the bowl and place on a lightly floured surface and knead into a ball. Cut the ball in half and place each half in a lightly oiled bowl and cover with a linen towel until doubled in size. This usually takes 40–60 minutes.

Optionally, age the dough by placing the divided dough balls covered with plastic film in the refrigerator for 12–18 hours. Remove from the refrigerator and let rest on the counter for 30–45 minutes before stretching. (This is good when you want to prepare the dough in advance.)

For very thin crispy pizza, use a pastry roller on a well-floured surface to stretch the dough to your preferred size.

Note: Bread flour will make a crisp dough, while all-purpose flour will make a softer, chewy dough. This recipe will yield 2 12- or 14-inch pizzas.

Raspberry Sauce

1 Package (12 Oz) Frozen Raspberries –thawed	**⅓ Cup Sugar**
1 tsp Cornstarch	**½ tsp Vanilla Extract**

Process thawed berries in food processor for about 30 seconds or until smooth. Press through a fine wire sieve into a saucepan. Press down with a spoon to get most of the juice and then discard the seeds and the pulp.

Stir together the sugar and cornstarch in a small bowl and then add to the pureed raspberries. Stir in the vanilla. Bring this mixture to a slow boil over medium heat, stirring often to make sure nothing is sticking to the bottom of the pot (about 3 minutes). Pour into a small bowl and chill at least 1 hour before serving.

Note: This makes a great dessert topping. It works well over ice cream, panna cotta, cheesecake, pound cake, and most chocolate desserts. It will make a plain dessert special. And sometimes I use almond extract instead of the vanilla extract.

Rouille

4 Large Garlic Cloves
1 Extra-Large Egg Yolk – room temperature
½ tsp Saffron – optional
1 Cup Extra Virgin Olive Oil

1½ tsps Kosher Salt
1½ Tbs Lemon Juice
¼ tsp Red Pepper Flakes

Mince garlic with salt and place in food processor. With motor running, add egg yolk, lemon juice, and pepper flakes. Process until smooth and add olive oil slowly to make a mayonnaise-like emulsion. Should make about 1 cup. Store in refrigerator until ready to serve.

Sangria

Our Penn State Football Game Beverage

1 Quart Hearty Burgundy
2 Shots Brandy
1½ Cups Orange Juice

½ Cup Sugar
Assorted Fruits – your choice

Mix all ingredients except the wine in a glass jug for at least 24 hours. Add wine 1 hour before serving. Good fruits to use are apples, peaches, cherries (pitted), and grapes (halved). When serving, you can leave the fruit in, as it will settle to the bottom, but try not to mash the fruit when mixing. Different fruits create a different flavor.

I can't make Sangria without thinking fondly of Penn State football games in State College, PA. Best tailgating ever! Tailgating actually started with breakfast, and for several years, there was a group who rolled a full-sized piano off the back of a truck. But, oh, the variety of foods! This Sangria was made by Marlene Sonko and we enjoyed it very much, way too much, at every game we went to. Toftrees Resort was the best place to stay, and I can't forget the buffet at The Corner Room in town. Great memories. Trying to forget Car-Mel Motel. We couldn't get reservations at Toftrees Resort because we waited too long. Never, ever, make reservations at a motel with a hyphenated name, and that's all I will say about that. We attended those games, meeting up each year with a group of friends from West Milford. Charlie worked for ETP and they had a plant in State College, thus the affiliation and our fondness for Penn State.

The Cosmopolitan

1½ Oz Citron Vodka
¼ Oz Freshly Squeezed Lime Juice
Orange Peel for Garnish

½ Oz Cointreau
1 Oz Cranberry Juice

Shake the vodka, Cointreau, lime juice, and cranberry juice in a cold shaker with ice. Pour into a chilled cocktail glass and garnish with an orange peel.

Note: The Cosmo was born out of an earlier drink called the Harpoon, but changed slightly in later years and made famous as the drink of choice in the TV program *Sex and the City*.

The Importance of Egg Creams

Beginning at a young age, I was very aware of the corner candy store. And for long before that the corner candy store was the focal point of neighborhood life. In my New York City "lifetime," there were two candy stores that were important to me. First there was Ray's on Second Avenue at Forty-Third Street. This is where my Dad and Sisters stopped for cigarettes; it was where we bought our three newspapers: The Daily News, The Daily Mirror, *and, on Sunday,* The Journal American. *It was where I stopped for some school supplies, penny candy, Dixie Cups (which was two-flavored ice cream and the inside of the lid had a picture of a movie star or baseball hero), and the occasional egg cream or Mello-Role (which was an odd-shaped sugar cone on which you unrolled a vanilla or chocolate ice cream). Ray also had the latest neighborhood news.*

The second candy store of importance in my life was Rudy's on Second Avenue at Forty-Eighth Street.

Egg creams, malteds, milk shakes, ice cream cones, a good greasy hamburger, grilled cheese sandwich, newspapers, and candy were also available here, along with a Pepsi, a Coke, a Cherry Lime Rickey, and a 2-Cent Plain! During Lent there was a tuna on toast sandwich. But it was much more than just a candy store to me and my friends as teenagers. In the booths in the back of the store, with the jukebox playing, dates were made and hearts were broken. Before the advent of personal phones, a daily stop into Rudy's was important to catch up on what was happening and have a few minutes with your boyfriend sharing an egg cream. You definitely wanted to be seen in the neighborhood candy store on Saturday with your hair in curlers and tied up with a kerchief. That meant you had a date that night!

The running joke at Rudy's was that when a gallon of milk went up a penny, egg creams went up 2 cents.

The Egg Cream

In a perfect world, you would make an egg cream with a seltzer-siphon bottle or seltzer cannister. Lacking that, there is an alternate suggestion. But a must-have is Fox's U-Bet Syrup, chocolate or vanilla.

Squirt ¾ inch of Fox's U-Bet syrup in a large glass. On top of the syrup, pour an inch or so of very cold whole milk. Fill the glass about halfway up with seltzer, aimed at the side of the coned-shaped paper cup, in the metal holder, or glass and stir. But only stir the bottom of the glass to make sure the syrup is well mixed with the milk. Then fill the glass with more seltzer until the foam reaches the top. Ahh, so good!

Toasted Garlic Bread

Olive Oil
Garlic Cloves – peeled

Italian Bread – thickly sliced
Salt and Freshly Ground Black Pepper

Toast the bread with a little olive oil spread over each slice. Then scrape a clove of garlic over the toasted, oiled side of each slice, letting the pulp and juice seep into the bread. Sprinkle with a little more olive oil. Now, if desired, you can sprinkle a little salt and freshly ground black pepper over each slice or maybe some grated cheese. However, it is delicious just with the garlic alone.

Note: There are unlimited ways to serve garlic bread. It is a great accompaniment for soups and fish stew, just to mention a few. For a variety, spread a little anchovy paste on the breads before toasting or grilling.

Pignoli Cookies

1 Lb Almond Paste
1 Tbs Honey
¼ tsp Lemon Extract
4 Egg Whites
Powdered Sugar – for dusting

1⅓ Cups Sugar
¼ tsp Cinnamon
½ tsp Vanilla
Pignoli Nuts

Preheat oven to 300° and line a baking sheet with parchment or wax paper.

In a large bowl, mix almond paste and sugar until well blended. Mix in honey, cinnamon, lemon, and vanilla extracts. Beat in egg whites a little at a time, beating well after each addition. Mixture will be sticky.

Line cookie sheet with parchment paper. Fit a pastry bag with plain round tip, and scoop dough into the bag. Pipe onto parchment paper or wax paper in small rounds the size of a half dollar. Leave an inch between cookies.

Press some pignoli nuts into each unbaked cookie, and then generously sift some powdered sugar over them.

Bake in an oven preheated to 300° for 16–20 minutes. Remove from the oven and let cool slightly. DO NOT REMOVE COOKIES FROM PAPER. Place cookies (still on the paper) in the freezer for about 1 hour. Remove from freezer and peel off the paper.

Index of Recipes

Pasta, Polenta, Rice

Sweets

This and That

About the Author

Chi mangia bene, vive bene.

My home is a very special place, and all because very special people live and gather here. I also have some cherished things that abide in my house, and a few of them are presented throughout the book.

I am contented in the kitchen, where I especially love to cook for my family, because they inspire me with the emotion and appreciation they show for many of the foods I prepare for them.

Times sitting around the table with my family are very special for me.

Dove c'e' amore, troverai la vita.
(Where there is love, you will find life.)